DEMON
POSSESSION
IN
ELIZABETHAN
ENGLAND

Chapter 1

Introduction

The young man falls to the ground and lies motionless. A few seconds later, his arms and legs begin to twitch, jerking ever more violently, until they are thrashing in the dirt. His head rolls back and forth. His back arches upward, into a deep curve. His teeth grind together; spittle foams from his mouth. A passerby, alarmed, stops and asks, "What's wrong? How can I help you?" The suffering young man, oblivious, cannot respond. His behavior continues to be fiercely convulsive, his body and mind obviously racked with pain. A crowd gathers and watches in dismay. A few in the crowd attempt to help, but they can do nothing. The young man's father arrives. He tries to calm and comfort his son, but his attempts are as futile as everyone else's are. The young man's agony continues, visible for all to see, its furious power intensely frightening the helpless crowd.

A local rabbi approaches the crowd and asks what is happening. The father says, "This is my son, who has been possessed by a demon for many years, ever since he was a little boy. The demon tears and wastes my son's body. It renders him deaf and mute. It makes him thrash, foam, and gnash. It causes him to cast his body into fire and into deep water. No one here has been able to help him today." The rabbi expresses impatience at the crowd's helplessness. Then, turning to the young man on the ground, he sternly addresses the evil spirit within: "Demon, I command you to leave this man's body and never to return."

The afflicted man immediately cries out in a loud, strange voice, a voice unlike his own. He shudders one last time, this final tremor shaking his entire body violently from head to foot. Then he lies still, completely motionless. The bystanders see no evidence that he breathes. Several people in the crowd murmur sadly, "He's dead." The rabbi, however, bends down and takes the young man's hand in his own. The young man begins to breathe. He opens his eyes and looks into the face of the rabbi. He allows the rabbi to help him stand up. His behavior is quiet and controlled. Slowly he walks away, his father's arm around his shoulder.

The rabbi in this story is, of course, Jesus Christ. The story is told in three gospels: Luke 9:37–42, Matthew 17:14–21, and Mark 9:14–29. It is one of many scriptural accounts attesting to Christ's power to cast demons out of afflicted human beings. Some of the other accounts appear in Luke 4:33–36 and Mark 1:25–26 ("In Capernaum, a man with a demon cried out at Jesus"); Mark 1:34 ("Jesus cast out many demons"); Mark 3:10–12 ("Jesus sternly warned the unclean spirits"); Luke 4:40–41 ("Jesus laid hands on many people and the demons cried out and came out of them"); and Matthew 8:28–32, Luke 8:26–33, and Mark 5:1–20 (Jesus and the fierce Gaderene demoniacs).

Anthropologists classify exorcisms as apotropaic rituals—that is, ceremonies intended to avert misfortune, which preindustrial cultures often ascribe to a personal, malevolent, intelligent force (evil). Because misfortune is universal, and because people's desire to avert misfortune is universal, exorcisms are ubiquitous. The Christian idea that evil can possess a human body originated many centuries before Christ in the religions of ancient Babylon and Assyria. Sophisticated demonologies developed as these societies graduated from a bare sub-sistence economy to a more stable prosperity. As these societies thrived, the malevolent forces that had formerly personified bad weather, failed crops, illness, stillbirths, and other negative natural phenomena gradu-ally came to represent negative social and political phenomena as well, such as wars, riots, murders, adultery, incest, drunkenness, and any-thing else that threatened the status quo. This expansion of the realm of evil greatly increased its power and importance, elevating it to a position challenging the dominance of the force of good. Such theological dual-ism posited the existence of an eternal battle between good and evil, between God and his adversary. The Jewish exile in Babylon in the sixth

DEMON
POSSESSION
IN
ELIZABETHAN
ENGLAND

Kathleen R. Sands

PRAEGER

Westport, Connecticut
London

Library of Congress Cataloging-in-Publication Data

Sands, Kathleen R.
    Demon Possession in Elizabethan England / Kathleen R. Sands
      p. cm.
    Includes bibliographical references and index.
    ISBN 0–275–98169–X (alk. paper)
    1. Demoniac possession—England—Case studies. 2. Demonomania—
England—Case studies. 3. Demoniac possession—England—History—16th
century. 4. Demonomania—England—History—16th century. I. Title.
BF1555.S26   2004
133.4'26'09420931—dc22   2004052156

British Library Cataloguing in Publication Data is available.

Library of Congress Catalog Card Number: 2004052156
ISBN: 0–275–98169–X

First published in 2004

Praeger Publishers, 88 Post Road West, Westport, CT 06881
An imprint of Greenwood Publishing Group, Inc.
www.praeger.com

Printed in the United States of America

The paper used in this book complies with the
Permanent Paper Standard issued by the National
Information Standards Organization (Z39.48–1984).

10 9 8 7 6 5 4 3 2 1

Copyright Acknowledgment

The author and publisher gratefully acknowledge permission for use of the following
material: Images from *Picture Book of Devils, Demons and Witchcraft,* Ernst and
Johanna Lehner. © 1971 by Dover Publications, Inc.

To the memory of those who moved on
during the writing of this book:

Steven E. Squire,
who loved history;

J. Douglas Canfield,
who loved writing;

Pauline M. Hicks,
who loved reading;

Rosemary G. Davis,
who loved me.

Peace to you all.

Contents

century before Christ presented an opportunity for this concept to be absorbed into Judaism, which began to evolve a demonology of its own, adapting the idea that the great adversary (*ha-Shatan,* Satan) sought to undermine God by harrying and afflicting God's dearest creation, mankind.

By the time of Christ, therefore, human afflictions of any type had come to function as confirmation of the existence of evil, both spiritual (sin) and physical (disease). Christ's ability to relieve these afflictions served as proof of his authority to forgive sins. Such authority, it was thought, attested to his divinity. It also attested to the falseness of rival claimants, such as Beelzebub, who was originally a Philistine god with the special function of driving away demons in the shape of flies. Christ's ability to compete successfully with rivals such as this demonstrated that he was strong where they were weak, that he was divine and they were not, that his was the true religion and theirs was false. His performance of a single exorcism, then, was not just the salvation of an individual soul; it was an expansion of God's kingdom, a diminution of Satan's. Exorcism therefore functioned as a sign of mankind's deliverance from sin, as both weapon and promise of victory in the eternal struggle between dark and light. From the very beginnings of Christianity, then, exorcism served an important function as religious and political propaganda.

Following Christ's example, early Christians practiced exorcism regularly, with contemporary Roman historians noting that these practitioners seemed to be more successful than their non-Christian rivals in this important endeavor. At first, the practice was open to anyone: laymen and clerics, men and women. It was routinely performed and considered normal among all social classes, who used it against the ubiquitous pagan gods that regularly manifested themselves as possessing devils. Indeed, one early church father observed that God's purpose in conferring the power to exorcise on humble people was to demonstrate "the meanness and weakness of evil spirits." When Christianity became the official religion of Rome in the fourth century, the political function of exorcism became even more important, now perceived as essential to propagandize for the true faith and increase the church's membership. In recognition of this fact, the church instituted an official clerical order of exorcists whose sole duty was to purge demons. This act assisted the church in controlling abuses of the practice and formally recognized the

E purgatoire sainct Patri=ce,

The Devil tempting St. Patrick. From *Le purgatoire Sainct Patrice*, Paris, 1530.

status of those who performed this important service. It also served as a demonstration of the sanctity of the exorcist.

This sanctity was reinforced over the next several centuries, as many saints earned their reputations for holiness by casting out devils. Saint Anthony of Padua, for instance, once exorcised a distinguished young man who was possessed by a demon that caused him to eat his own excrement. The saint rebuked the demon in God's name and commanded it to depart. The young man then attacked the saint, who interpreted this assault as a sign of the demon's departure. Saint Bernard of Clairvaux once exorcised a demon by displaying kindness and consideration for him, commiserating with him on his isolation from his brethren, and encouraging him to leave the woman he was possessing in order to rejoin his old friends, the other demons in hell. Saint Martin of Tours employed a less psychological, more physical approach in his exorcism of a demon that had possessed a man and was forcing him to bite anyone who approached. When the demoniac opened his mouth to bite the saint, the latter thrust his arm into the man's throat as far as he could, forcing the demon to exit from the man's anus, leaving "sad and foul traces behind." Saint Hilarion, the best known of the exorcist-saints, could discern demons by smell and cast many of them out of people (and, in one famous incident, a camel) during his long career. He once cured 200 demoniacs at one time. His power over demons was astonishing, as illustrated in the story in which a strong man named Orion was possessed by a legion of demons that caused him to break out in violent rages. When Orion was brought to Saint Hilarion, he broke his bonds and hoisted the old, weak, emaciated saint high up into the air. From this aerial position, the saint pulled the demoniac's hair, causing Orion to release his hold. The saint then stamped on Orion's feet, saying "Writhe! Writhe! Thou mob of demons! Lord Jesus! Release the captive! Thou canst conquer many as well as one." The demoniac opened his mouth, emitting a clamor of many voices, and the demons departed.

For fifteen centuries, the primary political function of Christian exorcism was to prove the superiority of Christianity over non-Christian religions, particularly Judaism. In the sixteenth century, however, after the Reformation split European Christianity into Catholicism and various Protestant denominations, the political focus of exorcism turned inward, and it became a weapon that Christians used against each other. The religious schism in England, as in many other countries, was sustained at a fairly desperate level of crisis for many decades following the Reformation. For instance, in 1536, Robert Aske, a London barrister from a good Yorkshire family, organized the Pilgrimage of Grace to protest Henry VIII's dissolution of the English monasteries, which had begun in that year, and the transfer of their income to the crown. This enormous Catholic revolt, which involved perhaps 30,000 insurgents, spread throughout northern England, from Lincolnshire, to Yorkshire, to Cumberland and Westmorland. The king authorized negotiations to placate the rebels and persuade them to disperse, but once the threat had disappeared, so did his promises of compromise and leniency. With the revolt safely crushed, Aske and more than 200 other rebel leaders were executed, and martial law was levied on Cumberland and Westmorland to justify a series of massacres. This rebellion involved most of those in the upper and middle classes in the affected counties, with the percentage of Catholics among these classes probably at about 75 percent.

This was just one of the first of dozens of hugely disruptive events attendant on the major shifts in England's official religion that occurred following the dissolution of the monasteries. Henry's successor, Edward VI (succeeded in 1547), instituted a much more radical Protestant agenda than his father's, accelerating the abolition of shrines and chantries, ordering the removal of images from churches, prohibiting kneeling during prayer, and mandating the compulsory use of the new *Book of Common Prayer* (which, incidentally, eliminated the role of exorcism in infant baptism). Edward's successor, Mary Tudor (succeeded in 1553), returned the country to fundamental Catholicism, ordering the beheading of the nine-day queen Jane Grey and the burning of several hundred Protestants (including the former archbishop of Canterbury), refounding the monasteries, revoking Edward's new prayer book, and instigating the flight to the continent of hundreds of Protestant refugees. Mary's successor, Elizabeth I (succeeded in 1558), swung the country back to a moderate Protestantism, prohibiting preaching and mandating the Acts of Supremacy and Uniformity compelling public repudiation of the pope and of traditional Catholic forms of worship. These acts underscored the ambivalence and schism rife among England's leaders and perpetuated continual dissension, uncertainty, and fear among the people.

Despite the fact that from the first year of her reign, Catholic plotters were many times arrested for conspiring against her life, Elizabeth began her rule with a fair amount of tolerance for her Catholic subjects, her primary concern being for the speedy settlement of religion within her realm. She wanted her church broadly defined in order to maintain as large a congregation as possible, so she aimed to keep everyone, if not happy, at least hopeful, even her many Catholic subjects. She did appoint some moderate reformers to bishoprics, but they all increasingly conformed after their appointments, opting not to argue with the queen over the wearing of vestments and other such matters of outward show. The Elizabethan Settlement of 1559 was a compromise requiring subjects to display an acceptable level of social conformity while allowing them the free use of their private minds in theological matters: outward religion, not inward, was what mattered most to the state.

The decline in clerical recruits that had begun in Edward's reign continued unabated in Elizabeth's, aggravated by higher standards for university admission, the unsettled role of the church, low status and pay coupled with high taxes for ministers, few chances for advancement in the church, and lucrative opportunities in other professions such as law. It was estimated that only about 600 out of the country's 9,000 clerical livings could actually support a minister. At Elizabeth's accession, perhaps 15 percent of clerical livings were vacant, and some of the new bishops had to resort to mass ordinations of poorly qualified candidates, accepting virtually anyone who had character references, even if he did not know Latin. Some of these makeshift ministers maintained their primary jobs as craftsmen or merchants while performing their church work on the side, thus publicly confirming their vocational unsuitability. Most bishops held multiple livings and rarely visited the parishes associated with those livings, and many churches went for years without adequate clergy. By the end of Elizabeth's reign, nearly half the revenue from the country's parochial livings went to the queen, church, and universities rather than to the resident ministers.

This initial phase of the Elizabethan government's attitude toward heterodoxy constituted the inertia preceding the action. Mary Tudor's reign had given new heart to English Catholics in many areas of the country, resulting in a stronger Catholic spirit during the early 1560s than had existed during the 1530s and 1540s. This spirit was sluggish, however; virtually no important Catholics exerted any serious, sustained effort to reinstitute Catholicism, to organize a sectarian Catholic underground, or to protest against Catholic conformity. They simply waited passively for the inevitable change of religion to occur again, for God to reassert the true faith over heresy, as he had done under Mary Tudor. Elizabeth's initial tolerance was thus fed by the fragmented and passive state of her Catholic subjects, and her government had every reason to expect that English Catholicism would soon die of inanition.

But it did not. Rather, the events of the late 1560s began to refortify Catholic determination. Mary Stuart's flight from Scotland placed within England itself the best hope of an English Catholic succession; young Catholic expatriates began training on the continent for the English mission; Catholic books smuggled from the continent began to circulate widely within England; and the northern earls led a massive rebellion in 1569. English Catholicism began to experience a revival, and Elizabeth's government felt compelled to enforce increasingly stringent measures against Catholics. Prominent Catholics began to be arrested for circulating forbidden books, possessing images, harboring priests, and celebrating secret masses. Reports of illegal and subversive Catholic activities were submitted to the Privy Council by bishops, magistrates, and spies, thus feeding the official perception that English Catholicism, formerly moribund, was now revivified and spreading like a spiritual cancer through the body politic.

Despite the government's measures, this cancer continued to spread during the following decade, with the government's treatment of it becoming accordingly more radical. In 1570, the pope issued a bull excommunicating Elizabeth and absolving her Catholic subjects from allegiance to her. The following year exposed the Ridolfi plot to assassinate Elizabeth and replace her with the joint rule of Mary Stuart and the Catholic duke of Norfolk. Parliament then enacted a stringent anti-Catholic bill defining as high treason the declaration of Elizabeth as heretic or usurper, the use of papal bulls, or any attempt to reconcile with Rome. The following year saw the arrival of the first missionaries to England from the continent and a new requirement that justices of the peace report all suspected or known Catholics. In 1574, the government replaced its formerly haphazard course of imprisoning and fining lay Catholics with a more stringent and consistent policy of penalties, one that lasted for the duration of Elizabeth's reign. By the end of the decade, Catholic priests were being imprisoned as a matter of course and, when they questioned the queen's legitimacy, executed.

The continuous political and ideological upheaval deriving from England's unsettled religion affected virtually every Elizabethan in some way. Some thrived on the country's instability, taking advantage of the socioeconomic shifts to aggrandize their families' positions and fortunes, to climb a few rungs on the ladder of social hierarchy, and to find new opportunities to acquire power and wealth. Others simply endured, riding out the changes as quietly as possible, maintaining their equilibrium as best they could. Some, however, could not find their way to either of these self-preserving courses of action, and they suffered for their failure. They fled the country to take up new lives in strange lands, some separating forever from family and friends. They forfeited generations' worth of wealth and traditional ways of life. They were imprisoned, tortured, and executed. A few, not surprisingly in this difficult religious climate, became possessed by demons.

Demon possession is a highly emotional experience in which a subject—the demoniac—displays behavior that manifests a state of religious distress. It is a public experience, validated by witnesses, that serves as a method of communication by which the demoniac can convey the nature and seriousness of this distress to others in mutually comprehensible language and concepts. It is a coping mechanism that allows the demoniac to express this distress without alienating him or her disadvantageously from other members of the community. It temporarily upgrades the demoniac's social status in the community by implying special divine attention to that one member of that community. It occurs in virtually every religious culture that believes in the literal existence of a malevolent intelligence, a conscious evil force that has the will and power to harm humankind. It is not necessary to believe in the existence of such a force in order to understand demon possession, but we must acknowledge that a great many people do hold this belief. Nearly all English Elizabethans did. The underlying theological principle derived from the same moral dualism that had originated two millennia previously in the religions of ancient Assyria and Babylon and had been subsequently incorporated into Judaism and then Christianity: good and evil define themselves against each other, and to dismiss one is to dismiss both. To most Elizabethans, educated or uneducated, disbelief in Satan was theologically ridiculous and conceptually disturbing, upsetting the balance of the moral universe and rendering Christ's sacrifice pointless. In fact, many perceived disbelief in Satan to be tantamount to atheism: "no devil, no God."

Those who were possessed by demons during Elizabeth's reign offered an opportunity for proselytizers on both sides of the religious schism to offer demonstrations of the legitimacy of their positions through exorcism, a vivid and immediate demonstration of the power of good over evil, of truth over falsehood. Exorcism was perceived as an irrefutable sign of God's continuing presence and influence in the fallen world of humankind. As a demonstration of God's unanswerable authority, exorcism (or dispossession, as the Protestants called it) functioned as social reassurance, forcing evil to emerge from its hidden lair and show itself, forcing it to name itself and admit its purpose. This act reduced and circumscribed the power of evil, showing it to be less significant, weaker, than it seemed when its limitations were unknown. Indeed, so weak was Satan's power in the face of God that even a mere sinful man, the exorcist, acting as God's agent, could successfully execute what was essentially a judicial investigation, judgment, and punishment against the demon.

Of course, in addition to the social and political advantages of exorcism, there was the medical advantage: exorcism often did relieve the sufferings of the demoniac, sometimes only temporarily, but other times permanently. Both illness and cure are often induced by the mind, as most educated early modern people realized. Even the most ardent early modern critics of exorcism admitted that the practice was frequently efficacious if the demoniac believed that it would be. For instance, Johann Weyer, a sixteenth-century physician, said, "That physician in whom more patients trust effects more cures. . . . It is the power of the confident mind [that cures]." Weyer reported a case of a girl whose protection against the devil consisted of a folded paper inside a leather bag worn around her neck. The paper was blank, but the girl's assumption that it bore a powerful word-charm against evil allowed her to recover, developing a good appetite and appearing cheerful and contented for the rest of her life. Another physician, Edward Jorden, made the same observation: "The confidence of the patient in the means used is often times more available [efficacious] to cure diseases then all other remedies whatsoever." John Webster, who practiced medicine for forty years and never saw a case of demon possession that he considered genuine, admitted that many of his patients were cured solely because of their faith in his procedures, not because the procedures themselves possessed any inherent efficacy. George Gifford, a minister, concurred, observing that "Imagination is a strong thing to hurt, all men do find, and why should it not then be strong also to help, when the party's mind is cheered by believing fully that he receiveth ease?" Modern studies show that recovery rates in patients who receive placebos *that they believe are effective* are higher than recovery rates in patients who receive no medication, thus proving that hope and confidence contribute to curative success. Exorcism was a form of what one medical historian has called "therapy of the word," a precursor of Freud's "talking cure."

The role of faith in alleviating mental distress was vital during the early modern era, when educated physicians were few and their attention expensive and often unpleasant. Most common people had no geographical or financial access to skilled medical care. When they did receive the attention of a physician, the prescribed course of treatment was sometimes worse than the disease. Virtually no early modern medical treatment would have had any effect other than temporarily sedating a violent or disturbed patient. The surgical approach to curing mental distress was bloodletting, either through the application of leeches or through cutting into the veins of the forehead. The only chemical alternatives to surgery were opiates such as oil of poppy or mandrake. No other drugs available at the time were pharmacologically effective, and virtually all other drugs were violent and dangerous purges or emetics, such as antimony and mercury. Both the bloodletting and the purges were intended to evacuate the excessive bodily "humors" whose vapors were thought to cause a "sick brain." The four elemental bodily humors (fluids) were widely perceived as the source of human health and temperament: blood, phlegm, yellow bile, and black bile. An excess of any one of these humors caused an imbalance in the bodily system, resulting in physical or mental distress. For instance, an excess of black bile produced a melancholic personality tending to depression, whereas an excess of blood produced a choleric personality tending to anger. Humoral theory was basic to the early modern logic of exactly *how* Satan could afflict mankind—what exactly was the physical mechanism at work here— and the answer, to an Elizabethan, was readily comprehensible: he simply perpetuated an imbalance in the humors of a human body. By overloading a man with blood, Satan could naturally induce that man to fits of violent rage. By overloading a woman with black bile, Satan could naturally induce that woman to commit suicide.

Thus, we see that early modern social, psychological, political, medical, and theological assumptions all contributed to the occurrence of demon possession and exorcism in Elizabethan England, and we will notice these assumptions recapitulated frequently in the following chapters.

Chapter 2
Anne Mylner

On October 18, 1563, 18-year-old Anne Mylner left her house on Bridge Street, in Chester, to herd her father's cows into a nearby field for grazing. Suddenly, she was stricken by fear when a "white thing" seemed to "compass her round about." Mylner returned home, very ill, and took to her bed for four months. During this time, she ate very little, only a tiny amount of bread and cheese once a day. She also slept very little, only about three hours a night.

The malevolent "white thing" approached Mylner as a formless cloud, enveloping her. This approach reflected the idea that Satan had a body but no inherent form. True, his body was much more tenuous than a human's, accounting for his great swiftness and his ability to pass through tiny portals, but he was no less material. Because he was corporeal, it was generally presumed that possession could occur only when Satan entered a human body through an orifice, such as a nostril, an ear, a wound, or a skin pore. And as Satan entered, so he exited: a would-be exorcist had to be prepared to "force absolute garlands of demons to stream out the natural openings of the body in single file." One of Satan's favorite targets was the mouth, as was shown when he implored Helen Fairfax "to open her mouth and let him come into her body," or when he tried to repossess William Somers by entering his mouth as a rat. Demoniacs often became possessed by consuming unblessed lettuce, apples, or bread that an invisible demon happened to be lurking upon at the moment of

Demons, designed by Hans Holbein the Younger, from Historiarum Veteris Testamenti icones, printed by Johan and Franciscus Frellon, Lyons, 1543.

ingestion. The mouth also afforded a demon the perfect opportunity to enter a body through a kiss.

The vulnerability of the mouth to demonic violation was mirrored by the vulnerability of the nether mouth. Tales of possession and exorcism via the anus were extremely common, as we have already seen with Saint Martin of Tours, who exorcised a demoniac by thrusting his fingers into the man's throat, forcing the demon to exit from the anus. The scatological potential of this situation lent itself easily to attacks on heretics: political philosopher Jean Bodin reported that in 1554 some Jewish Roman demoniacs were possessed by devils that spoke "through the shameful parts." Similarly, Protestants were fond of relating the story of how

a famous [Catholic] expeller of devils, having cast out an evil spirit from a man in a monastery at Cologne, and being politely asked by the Devil for some place of retiral, jokingly told him to go to the privy. The ejected one having established him in that place of resort, was enabled at the first visit of the facetious brother to most effectively attack him during the temporary absence of his rear guard.

To dislodge a demon so ensconced, the quickest means of relief was to break wind. The best-known exponent of this form of self-help was Martin Luther, whose repulse of Satan in this manner was frequently retold by both admiring friends and disgusted enemies. In reading the report that the malevolent "white thing" enveloped Mylner's body, therefore, we are meant to understand that the objective of the act was for the formless but corporeal demon to find an open doorway—an orifice—into that body.

After her possession by the "white thing," Mylner returned home and attempted to dislodge the parasitic evil from her body by fasting, an ascetic religious practice with a very long history. Religious fasting in Western Europe dates at least as far back as ancient Greece. The Pythagoreans, for instance, believed that the body was the prison of the soul and had to be weakened by fasting in order to liberate the captive. In the Christian tradition, scriptural precedent authorized the practice of fasting, as, for instance, in Daniel 10:11, which says that Daniel chastened himself by eating no bread and drinking no wine. The most famous scriptural fast, of course, was Christ's 40-day fast in the wilderness.

The Christian view held that fasting yielded many spiritual benefits: it rendered the soul receptive to divine truth, it assisted one in focusing on prayer rather than sleep, it curbed sexual appetite. A Cistercian monk, Gunther of Paris, said, "Fasting is useful for expelling demons, excluding evil thoughts, remitting sins, mortifying vices, giving certain hope of future goods and a foretaste . . . of celestial joys." Both Maximum of Turin and Saint Thomas Aquinas had observed that Christ's (and therefore a Christian's) renunciation of food compensated for Adam's greed in eating the forbidden fruit. Saint John Chrysostom had seen fasting as abstinence, not merely from food, but from sin itself. Saint Cyprian believed that fasting cleansed and strengthened the flesh to render it "morally pure."

One of several early modern English books published on the spiritual benefits of fasting, Henry Mason's *Christian Humiliation, or the Christian's Fast* (1627), is a complete treatise on fasting as a Christian's duty, addressing definitions of fasting, types of fasting, reasons for fasting, effects of fasting, authorities for the efficacy of fasting, and so on. In this book, Mason observes that physical satiety conduces to spiritual faults like rebellion and pride:

For as horses, which provender and high keeping do make proud, do kick and strike and throw down their rider; so this people, being pampered and fed to the full, grow stubborn against God, and contemn his word and ministers, and cast away his yoke from them. . . . [F]ull feeding is apt to puff up the best men, and to make them kick and spurn against God and all good admonitions.

Therefore, fasting helps a person to "tame the flesh by subtracting its food, may elevate the mind towards God by estranging it from the sense of worldly things, and may both show and increase our humiliation and sorrow by chastening the body for the sins of our souls." Mason goes on to say, "Fasting comes nearest to blood-letting in force and virtue" by dispersing and evacuating humors and "all kinde of excrements." Nature is freed thereby and consequently promotes health: "By these means, the whole body is eased, being disburdened as it were of its load, the breathing is made free and easy, the mind and all the senses become more ready and cheerful."

Because of the widespread perception of fasting as beneficial to the soul, it was believed to be a useful weapon against demon possession. Physician Johann Weyer believed that fasting was called for if "perchance the flesh has grown insolent in its excessive self-indulgence—thereby making room for the demon." Demons, it was thought, loved blood, which increased with food consumption. Fasting, therefore, mortified Satan at the same time that it mortified the flesh of the possessed person. On "the highly lauded power of fasting as a most excellent antidote," Saint Athanasius had observed,

Fasting heals disease, dries up rheum, routs demons, banishes evil thoughts, and makes the mind clearer, the heart purer, and the body healthier, setting man beside the throne of God. . . . Whoever, then, is troubled by an unclean spirit, should rest assured that by this remedy—namely fasting—evil spirits will at once depart in confusion, fearing the power of fasting. For demons delight exceedingly in drunkenness and bodily inactivity.

To achieve its spiritual purpose, however, fasting had to be moderate, controlled, purposeful, and of a limited duration. Unfocused, uncontrolled, or purposeless fasting had no scriptural precedent and was merely a show of vainglory. Since the earliest days of the Christian church, however, zealous practitioners had sometimes ignored this principle of moderation, operating on the assumption that, if moderate fasting indicated moderate sanctity, then extreme fasting must indicate extreme sanctity. For instance, in the seventeenth century, some Quakers engaged in marathon fasts in which survival was considered a miracle. Even Quaker children fasted for ten to twenty days, trusting that they would be sustained by God. Quaker leaders also challenged sectarian opponents to competitive fasts, as in 1655, when Richard Farnsworth proposed a competitive fast to a group of Manifestarians to see who could preach the best sermon after fasting. Similarly, George Fox challenged all the Catholics in the world to a competitive fast to prove that their "bellies be not [their] god"—a challenge that was apparently not accepted. As with other privations and self-mortifications, extreme fasting frequently resulted in a trance state, a condition characterized by the absence of voluntary movement and the presence of involuntary movement, sometimes very forceful. This was the case with Anne Mylner.

During Mylner's four months of illness, several symptoms manifested themselves, primarily recurring trances. In this state, Mylner lay in her bed "as still as a stone" with her eyes and mouth half open, her tongue "doubling between" her teeth (curled back and protruding), her face unnaturally red, and her head as "heavy as lead" for a bystander to lift. To the bystanders, she appeared "aghast" (as though she had seen a ghost). Mylner also suffered from convulsions that occurred intermittently between her trances. Lying on her back in bed, Mylner would suddenly arch her back and lift her torso up, bending her legs backwards beneath her so that they almost touched her head, thus "casting herself (her belly being upward) into the shape of a hoop." Not only was Mylner's belly on prominent display because of this hooped posture, it also swelled "up and down, sometimes beneath her chest, sometimes up to the throat, in such vehemence that a man would have thought she would have burst."

Convulsions and contortionism would figure prominently in several later cases of demon possession, such as that of William Somers of Nottingham (1597), the Meredith children of Bristol (c. 1675), and Richard Hathaway of Surrey (1701). The commentator on one of these cases, that of the Meredith children, asserted that the four children's violent distortion of their faces and limbs was a sign of demon possession because, as he believed, children of such a young age (eight to fourteen years old) were not naturally capable of such extreme convulsions, an assertion that many parents would dispute. In all these cases, it seems clear that the putative demoniacs were largely or entirely faking their symptoms, including their convulsions. In the case of Anne Mylner, however, the convulsions may well have been the result of a disease, such as epilepsy, meningitis, encephalitis, Reye's syndrome, or some other illness characterized by convulsive episodes causing extreme rigidity of the torso and limbs. At the time of Mylner's experience, of course, the initial diagnosis of most of these diseases was still in the future and therefore not available to the bystanders as a culturally acceptable explanation of what they were seeing.

The exception to this generalization was epilepsy. Since at least Aristotle's time, ancient physicians had diagnosed epilepsy and had differentiated it from demon possession. Most uneducated people, however, associated the two afflictions, and educated people began associating the two more closely during the Middle Ages. The scriptural tales of Christ's casting out of demons wrought the major change in attitude: the young man whose story is told in the introduction to this book is described in terms that clearly identify him as an epileptic, yet Christ treats him as possessed, rather than ill. Church fathers such as Origen therefore interpreted this story supernaturally: the boy's affliction "is obviously brought about by an unclean deaf and dumb spirit." Thus, the belief in possession and exorcism changed from the polarizing idea between educated and uneducated to that between Christian and pagan. Epilepsy therefore had a long tradition as a "sacred disease," provoked by supernatural causes and susceptible only to supernatural treatment—a punishment for sin. Following logically from this belief was reluctance on the part of most onlookers to touch or otherwise interfere with the demoniac during an attack because of his or her perceived uncleanness. The description of Mylner's symptoms implies that she may have been experiencing epileptic seizures, possibly triggered or aggravated by her extreme fasting and insomnia.

Although generalized convulsions occurred in both male and female demoniacs, a swelling belly in a semi-naked, 18-year-old woman such as Anne Mylner very distinctly conveyed the idea of pregnancy—important because early modern Europeans perceived many parallels between pregnancy and demon possession. This per-

ception was made explicit in other cases with young female demoniacs of childbearing age, such as Mary Cooper, sister of the famous
demoniac William Somers, and Sarah Williams, one of the Denham
demoniacs. The perception of these parallels derived partly from mis-
conceptions about pregnancy. It was commonly believed that a
woman could not become pregnant unless she experienced sexual
orgasm, an event thought to release the "female seed" necessary for
conception to occur. Not until the eighteenth century did modern
symptoms of pregnancy become widely known, such as the cessation of
menstruation, the darkening of the aureola, and nausea. Thus, Elizabethan women who were pregnant frequently believed themselves not
to be, and they therefore looked for alternative diagnoses, including
possession. Indeed, women sometimes pretended to be possessed in
order to cover up unwanted pregnancies, such as the woman who
tried to hide her affair with a priest who routinely exorcised her. The
sixteenth-century physician who commented on this case drily concluded that this woman finally gave birth to "a little female spirit"—
that is to say, a daughter fathered by the priest.

Young women were thought to be more attractive to demons than
old women, men, or children, implicating female sexual receptivity as
a condition for possession. The behavior of women deemed possessed was frequently interpreted by onlookers as similar to the
behavior of sexually aroused women. For instance, two possessed
nuns in the convent of Nazareth at Cologne in 1564 "were frequently
thrown to the ground and their lower torso was made to thrust up and
down in the way usually associated with sexual intercourse. During this
time, their eyes were shut, and later they opened them with shame,
panting as though they had undergone a great labor." This behavior was
interpreted as the women's copulation with an invisible demon. Phan-
tom pregnancies were considered a symptom of possession or sexual
activity with an incubus, a male demon who copulated with human
females and pretended to impregnate them but who possessed no
seed. A sixteenth-century work on demonology explained that, in
such women, "their bellies grow to an enormous size; but when the
time of parturition comes their swelling is relieved by no more than the
expression of a great quantity of wind."

Not only did parallels exist between possessed women and pregnant women, they also existed between fetuses and possessing

demons. Early modern Europeans generally believed that ensoulment occurred during the second month of gestation; thus, a month-old fetus possessed no soul at all. The uterus and birth canal were widely perceived as the sink and conduit of evil, since the "bad humor" of menstrual blood was evacuated from it. Furthermore, during gestation, parturition, and until baptism, the child was perceived as the embodiment of original sin, which was believed to be the natural condition of every newborn. In fact, the centuries-old Catholic practice of baptismal exorcism was premised on the assumption that a child who had not been baptized still lodged the evil spirit with which it had been born. Before the child could receive God's grace during baptism, this evil spirit had to be evicted. Any human being not possessed of the Holy Spirit was necessarily possessed of Satan; moral neutrality was impossible. God's creation was structured by oppositions: dark and light, health and sickness, birth and death. The world was perceived as organized according to contrariety. This principle was implicit in one early modern cleric's denial of the possibility of a vacuum: "God hath so ordained that in this whole world there cannot be [a] vacuum, that is to say, any place void or empty, but it must needs be filled with somewhat; there is no power in man to make such empty place, so much as a pin's head." Like the universe itself, a human being was a plenum rather than a void, either good or evil, but never impartial. In the unbaptized infant, the expulsion of the evil spirit was accomplished through *exsufflatio* and *insufflatio*, the ritual breathing out of the demon and breathing in of the Holy Spirit. This practice had been authorized by Saints Cyril and Augustine and used since ancient times, perhaps even as far back as the time of Christ.

The practice of baptismal exorcism, however, became controversial in England after the Protestant Reformation. One early attack (1533) described this ritual as "plain sorcery, devilry, witchcraft, juggling, legerdemain." Unlike the Catholics, who had perceived baptismal exorcism as part of an essential act of salvation, the new English Protestants came more and more to perceive baptism as Calvin had defined it, "a badge and attestation of the divine grace and seal of the divine promise"—that is, a signifier of entrance into the earthly Christian community, not an act of salvation. In 1552, the government-authorized prayer book was changed to omit the exorcism prayer and to shift the making of the sign of the cross to after the baptism ritual so that this gesture could not be construed as an act of exorcism. During the last half of the century, the entire baptism ritual was so controversial that many dissenting parents allowed themselves to be imprisoned rather than subject their infants to it. Still, some country folk continued to view baptism as exorcism as late as the seventeenth century, with some Puritan ministers at this time preaching that unbaptized children were the devil's spawn.

Another parallel between the unborn fetus and a demon inside a human body was that the remedy that had been used for centuries to expel such a demon—exorcism—was also used to induce childbirth. This remedy made sense in light of the common view that the emergence of the fetus from the womb resulted from an act of volition on the part of the fetus, which was perceived as having an active and conscious role in its own birth. If labor went well, the fetus was presumed to be strong; if not, the fetus was presumed weak. Infants born spontaneously after maternal death were thought to have achieved their own births against great odds. Not only were similar prayers used to induce both demons and fetuses to leave human bodies, the same herbs, ligatures, stones, amulets, and so on were used in both cases. Rue, for instance, an abortifacient and contraceptive well known and much used until the nineteenth century, was employed by early modern Europeans for both childbirth and exorcism on the same principle: the fetus or demon, repulsed by the herb's bitterness, would flee its warm berth. Similarly, natural amulets such as diamonds and garlic (both reputed for their "binding" properties) were removed from the presence of both women in childbed and demoniacs to give the fetus or demon free rein to leave.

During the four months that Mylner was bedridden with her distressing symptoms, friends and neighbors frequently visited her house to commiserate with the family, offer charity, pray, or simply watch the show. Among Mylner's visitors were several important local people, including John Pierce, one of the canons of Chester Cathedral and reader of the divinity lectures there. His visit to the afflicted woman so moved him that in December, while conducting a service at the cathedral, Pierce asked his congregation to kneel and say a special prayer for Mylner's deliverance from her suffering. The effect of this request was naturally to ensure that virtually everyone in Chester knew of the situation. A month later, near the end of

January, John Lane, a fellow of Christ Church, Cambridge, and a "famous and godly preacher of the gospel," happened to be preaching at a town near Chester. Lane was reputed for his ability to help those with mental afflictions: "it is well known to diverse credible persons . . . what rare and singular remedy God hath wrought by Master Lane in some that sustained of late no small decay of mind and memory." At this time, Lane was approached by two men of Chester, who described Mylner's affliction to him. These men were among those whose religious beliefs caused them to "seek miracles to confirm God's word." When, therefore, they told Lane that they thought Mylner was possessed with evil spirits, "as in times past," the miracle they sought was clearly a dispossession—the Protestant alternative to a Catholic exorcism.

When the assize session opened in Chester two weeks later, Lane came to town and lodged with a local knight, Sir William Calverley. That day, the same two Chester men who had importuned Lane to visit Mylner the previous month did so again. Lane therefore went to the Mylner family's house on February 16, accompanied by his host and his host's wife, Lady Calverley; another knight, Sir William Shepherd; and other important guests. Arriving at the Mylners' house, Lane and his entourage were taken to see the afflicted woman, who was lying in bed wearing only her undergarment. Before the eyes of these important guests, Mylner's belly began to swell and her body began to contort into a hoop. Observing this, Lane asked whether Mylner's attendant had ever tried to force Mylner's body down when it was in its hooped posture. The attendant said that she had indeed tried but without success. Mylner was too strong for her, she said, but Lane was welcome to try to do it himself.

At this point in the conversation, Mylner had contorted her body into a hoop four or five times before the amazed eyes of her guests. Lane grabbed her ankles, yanked her feet out from under her, forcibly straightened her legs, and sat on them. He then leaned over her body and held her hands down as well. During this, Lane's first physical confrontation with Mylner, he found her strength so prodigious that he was convinced that she was, as he said, possessed. While he sat on her legs, the bystanders pressed Mylner's belly down with as much weight and strength as they could muster and observed that she "was very like to have thrown them over."

Lane sat on Mylner and restrained her for two hours, preventing her belly from swelling and her body from arching. The observers, noting the sweat dripping down Lane's face, begged him to release her, fearing that the ordeal was too difficult for both minister and demoniac. Lane, weakening, considered giving up, but he persevered, gaining renewed strength from the prayers of the onlookers as well as his own. He prayed silently, repeating the fiftieth psalm in his mind and asking God to deliver Mylner "through the blood of his son Jesus Christ."

At the end of the two hours' stalemate, his strength exhausted, Lane finally called for vinegar. The bystanders objected, pointing out that this age-old remedy had already been tried several times and had always failed. Lane insisted. The vinegar was brought and poured into Lane's mouth. Still sitting on Mylner's legs, still leaning over Mylner's prone body to hold down her wrists, Lane forcefully expelled the vinegar from his mouth into Mylner's nostrils.

When Lane spat the vinegar into Mylner's nostrils, the girl cried out her first words in four months: "Ah, Lady, Lady," an appeal to the Virgin Mary to rescue her from the stinging, burning pain. Lane immediately reprimanded Mylner for this outcry. Her prayer, he said, ought to address God and "the blood of Christ," not any saint, not even the Virgin. Mylner was silent in the face of this reprimand. Lane therefore called for more vinegar, whereupon Mylner cried out, "No, no, no more, for God's sake." Lane then ordered Mylner to say the Lord's Prayer and the Te Deum after him and to continually call upon God's name. She complied.

When Mylner cried out her appeal to the Virgin Mary, Lane admonished her to call on God's name instead. This brief exchange illustrates one of the most controversial theological prohibitions levied by the English reformed church on its parishioners: the prohibition against praying to saints. The practice of invoking various holy names in the expulsion of demons predated Christianity, originating in ancient Babylonian and Jewish rituals, and had constituted an important part of the Christian exorcism ritual since the origin of such ritual in the second century. The most important names, of course, were those of God (who had many such names) and Jesus, but hundreds of other holy names were available for the purpose. In Yorkshire alone, the saints invoked during exorcisms included Mary, Andrew, Nicholas, Margaret, Peter, Paul, Matthew, Bartholomew, and Brigit. The thirteenth-century

Ingleby Arncliffe crucifix, which contains a parchment inscribed with an exorcism formula, invokes dozens of holy names:

> Agla. In the name of the Father and of the Son and of the Holy Ghost. Amen. I conjure you, ye elves and demons, and every kind of phantom, by the Father and the Son and the Holy Ghost, and by Saint Mary, the mother of our Lord Jesus Christ, and by all the apostles of God, and all the martyrs of God, and by all the confessors of God, and by all the virgins of Jesus Christ our God, and the widows, and all the elect of God, and by the four Evangelists of our Lord Jesus Christ, Mark, Matthew, Luke, and John, and by the incarnation of our Lord Jesus Christ, and by God's passion, and the death of our Lord Jesus Christ, and by God's descent into hell, and by the resurrection of our Lord Jesus Christ, and the ascension of our Lord Jesus Christ into heaven, and by the four evangelists of our Lord Jesus Christ. Agla. Mark. Agla. Matthew. Agla. Luke. Agla. John. Agla. and by the virtue of our Lord Jesus Christ, and by the great names of God + a + g+ l+ a + on + tetra + grammaton + Sabaoth + adonai + and all names, that thou hurt not this servant of God, Adam, by night nor by day, but by the exceeding mercy of Jesus Christ our God, with the help of Saint Mary, the mother of our Lord Jesus Christ, he may rest in peace from all the aforesaid evils and all else. Amen. + Agla. In the name of the Father and of the Son and of the Holy Ghost. Amen. And his folk may rest, and this servant of our God Jesus Christ, Adam, may rest, through the help of Saint Mary, mother of our Lord Jesus Christ, from all the aforesaid evils, and all others. Amen. + Agla. // Agla. Agla. Agla. Agla. The five wounds of our Lord Jesus Christ, and five joys of Saint Mary of Osanna, Saint Dunstan, Saint Andrew, Saint Nicholas, Saint Margaret, Saint Peter, Saint Paul, Saint Matthew, Saint Bartholomew, the five holy wounds of our Lord Jesus Christ, thee Saint Brigit. Agla. Christ is King. Agla. Christ reigns as ruler, and may Christ defend Adam from all harm. Amen.

Church fathers such as Origen had explained that the invocation of such names was an infallible weapon against a possessing demon: the actual pronunciation of a holy name constituted a magic charm, a "name-spell," against which evil was powerless. Magic language was assumed to operate on the principle that the names of things were somehow extensions of the things themselves; thus, the name of a great person was *in itself* deemed more potent than the name of a lesser person. The Catholics of early modern Europe had a long history of using hundreds of saints' names in exorcisms, such as that of Baptista Peruso, the invocation of whose name was reputed to cast out devils, cure natural illness, calm storms, and ease childbirth. The efficacy of pronouncing such names resulted from the faith of the sufferer in that efficacy, a phenomenon recognized at the time by at least one early modern physician, who observed that the "physician in whom more patients trust effects more cures. So important is it when one has an intense mental image of being healed. . . . [I]t is not charms, it is not characters, that can do such things [as cure illness]; it is the power of the confident mind in accord with [the mind of] the patient."

To most early modern Protestants, however, the use of saints' names in this fashion was deemed "Popish" and "superstitious." This position is clearly implied in the report of another case of demon pos-session, that of Alexander Nyndge: "Then all that were there present [around the bed of the demoniac], to the number of twenty persons and more, fell down and said the Lord's Prayer . . . and one of the company uttered words joining God and the blessed Virgin Mary together." The Protestant cleric who was attempting to cast out the demon rebuked the speaker, saying, "You offend God." This rebuke was answered by the demon itself (from inside the demoniac) in an attempt to induce the bystanders to use an illegitimate form of prayer: "There be other good prayers" (besides prayer to God and Jesus). The cleric then responded, "Thou liest, for there is no other name under heaven whereby we may challenge salvation but the only name of Christ Jesus."

To the more radical Protestants, however, even the use of the names of God and Jesus in this manner was neither efficacious nor legitimate, and they amassed several arguments to bolster this position. First, they observed that Scriptures quote Satan himself as pronouncing the names of God and Christ on several occasions. Second, they argued that the name "Jesus" was a very common name among the ancient Jews and that in itself it possessed no intrinsic power. Its value was con-notative: "By the name of Jesus is meant the authority and power that hath given him over all things in heaven and in earth and under the earth." Third, they pointed out that the seven sons of Sceva (Acts 19:13) who tried to exorcise demons in Christ's name failed because they "did

mightily offend the majesty of God in so profaning of the most holy
name of Christ Jesus, by making thereof a charm or enchantment, and
abusing it to their own private fame and commodity without any such
commission or authority from God." They concluded, in fact, that the
use of the names of God and Christ in this manner was a form of
blasphemy:

> They which do use the name of God as it consisteth of letters and
> syllables in these cases [of working miracles], whether pronounced
> in the mouth, or written, do exceedingly abuse and blaspheme the
> name of God against the third commandment, "Thou shalt not take
> the name of Lord thy God in vain," using it unto another end than
> he hath ordained it. For God hath not appointed his name for men
> to work wonders by it but that thereby he might be known and
> glorified.

After her deliverance, Lane ordered Mylner to pray, not generally
to Christ, but specifically to "the blood of Christ," as he himself had
done earlier. Traditionally, the wound in Christ's side functioned as a
powerful focus of devotion because of its proximity to the sacred heart.
Because of this proximity, it symbolized the well of everlasting life,
man's refuge from the consequences of his own sin. Dame Julian of
Norwich had envisioned this wound as a "fair and delectable place, and
large enough for all mankind that shall be saved and rest in peace and
in love." One traditional prayer attributed to Saint Bridget was "O Jesus,
most profound abyss of mercy, I beseech you by the depth of your
wound, which pierced your flesh to the heart and very marrow of your
bones, draw me out from the depths of sin into which I have sunk, and
hide me deep in the hole of your wound from the face of your anger,
Lord, until the judgment is past." Similarly, Saint Bernard had said of
the crucified Christ, "Take heed and see . . . his side opened to love
thee." It was widely believed that when Christ appeared at the Last
Judgment, he would display his wound as a pledge of his love for
humankind.

This image of the wound of Christ as a well of salvation appeared
prominently in other cases of demon possession as well as in Mylner's case. In the case of Robert Brigges, for instance, this image
functioned as a central recurring symbol for the demoniac. In his
arguments with Satan during his affliction, Brigges asserted, "I have
told thee oft that the least wound which he [Christ] suffered shall

swallow up all my sins though they were so many as all the sins of the world." Far from being an object of repugnance, Christ's wounds were an object of longing and admiration to Brigges: "I see him crucified . . . and his wounds sweetly bleeding, gaping wide to receive and swallow up the sins of all them that believe in him." In fact, repugnance at the sight of Christ's wounds was a characteristic of Satan, as we see when Brigges accosted the latter: "Why tremble you? . . . Here are dragons of hell gaping, but behind me are the wounds of Jesus Christ, fresh bleeding." The blood from Christ's wounds was described as legal tender with which Brigges' soul could be redeemed from Satan: "I tell thee, [my soul] is not mine; it is his who hath paid his heart's blood for it."

Shortly after Anne Mylner's deliverance, Lane asked the women of the house to bring food and clothes for Mylner. After eating a few bites, she allowed the women to dress her while Lane modestly withdrew from the room. He then returned and ordered her to get up from her bed and walk, as Christ had commanded those whom he had cured. At this command, the bystanders protested, pointing out that she had been bedridden for four months and was much too weak from illness and fasting to be expected to walk. Lane responded, "If God can make her talk, he can make her walk." He again commanded Mylner to leave her bed and walk to him, and he went to stand on the other side of the house. Mylner did as she was told. When she finally reached Lane, he admonished her once more to maintain faith in Christ and to occupy herself in prayer. He then left the house.

The day after Mylner's deliverance, Lane preached a sermon at Saint Mary's in Chester. In the congregation was Mylner herself, behaving decorously in public for the first time in months. Also in the congregation was John Throgmorton, Esq., the Queen's Majesty's High Justice in the County of Chester, who was so impressed with Lane's sermon and Mylner's demeanor that he invited the girl to visit him so he could converse with her about her astonishing experience. Two weeks later, on March 4, Master Rogers, Archdeacon of Chester, preached another sermon on the subject, this time in a more prestigious venue, Chester Cathedral, before an even more important congregation, including the mayor of Chester, two bishops, and a great multitude of citizens. In this sermon, Rogers asserted that "whatsoever

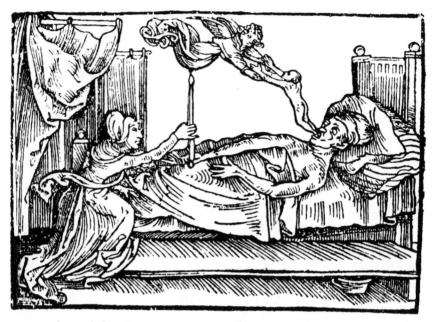

The Angel of Death taking the soul, in the form of a child, from a dying man.
From Reiter's Mortilogus, printed by Oegelin and Nadler, Augsburg, 1508.

was the original cause of so great and strange a disease, yet was the cure wonderful, and wrought by God, either to the great commodity, or else for the great plague of the City of Chester, and the country adjoining."

Less than three weeks later, on March 24, an account of Mylner's affliction and deliverance was published by John Fisher, a gentleman who had been one of the witnesses to Lane's treatment of Mylner. In addition to Fisher, other important witnesses to the event who signed their names to the account, including Sir William Calverley, knight; and Richard Hurleston, Esq. Fisher explained that his motivation for publishing the account was that the event was "so rare and notable that it should not be kept from posterity."

Chapter 3

Edmund Kingesfielde's Wife

Edmund Kingesfielde had been a mason working in the West Country before he moved to London. After his move, however, he decided to change his profession and so established an inn in the parish of Saint Sepulchres. To advertise his new business, he commissioned a sign to be painted and hung outside his inn around August 24, 1564. This sign was so unusual, so "full of merry conceits," that it created considerable controversy in the neighborhood. Painted in many bright colors on both sides, the sign displayed "a hoop drawn round about the painting, with a cock standing thereon, and in the midst of the hoop an image of the devil and of a man also with a sack on his back." The sign was also furnished with two "posies," brief verse stanzas intended to assist the viewer in interpreting the images. These posies were composed by Kingesfielde himself, who was known for his skill in "crossing rhymes." The posy on one side of the sign read, "Whippet awhile / And fill the can / Set cock on hoop / The devil pay the malt man." On the other side, the posy read, "Go no farther / Your matters to scan / Here is good ale / Where the devil pays the malt man." Kingesfielde was so pleased with his sign that he frequently sat at the door of his inn, singing its praises to his friends and offering pots of ale to passersby who stopped to admire it. Indeed, the sign seemed to contribute to an increasingly brisk business: the pots of ale "walked within more merrily than before."

Not everyone, however, liked the sign as much as Kingesfielde did. Popular opinion was divided: "so diversely was this sign judged and talked of by the passersby, some praising the man's merry wit, some musing what the meaning of it should be, and others misliking that kind of jesting." The reason for the "misliking" of this last group of people was their belief that the depiction of the devil on the sign was a pictorial variation on "Speak of the devil, and he appears"— that the sign showed Kingesfielde's casual, perhaps even jocular, attitude toward sin. Such a sign was clearly offensive to God, its manner of jesting commonly causing God "to deal in good earnest" with the jester. To be sure, for a time after the erection of the sign, God seemed "awhile to be asleep or . . . wink at the matter." Rather than recognizing this divine indulgence, however, and reciprocating it through godlier thought and behavior, Kingesfielde, like so many other wicked people, was emboldened to heap sin upon sin, allowing his conscience to lie dormant. For some months, the Kingesfielde family "passed their time in great security as though there had been no God."

This account demonstrates a common early modern intellectual tendency to perceive metaphysical significance in physical objects, to see natural phenomena as signs of supernatural presence, to render the invisible visible. The early modern English possessed highly pictorial imaginations, and these imaginations habitually translated moral abstractions into emblems. Emblems were culturally ubiquitous, appearing in books and broadsides, painted and carved portraits, architecture, tapestry, jewelry and clothing, armor and weapons, monumental funerary sculpture, and wall and ceiling decoration, among others. University students neglected Aristotle in favor of fashionable continental emblem books, and the taste for embellishing houses with emblems extended from the monarchy and aristocracy to the landed gentry and the rising middle class. The psychological impact of emblems on the early modern mind was as immediate and graphic as illustrated advertising is to us today.

Emblems were educational, exemplary, and morally illustrative. Emblem books were used in English grammar schools to assist in the teaching of composition and oratory. They were also used in religious education as supplements to sermons and foci for meditation. Early modern educational theorists such as Francis Bacon and John Willis explained that emblems assisted people to learn by reducing intangible concepts to concrete images. The latter impress the mind more deeply than the former, and thus they are retained longer in the memory. Teachers and students trained themselves to remember and organize abstract ideas by translating those ideas into concrete images (such as flowers or statues) and placing them within a concrete setting (such as a garden or a castle). This centuries-old emphasis on visual learning was shown by the illustrated title pages for many of the thousands of books that poured from the press every year.

Not surprisingly, then, many cases of demon possession document the existence of revelatory signs, concrete images whose significance was culturally determined and generally understood by the witnesses in those cases. For instance, in the case of Robert Brigges, the demoniac hallucinated a disturbing apparition of a "great spotted clout [cloth] . . . of such diverse colors and so red in diverse places." This soiled and bloodied cloth, we discover, represented Brigges' soul spotted with his countless and varied sins. These sins further metamorphosed into another concrete symbol: a body of water symbolizing eternal damnation. Satan, attempting to induce Brigges to enter the pond, lied to him, asserting that the water was only knee deep and would not harm him. At first, Brigges resisted, suspecting the lie: "If it be deeper than my height, what then? What shall I gain if for all I lose mine own soul? What gained Judas, that for a paltry sum of money, lost his own soul? Nay, surely thy purpose is that I should drown myself in sin, as thou persuadest Cain." Finally forced into the pond, Brigges refused Satan's assistance to get out again, calling instead on Christ: "O Lord Jesus, now I am in the pond. Show thy power, help me, for he hath plucked me into it by violence. . . . He that helped Daniel and Peter shall and will help me; I will never have help of the devil." Such instances of the revelation of an invisible truth though a visible sign were a fairly common occurrence, but only in the case of Edmund Kingesfielde's wife do we see a literal sign functioning in this manner.

The unholy state of affairs in the Kingesfielde household, of course, could not last. Kingesfielde's complacency was shattered when God "awoke as a giant refreshed with wine and smote his enemies," trapping the wicked in the "work of his own hands." God's punishment for Kingesfielde's irreverent behavior finally lit, not on Kingesfielde himself, but on his wife. Mistress Kingesfielde was judged by her neighbors to have been "not the worst of that family, yet infected . . . with the disease of the rest," carelessness in the honoring of God. She had, after all, allowed her household to lapse into great negligence in attending church and receiving communion. So, bearing the punishment for her husband and the rest of her household, she became "sore troubled in mind and assaulted with continual temptations."

Wishing to redress her offense and that of her household, Mistress Kingesfielde attended church one morning, a duty she had long neglected. During the service, however, she suddenly cried out loudly that she was destined for eternal damnation. The rest of the congregation, much amazed, attempted to calm and comfort her. After she had become a little quieter, she explained to the congregation that she had cried out because it seemed to her that "a smoke or mist came before her eyes with an extreme air of brimstone in her nose," a phenomenon that both she and her husband interpreted as the moment of her possession by a devil.

Like Anne Mylner, Mistress Kingesfielde was possessed in the moment that a corporeal but shapeless form ("a smoke or mist") enveloped her. In Mistress Kingesfielde's case, however, this cloud of evil had a definite smell, "an extreme air of brimstone." The idea that evil had a bad smell was the converse of the idea that goodness had a pleasant smell. The corpses of saints, for instance, were often reported to smell like roses. When Saint Hilarion died, his body reputedly emanated odors so fragrant that it was as if the corpse had been scented with sweet ointments. Because the early modern universe was organized according to principles of opposition, this odor of sanctity was balanced by the odor of evil, an odor that empirically demonstrated Satan's inherent uncleanness. As a creature completely corrupt and impure, Satan was presumed to delight in all types of filth and uncleanness, both physical and spiritual. His presence in the world, therefore, was often assumed to be signaled by the presence of some foul and noisome stench, often resembling that of excrement or putrefaction.

Demon possession, therefore, could sometimes be suspected or confirmed by the presence of unpleasant odors. Saint Anthony once discerned the presence of a demon within a sailor by smell alone. (Everyone else on the ship thought the stench emanated from the pickled fish in the cargo.) After the saint rebuked the demon in the name of Christ, the other sailors realized that the demon was the source of the stench. Saint Hilarion, he whose corpse was so fragrant after his death, was, in his lifetime, a famous expeller of demons. Not only could he detect the presence of a demon merely by the smell of a human body or its clothing, he could actually discern the identity of the particular demon and the nature of the demoniac's specific sin from that same smell. This particular mode of diagnosis is not surprising when we realize that the source of the stench was frequently identified as the demoniac's breath. One early modern French scholar of demon possession documented a group of possessed women, every one of whom, he reported "gave off a strongly stinking breath." In the later case of the possession of some members of the Starchy household, Margaret Byrom's breath stank so badly that she herself could not endure it, and no one could bear to come near her. During the seventeenth century, George Fox documented a woman who had been possessed for thirty-two years, reporting that her breath was so foul that "there were many Friends [Quakers] almost overcome by her with the stink that came out of her."

Returning home, Mistress Kingesfielde continued to experience "temptations and conflicts . . . and strange things befalling her." One of these strange events was an incident in which her kerchief floated above her head so that "she had much ado to keep it down," a phenomenon witnessed by her husband. More serious were her suicide attempts, in which she several times attempted to "cast herself . . . into a privy or otherwise to dispatch herself." These suicide attempts resulted from her "great grief of mind," a grief that expressed itself in a loathing and abhorrence of her own children. Eventually she became so weak in both body and mind that she took to her bed "in great extremity and peril," growing more miserable every day.

That Mistress Kingesfielde should bear the brunt of her husband's sin may seem a little unfair to us. Elizabethans, however, perceived husband and wife as one person under the law of both God and man, equally culpable in guilt. This woman's torment, as the author of the account reminded his readers, was not to be interpreted as God's punishment specifically of her, but of her household, her community. Today, psychiatrists often interpret apparent demon possession as a form of rebellion against social emphasis on restraint and self-control. The behaviors of early modern English demoniacs were largely contrary to acceptable social conduct, involving public shouting and

Hanging of a farm woman declared by the Inquisition to be possessed by demons.
From *Rappresentatione della Passione*, Florence, 1520.

raging, sexual exhibitionism, and iconoclastic or egotistic speech and behavior. Since the possessed were not held accountable for their actions, their condition liberated them from social regulation without fear of punishment. Because the new English Protestantism enabled all believers to participate directly in the spiritual life and encouraged them to express that life individually, it exerted a subversive potential in encouraging religious dissidence and social rebellion in those who normally experienced a high degree of social repression, such as women.

Women have long been perceived as particularly susceptible to ecstatic religious experiences, deriving from their contact with the supernatural world a degree of prestige and power otherwise unavailable to them. Capitalizing on widespread social perceptions of feminine weakness and passivity, demon-possessed women received attention, respect, and deference. Women were often under more social and psychological stress than were men because of patriarchal limitations on their social power. In general, women in post-Reformation England had even less social power than before the suppression of the monasteries. Although the reformers believed they had liberated women from sexual (clerical) domination by limiting their social sphere to the home alone, unmarried women essentially had no social location.

Married women endured additional stresses peculiar to wives and mothers. The infant mortality rate was very high, with one-third to one-half of all children dying before the age of five. Reformed wedding services emphasized the penitential nature of marriage, its labor and toil, in commemoration of the guilt brought to humankind through the first marriage. With marriage now perceived as the stabilizer of both individuals and society, wives shared responsibility for the bodily health, preservation of property, and intellectual and moral training of their families. The psychological burden of these responsibilities was compounded by pulpit admonitions against developing close emotional attachments in rebellious protest against the ephemeral nature of a man's life on earth ("All flesh is grass"). Early modern preacher William Gouge warned wives not to address their husbands by affectionate nicknames such as "Sweetheart" or "Dear."

Mistress Kingesfielde's suicide attempts and abhorrence of her own children appear to our modern eyes to be symptoms of postpartum depression or, particularly in light of her other manifestations, of postpartum psychosis. These diagnoses and their conceptual backgrounds, of course, would not be developed for many years to come and were therefore not available as explanations to Mistress Kingesfielde or those who cared about her. The explanation more readily available to the English Elizabethan mind was "melancholy." Copiously documented in various early modern journals and other contemporary accounts, this form of despair (which often manifested itself in a feeling that one's body was inhabited by demons) afflicted many early modern people.

As defined in early modern usage, melancholy was a condition characterized by anxiety, depression, fear, chronic fatigue, or any combination of these symptoms. It was thought to be precipitated by an excess of black bile, one of the body's four vital humors. The ultimate cause, however, was often suspected to be supernatural rather than natural. Whereas the proximate cause of any mental disorder such as hypochondria, mania, delirium, and melancholy might be humoral imbalance, the ultimate cause might be Satan. By working through nature, by controlling the body's natural processes, Satan perpetuated the illusion that he did not walk on the earth, that he did not interfere with men's lives, that he, in fact, did not exist. In perpetuating this illusion, he created earthly disorder while encouraging men to turn away from God—for, after all, if no Satan, no God.

For an individual to articulate a sense of psychological distress and communicate it to others, language is essential—language in an idiom understood by those others, whether that idiom is "ego" or "Satan." To some extent, manifestations of mental disorder and the language used to discuss it are culturally conditioned. In analyzing early modern mental disorders such as melancholy, we must remember that the vocabulary with which people discussed those disorders was considerably different from the extensive and specialized medical lexicon of modern clinical psychology. Medical explanations of mental disorder in secular terms were rare and generally focused on the people in the very highest social echelon, people who understood Latin terminology and could pay for care. Everyone else had to make do with religious explanations in terms of spiritual affliction. The early modern language of symptom description often blurred the distinction between metaphor and literal reality; to articulate a distinction between feeling *as though* a rat *were* moving around inside one and feeling *that* a rat *was* moving around inside one requires some linguistic sophistication.

Early modern melancholy frequently precipitated suicide attempts, as it did with London turner Nehemiah Wallington. This man, suffering from religious despair, reasoned that the longer he lived, the more he would sin, and the greater his eventual punishment would be. Therefore, he saw no logical reason to continue his life and a very logical reason to hasten his death. He attempted to kill himself by poison, jumping from a window, hanging, cutting his throat, and drowning. He documented stories of others' suicides as warnings particular to him, one of that class of "melancholic and solitarious" people who were most prone to the temptation of suicide. He especially noted the suicides of godly men such as the minister at Saint Mary le Bow, who hanged himself, and a Master Monk from a neighboring parish, who cut his throat because he believed that he was damned and hated by God.

Early modern minds considered suicide a heinous offense against God and thus an act of apostasy. A felony in law like any other murder, suicide was generally presumed to have been committed by a sane person at the instigation of the devil. As explained by New England minister Cotton Mather, "A self-murder, acted by one that is upon other accounts a reasonable man, is but such an attempt of revenge upon the God that made him, as none but one full of the Devil can be guilty of." Several entries for 1590 in the diary of Queen Elizabeth's court astrologer, John Dee, recount the course of the demon-induced despair and grisly suicide of a nursemaid in Dee's household, Ann Frank:

> Aug. 22, Ann, my nurse, had long been tempted by a wicked spirit, but this day it was evident how she was possessed of him. God is, hath been, and shall be her protector and deliverer! Amen. Aug. 25, Ann Frank was sorrowful, well comforted, and stayed in God's mercies acknowledging. Aug. 26, at night I anointed (in the name of Jesus) Ann Frank her breast with the holy oil. Aug. 30, in the morning she required to be anointed, and I did very devoutly prepare myself and pray for virtue and power and Christ his blessing of the oil to the expulsion of the wicked, and then twice anointed [her]. The wicked one did resist awhile. . . . Sept. 8, nurse Ann Frank would have drowned herself in my well, but by divine providence I came to take her up before she was overcome of the water. . . . Sept. 29, nurse Ann Frank most miserably did cut her own throat, [in the] afternoon about four of the clock, pretending to be in prayer before her keeper, and suddenly and very quickly rising from prayer and going toward her chamber, as the maiden her keeper thought, but indeed straight way down the stairs into the hall of the other house, behind the door, did that horrible act; and the maiden who waited on her at the stair foot followed her and missed to find her in three or four places, till at length she heard her rattle in her own blood.

Naturally, it was deemed urgent to treat melancholiacs and demoniacs before they reached the point of self-murder. Because melancholy could have both natural and supernatural causes, some believed that the best course of treatment was both physical and spiritual. Robert Burton, observing that "melancholy persons are most subject to diabolical temptations and illusions, and most apt to entertain them, and the Devil best able to work upon them," summarized opinions advocating both physic and prayer. On the one hand, he said, some authorities believed that demonic possession could be cured by medical approaches designed to rebalance the body's humors, such as purging and bleeding. On the other hand, he cited Paracelsus as saying that "spiritual diseases . . . are spiritually to be cured, and not otherwise. Ordinary means in such cases will not avail: we must not wrestle with God. . . . No striving with supreme powers, no use to make great offers to the physician. Physicians and physic can do no good, *we must submit under the mighty hand of God,* acknowledge our offenses, call to him for mercy."

The latter viewpoint was shared even by practicing physicians such as Johann Weyer, who recommended that melancholiacs and demoniacs first resort to a physician who could administer a mild purgative to rid the patient of black bile, the humor "into which the demon loves to insinuate himself, inasmuch as it is a material suited for his activities." Then, when the body has been "disburdened," a clergyman should be consulted for "the remaining steps of the cure." These steps involved the correction of the patient's spiritual faults: the reform of the dissolute person, the uplifting of the fainthearted, the conformity of the heretic, and so on. Both Burton's and Weyer's positions implied that a purely physical approach to the problem was, by itself, insufficient. This presumption of the insufficiency of earthly medicine undoubtedly derived from the poor success rate of early modern physicians in dealing with mental afflictions. Ultimately, these courses of treatment would necessarily prove useless, and their failure was probably expected.

This last blow to his wife's mental and physical health opened Edmund Kingesfielde's eyes. He now realized that his wife's affliction was God's just punishment for the ungodly behavior of him and his household, and he understood that nothing less than his own true reformation could save Mistress Kingesfielde. He therefore "devoutly gave himself to prayer, sitting sometimes the most part of the night . . . on his bare knees in his shirt." He also sought counsel from others, presumably clerics or physicians or both. Mistress Kingesfielde, however, continued in her miserable condition, lying in a perpetual sweat. Sometimes she welcomed the prayers of those who gathered at her bedside, but other times she could not bear to hear such language pronounced, so that the bystanders were forced to cease their prayers in order to relieve her physical suffering.

Aside from the literal tavern sign, another sign in this case that would have been clear to the witnesses was the fact that Mistress

Kingesfielde could sometimes not endure the sound of prayer, that her witnesses were sometimes forced to cease their praying in order to ease her physical torments. A person possessed by a demon was generally presumed to be unable to tolerate the presence or evidence of godliness. Such a person manifested this intolerance by screaming if the name of Christ were pronounced, by throwing or tearing a Bible, by insulting or striking a cleric, by denying God's existence, or by exhibiting other outrageously impious or blasphemous behavior. Since, unlike most other symptoms of demon possession, this symptom could have no medical explanation, its display was considered by many to be a certain indication of the presence of a demon. For instance, in the Throckmorton case of 1589–93 the five young daughters and seven maidservants of the household were apparently possessed for over three years. During this time, the demoniacs repeatedly manifested horror at religious activities and the presence of holy men. They could not pray or endure to hear prayers spoken (but they had no trouble playing cards). To modern eyes, such a vigorous repudiation of holiness looks like a form of protest against the endless prayers, sermons, admonitions, and catechisms of the pious Elizabethan Puritan household—households in which children were constantly steeped in the Bible and its imagery from the moment they were born. But to many early modern eyes, such a repudiation of God seemed clear evidence of the presence of Satan.

Mistress Kingesfielde's torments continued despite the prayers of her husband, household, and neighbors, and Edmund Kingesfielde was finally forced to admit what some of his critics had said all along: that his impious tavern sign had provoked God's wrath, thus unleashing a demon to possess and torture his wife. This admission made, Kingesfielde pulled down his sign. Little by little, his wife began to recover, and at the time the account of this affair was published, she was living at peace with her husband, well in body and mind. The sign that had brought so much custom to Kingesfielde's inn once more hung proudly outside the inn, enticing passersby to stop and spend some time and coins. Before being hung up again, however, it had been repainted. Instead of an image of the devil, the new sign bore an image of a woman, and instead of the "lewd posy" flaunted by the original sign, the repainted version proclaimed, "God by his word / Hath driven the devil away / Here in his stead / A woman the malt man to pay."

The anonymous writer who documented this case expressly wished his account to serve as "a bridle to stay us from wickedness, considering that those who will not be made to repent with God's great and plentiful goodness and forbearing do through the hardness and impenitence of their hearts nothing else but heap up unto themselves wrath and vengeance against the day of vengeance." Examples such as this demonstrate God's general detestation of the sin inherent in all humankind, not merely the sin of the afflicted person. We must not, says the writer, despise Mistress Kingesfielde or any other person "afflicted with God's visitation." Rather, we should understand that we are "subject to the like danger . . . and be the more careful to serve and please so mighty a God as is the God of heaven."

Chapter 4
Alexander Nyndge

A t about seven in the evening on January 20, 1573, young Alexander Nyndge of Herringswell, Suffolk, began to exhibit strange behavior in the presence of his parents, his three brothers, and other members of his household. His chest and belly began to swell, his eyes began to stare, and his back began to arch in a manner that "did strike the beholders into a strange wonder and admiration." One of his brothers, Edward, who held a Master of Arts degree in divinity from Cambridge University, immediately declared that he suspected the presence of an evil spirit. Addressing this spirit directly, Edward charged it "by the death and passion of Jesus Christ" to declare its purpose in tormenting Alexander. The spirit did not respond immediately, and its silence encouraged the tormented Alexander, who said to Edward, "Brother, he is marvelous afraid of you; therefore I pray you, stand by me." The spirit's silence and Alexander's supplication emboldened Edward, who said to his brother, "My life for thine" and "I will go to hell with thee." With this promise, the two brothers faced the enemy together.

In response to the threat of Edward's presence, the possessing spirit began its tormenting of Alexander in earnest. It racked his body "in a far more cruel manner" than before, forcing him to perform

> such strange and idle kinds of gestures in laughing, dancing, and suchlike light [frivolous] behaviors that he was suspected to be mad. Sundry times he refused all kinds of meat [food] for a long

space together, insomuch as he seemed to pine away. Sometimes he shaked [sic] as if he had had an ague. There was heard also a strange noise, as flapping from within his body. He would gather himself in a round heap under his bedclothes, and being so gathered, he would bounce up a good height from the bed and beat his head and other parts of his body against the ground and bedstead in such earnest manner that the beholders did fear that he would thereby have spoiled himself if they had not by strong hand restrained him, and yet thereby he received no hurt at all. In most of his fits he did swell in his body, and in some of them did so greatly exceed therein as he seemed to be twice so big as his natural body. He was often seen to have a certain swelling or variable lump to a great bigness, swiftly running up and down between the flesh and the skin.

This racking of Alexander by the evil spirit continued periodically for six months. Finally, on July 23, 1573, Edward determined to attempt to cast the spirit from his brother's body. To prepare the afflicted Alexander for the dispossession, Edward directed the men of the household to remove Alexander from his bed and set him in a chair. This done, Alexander was repeatedly "cast headlong upon the ground or [fell] down, drawing his lips away, gnashing with his teeth, wallowing and foaming, and the spirit would vex him monstrously and transform his body and alter the same by many violences." After each such episode, the men of the household would "lay hands on Alexander and set him in the chair again, and there hold him," at one point even binding him to the chair.

The use of physical violence against a demoniac had been a widespread practice for centuries. Mental distress of all types had often been treated with corporal discipline and punishment, such as whipping, beating, binding, and ducking. Such practices had often proved efficacious in halting the objectionable behavior of the patient, at least temporarily. These practices were also considered by many to be pious remedies, scourging the body for the sake of the soul. Since sickness was widely perceived as a manifestation of sin, the scourging of the sickness was tantamount to a scourging of the sin. What may seem a harsh treatment of others to us was no more than many practiced on themselves for the sake of their own souls, taking it upon themselves to inflict upon their own bodies the punishment that they knew they deserved in the eyes of God. Flagellant groups were common throughout Europe from the thirteenth through the seventeenth centuries. Some exorcists doubted the efficacy of corporal punishment, perceiving the demoniac's protests as pretence on the demon's part to ridicule the exorcist's impotence and cause the demoniac even more pain. Many, however, believed that such physical violence was efficacious in humiliating the demon.

Such practices were rare in English Protestant dispossessions, so the binding of Alexander Nyndge to his chair was an unusual feature of this case. But Catholic exorcists who continued to perform secret exorcisms in England throughout the early modern era sometimes continued the practice. The best-known case was that of the exorcisms conducted at Denham in 1585. During the many months that these exorcisms continued, Father Robert Dibdale many times bound Sarah Williams, Fid Williams, and Anne Smith into their chairs so that they could not move while the exorcists went about their work. Indeed, Anne Smith later claimed that she was bound so tightly during this experience that for three years afterwards she was forced to swaddle her body against the chronic soreness created by the priests' ligatures. As late as 1663, a demon thought to be possessing the body of a woman ridiculed this practice, thus indicating that it was still in use, by asserting, "Doctor Woodhouse would have cast us out, but he could not; . . . let not him think a few slaps will expel Satan."

Once Alexander was secure, his brother Edward initiated his interrogation of the possessing demon. "Thou foul fiend," said Edward, "I conjure thee, in the name of Jesus our savior, the son of almighty God, that thou speak unto us." The demon remained silent but showed his displeasure by transforming Alexander "very ugly against his chest, swelling upwards to his throat, [and] plucking his belly just to his back." The tormented Alexander said that the demon was trying to speak to him (Alexander) alone, and he begged his brother and the others present to prevent this from happening by prayer, which they did.

In his account, Edward Nyndge three times used the word "conjure" to refer to the act of ordering the demon to leave his brother's body. At this time the account was written, the year 1573, the study and practice of conjuration and other magical arts were fashionable topics of debate among some of the young men attending

Oxford and Cambridge, with some of the students advocating such study for the advancement of human knowledge and others opposed to it as contrary to God's will. Edward Nyndge probably picked up his use of the word "conjure" in this environment. It had, however, a long history of association with the practice of exorcism.

To the Protestant eye, conjuration and traditional Catholic exorcism were nearly indistinguishable practices. Both were usually practiced by priests who addressed demons with formal commands, adjuring those demons to perform specific acts. The difference between the two practices lay in the nature of those acts. Whereas the formal command in an exorcism was for the demon to depart the body of the demoniac, the formal command in a conjuration was for the demon to perform some other act, such as revealing the location of buried treasure or afflicting an enemy with misfortune. The words generally used in the formal commands for both practices—*conjuro, adjuro,* and *exorcizo*—were virtually interchangeable with each other and with other words meaning "I command." Both practices used the same form, beginning with the declaration ("I conjure you"), the address to the evil spirit, the invocations of holy names, and the instruction to the spirit. Thus, we see that, whether the intent was to summon or evict the demon, the practices of conjuration and exorcism were practically identical. Simply put, conjurors and exorcists seemed the same because both claimed to command the devil.

In 1561, Francis Coxe published a treatise on the recent history of the practice of the black arts in England. In this treatise, Coxe assumed that his reader would agree with his premise that popular interest and belief in magical arts had grown considerably since the accession of Elizabeth two years previously because of the popularity of the prophecies of Nostradamus. Coxe observed that during the previous (Catholic) regime, the "godly and wholesome law" against conjuring had not been enforced; indeed, many made their living openly by conjuring. In this treatise, Coxe uses the terms "conjurer" and "exorcist" interchangeably, deeming both practitioners of "necromancy." Furthermore, Coxe cited Leviticus as his authority for defining conjurers as "rebellious traitors" who deserve death. Coxe's list of activities performed by "conjurers" included fumigations, invocations, and maledictions, all of which had been part of the Roman Catholic arsenal against demons for centuries.

To many post-Reformation English ears, therefore, the Catholic connotations of the practice of conjuration implicated it as an unlawful, heretical, and treasonable activity. After all, a demon conjured by a Catholic priest might reveal the location of buried treasure to fund a Spanish or French (i.e., Catholic) war against England. Indeed, the relationship between conjuration and treason was so clear in the eyes of the Protestant establishment that a statutory felony adopted in 1563 made the conjuring of spirits punishable by death on the first offense. In 1606, this statute was interpreted by the author of a popular legal handbook in this way: "To consult, covenant with, entertain, employ, feed, or reward, any evil spirit, is felony." Two decades later, however, the definition had become much broader: "A conjurer is he that by the holy and powerful names of Almighty God invokes and conjures the devil to consult with him, or to do some act"—this last phrase clearly encompassing the act of exorcism.

The demon within the body of Alexander Nyndge, angered at the opposition of Edward Nyndge, finally spoke. In a "bass sounding and hollow voice," it asserted that it would speak to Alexander: "I will, I will, I will." Edward responded, "Thou shalt not, and I charge thee in the name of Jesus Christ that thou speak unto us and not unto him." The spirit responded in its hollow voice, addressing Alexander, "Why did you tell them? Why did you tell them?" Edward, as before, charged the spirit to speak to him, not to the tormented Alexander, and commanded it to declare the reason for its action. The spirit, rather predictably, said that it had come for Alexander's soul. Edward responded, "We have a warrant in the holy Scriptures that such as do earnestly repent them of their sins and turn unto God with the only hope of salvation through the merits of Jesus Christ, you may not have them, for Christ is [their] redeemer." The spirit replied, again in "in a bass hollow-sounding voice, 'Christ, that was my redeemer.'" Edward immediately took up the shift in pronoun and verb tense, saying, "Christ, that is his redeemer, not thy redeemer, but my brother Alexander his redeemer."

The demon, even more angered, responded, "I will have his soul and body too," and began to rack Alexander more horribly than ever before, "forcing him to such strange and fearful skriking [screeching] as cannot be uttered by man's power." In this new fit, Alexander exhibited "such strength as sometimes four or five men, though they

Witch turned werewolf attacking travelers. Woodcut by Hans Weiditz. From Dr. Johann Geiler von Kaysersberg's Die Emeis *(The Ants), printed by Johann Grüninger, Strassburg, 1517.*

had much advantage against him by binding him to a chair, yet could they not rule him." In his struggles against these men, Alexander was never perceived to "pant or blow," seeming not to strain his strength or to struggle at all. He wept copiously, producing tears "in great abundance." He laughed loudly through his closed mouth. Sometimes he was "heaved up from the ground by force invisible," despite having six grown men trying to restrain him.

When the strength of the evil force waned temporarily and the men were again able to confine Alexander to the chair, one of his other brothers cheekily addressed the demon, "We will keep him from thee, thou foul spirit, in despite of thy nose." The demon responded, "Will you, sir? Will you, sir?" Edward replied, "Not I, sir, but the merits of Jesus Christ will," and the entire company of twenty or more knelt to say the Lord's Prayer, Edward insuring that no saints' names were invoked. The spirit roared "with a fearful voice," at which Edward asked the town's curate, Peter Bencham, to "conjure and charge" the demon in the name of Christ to tell them where it came from and what its name was.

Through Alexander Nyndge, the demon spoke in a hollow, bass voice, occasionally roaring or barking. Voice alterations of various types were a common characteristic of early modern demon possession, with one of the most common of these being the creation of animal noises. A few early modern physicians were able to offer medical hypotheses to explain such behavior in psychophysical terms. For instance, sixteenth-century physician Levinus Lemnius attributed this behavior to latent memories aroused by vehement cerebral stimulation. Such explanations, however, were not widely known or accepted.

Before the development of modern taxonomic systems for classifying biological species, the early modern mind perceived the boundary between man and beast to be fragile and easily violated. The perceived fragility of this boundary was demonstrated in the great number of published accounts reporting the birth of hybrid offspring to humans who had allegedly coupled with dogs, rabbits, pigs, or other non-human animals. Such boundary violation had serious implications for the future of man's salvation, because only human beings, no other earthly creatures, were thought to possess immortal souls. For a person to behave bestially, as if subhuman, was an indication of spiritual danger—not necessarily just for the person exhibiting the behavior but also for that person's family or neighbors. Thus, when Alexander Nyndge's possessing demon roared and barked, this noise could have been interpreted by Nyndge's witnesses as a significantly negative comment on the sad spiritual condition of their whole community.

Unresponsive but apparently uncomfortable with its situation, the demon mumbled, "I would come out, I would come out." Again, Edward charged it in the name of Christ to say its name and home, and, for the first time, it answered his questions: its name was Aubon, it said, and it came from Ireland. The demon's French name and Irish origin confirmed what the brothers had suspected all along: this was a Catholic demon using all his power to bludgeon Alexander into capitulating to "Popish" superstition.

One of the most striking features of this account is Edward Nyndge's lengthy interrogation of the demon. This interrogation derived from a practice of great antiquity—the "questioning and rebuking" of the demon—that dated back at least as far as the Roman practice of exorcism in the second century. Later, in medieval Catholic exorcisms, the questioning of the demon by the exorcist was still considered a form of judicial inquiry, as hostile and savage as necessary to intimidate the demon into confessing the truth of God's power. Even today, both Catholic and Pentecostal exorcists routinely interrogate a possessing demon, believing this course of action—the exchange of speech—to be a necessary concession to the idea that the exorcist's adversary is an intelligent presence. One example of an early modern Catholic exorcism in which such an interrogation was carried out involved a French noblewoman. From her possessing demon the exorcists successfully elicited the following information: his name (Mahonin); his rank (third hierarchy, second order of archangels); his primary divine adversary (Saint Mark), his place of birth (Beziers, a town in Languedoc); when he had entered the body (on the third Tuesday of the previous Easter); and what sign he would give when he departed the body (he would throw a stone from the tower into the water of the moat). It was particularly important for the exorcist to learn the rank of the possessing demon. That rank not only contributed to the prestige of the exorcist (the higher the demon's rank, the more prestigious its exorcism was), it also determined the conditions under which the demon might be expelled: "Marquesses may be bound from the ninth hour till compline and from compline till the end of the day. Dukes may be bound from the first hour till noon [if] clear weather is to be observed. . . . Counts or earls may be bound at any hour of the day, [as long as] it be in the woods or fields where men resort not."

One of the primary purposes of such an interrogation was to trick or force the possessing demon into revealing its name. The idea that an evil spirit's power lay largely in the secrecy of its name was a very ancient one, documented in many cultures and religions since before the time of Christ and manifesting itself more recently in fairy tales such as "Rumpelstiltzkin." For a person to discover the name of any supernatural being was to gain control over that being and force it into submission. A demon's confession of its name was, therefore, tantamount to a confession that it was of Satan's party, not God's, and that its goal was malign rather than benign. After such a confession, a demon's influence over its listeners would be greatly diminished, so an exorcist who forced a possessing demon to admit its name was perceived to have won a significant battle in the war with that demon. The exorcist's response to such a confession was generally to ignore or parody the name, thus undermining the demon's identity, instead bestowing on the demon a long list of pejorative epithets intended to wound his pride, which had been Satan's worst sin in his challenge to

God. An early modern book of exorcisms listed several pages of such epithets from which an exorcist might choose in his attempt to humiliate a possessing demon: "lustful and stupid one . . . lean sow . . . famine-stricken and filthiest . . . thou wrinkled beast, thou mangy beast, thou beast of all beasts the most beastly . . . thou bestial and foolish drunkard . . . most abominable whisperer . . . filthy sow . . . envious crocodile . . . swollen toad . . . lowest of the low . . . cudgelled ass!"

Besides addressing the demon with demeaning epithets, exorcists used other forms of taunts and insults to accomplish the task of undermining the demon's pride and self-confidence. An exorcist might, for instance, draw a caricature of the demon on paper (identifying the caricature with the demon's hard-won name, of course) and then burn the paper, spit on it, or defile it with excrement. In the case of the later demoniac Richard Dugdale, who danced wildly as a manifestation of his possession, the ministers attempting Dugdale's dispossession belittled the possessing demon in this manner:

> Canst thou dance no better, Satan? Ransack the old records of all past times and places in thy memory; canst thou not there find out some other way of finer trampling? Pump thine invention dry! Cannot that universal seed-plot of subtle wiles and stratagems spring up one new method of cutting capers? Is this the top of skill and pride to shuffle feet, and brandish knees thus, and to trip like a doe, and skip like a squirrel, and wherein differs thy leapings from the hoppings of a frog, or bounces of a goat, or friskings of a dog, or gesticulations of a monkey? And cannot a palsey shake such a loose leg as that? Doest not thou twirl like a calf that has the turn?

This ancient Catholic practice of demeaning the demon continued even in some early modern English Protestant cases, in which the dispossessors or the demoniacs themselves carried on long exchanges with their possessing demons, exchanges that demonstrated the strong faith and correct theological understanding of the questioner. For instance, the demoniac Thomas Darling engaged in considerable conversation with his possessing demon:

> I charge thee by the living God to tell me who sent thee. Dost thou tell me thy mistress sent thee? What is thy mistress's name? Dost

thou say thou wilt not tell me before tomorrow? And why, I pray thee, wilt thou not? Dost thou say thou wilt torment me twice more? Do thy worst; my hope is in the living God, and he will deliver me out of thy hands. . . . And dost thou say my faith is but weak? Sathan, it is too strong for thee to overthrow. Dost thou say thou wilt torment me worse then ever thou hast done? Do thou thy worst; my trust is in the Lord my God.

Darling then thanked God "for that he had somewhat revealed his enemy Satan unto him, and beseeching him to continue his goodness in manifesting him more plainly." The theatrical advantage of such a conversation, of course, was to reveal the situation to the bystanders, who did not have the advantage of hearing Satan's voice.

Most early modern Protestants, however, were deeply suspicious of carrying on such an interrogation. What was the point of asking questions of Satan? He was the father of lies, so his answers would clearly be designed to mislead and entrap the listeners into further sin. For this reason, Thomas Darling's own pastor tried (unsuccessfully) to persuade Darling to refrain from conversing with his possessing demon. This conduct of an interrogation of the demon during a dispossession was considered by many Protestants to be impious, abominable super-stition. To discuss any point of religion or truth with the devil was an illegitimate activity, one that Christ never conducted during his many exorcisms. Satan, they thought, *wanted* men to call upon him, to beseech him for favors, to worship him. The more theologically educated Protestants even cited Catholic authorities on this point, observing that Origen and Chrysostom discouraged the interrogation of devils, an act that implicitly awarded them more respect than was their due. Rather than treat demons as intelligent beings whose say deserved a hearing, the dispossessor should treat them as mere vermin, as pests, by refusing to acknowledge them to their faces and asking God to dispel them as one might ask him to dispel any other plague.

When Edward Nyndge "laid the fourth chapter of Saint Matthew against" the demon Aubon, reminding him that he should worship God alone and not Satan, Aubon defended the latter: "My master, my master; I am his disciple, I am his disciple." Edward responded, "Thy master we grant he is, but thou liest; thou art none of his disciple. Thou art only an instrument and scourge to punish the wicked so far as pleaseth him." When Edward reminded Aubon that Christ had cast many devils out of afflicted people, Aubon contemptuously replied, "Bow-wow, bow-wow," causing Alexander's body to transform "monstrously . . . much like the picture of the Devil in a play, with a horrible roaring voice, sounding [like a] hell-hound."

Aubon's barking reminds us that Elizabethans viewed dogs rather differently than we do. As an early modern emblematic common-place, the dog immediately and graphically conveyed to the Nyndge brothers and their contemporaries a range of negative abstractions such as greed, idleness, lust, discontent, fear, revenge, and anger. No doubt, these negative associations derived partially from fears for public health and safety. Dogs were extremely numerous in early modern towns, creating noise and stench, harassing and attacking passersby. The great majority of these dogs were not pets trained to behave civilly but guard dogs, bull-baiters, turnspits, and strays. When these urban dog populations got out of hand, the authorities routinely ordered mass slaughters of dogs, particularly during out-breaks of plague. Although other animals, such as cats and pigs, were also theoretically regulated in the same way and for the same reasons, in practice dogs were often singled out, with enormous numbers killed. For instance, in London during 1584–86, nearly 1,900 dogs were killed; during the high-plague summer of 1636, about 3,700; during the last major London outbreak in 1665, nearly 4,400. This singling out of dogs for slaughter also owed something to scapegoat psychology as well as to public health concerns. Dogs served as a focus for social anxiety more than other animals did. They personified human beings as they shared human spaces, food, and names. Dog slaughter was thus a symbolic suppression of bestial behavior in people, a suppression that was a primary goal of both religion and government. This symbolic substitution of dogs for people was emphasized by the fact that ladies' lapdogs and the hounds of the gentry were excluded from the dog slaughters, thus reinforcing human social stratification and authority. The dog massacres symbolized people's fear of, and desire to control, the more bestial aspects of their own social relationships.

In several cases of demon possession, dogs figured prominently as symbols of human bestiality. In the case of Robert Brigges, for instance, the demoniac was persecuted by an eerie black dog that followed and stared at him. This dog was described as ugly, shaggy-haired, "of a dark fusky color between black and red," with "terrible sparkling eyes," and possessed of an uncanny intelligence and life force. Brigges kicked the dog, hurled stones at it, and had a nearby laborer hit it with a spade, but it refused to go away. Brigges fled into a nearby house and hid for an hour. But when he emerged, the dog was still waiting. Terrified, Brigges got a boat to go back home, and the dog vanished. Furthermore, in Brigges' case, Satan himself was frequently the subject of simile or metaphor comparing him to a dog: his speech was "as the barking of a dog"; he knew only "as much as a dog touching the secrets of God"; he was a "dog's snout," "a stinking dog," a "kennel raker." He used dogs to hunt down Brigges' soul, threatening Brigges with his kennel of fearful "bandogs" (fierce bloodhounds or mastiffs) and fire-spitting "tykes" (mongrels), a kennel that included even Cerberus, the three-headed watchdog of Hades: "For here are good store of dogs of all sorts, long-tailed tykes, trundle [curly-tailed] tykes, and tykes of a size . . . This is a dog of all dogs, a triple-headed dog," a dog that, according to Eliza-bethan divine Edward Topsell, signified a "multiplicity of devils." The symbolic dogs of Elizabethan demoniacs existed within a widespread folklore tradition of terrible supernatural dogs, a tradition embracing the church grim, the skriker, the padfoot, the dandy dog, the gabriel ratchet, the wish hound, and many others—all dogs associated with Satan and his quest for souls.

At this point in the possession of Alexander Nyndge, about 11 P.M. (after the company had been assembled for four hours), Edward Nyndge ordered the window to be opened, saying, "I trust in God . . . the foul spirit is weary of our company"—a theatrical rather than a necessary gesture, given that the demon was tenuous enough to leave the house through any tiny chink in roof, floor, or wall. Two minutes later, Alexander's body and behavior returned to normal, and he leaped up, holding up his hands in joy, crying, "He is gone, he is gone! Lord, I thank thee." The company fell on its knees, praised God for Alexander's deliverance, and went to supper.

The struggle was not over, however. At about 4 A.M., Alexander was heard to speak to Aubon in apparent capitulation: "I will go, I will go." Edward, presumably sleeping in the same room, awoke and admon-ished Alexander, urging him to repeat the prayer, "Speak for me, my savior Jesus Christ," whenever he felt the approach of the demon. Alexander, trembling and fearful, repeated this prayer many times, his belly swelling a little for about thirty minutes. The two brothers prayed together for a while, and finally Alexander slept again.

Aubon was not yet defeated. At about 8 A.M., Alexander once more manifested his painful symptoms and cried out, "Help me, brother Edward, and all you that be my friends, and pray for me, for this foul fiend will come into me, whether I will or no." At this point, he "made an horrible spitting, his belly being swelled as before" and the terrible voice roared from within him while the assembled household again prayed for his deliverance. Finally, the company witnessed a sign: Alexander's left ear, into which Edward had been whispering his prayers and encouragement all along, "suddenly wrinkled like a clung walnut which falleth from the tree before it be ripe." Undaunted by this loss of his conduit to Alexander's consciousness, Edward moved around to the right side of Alexander's head and continued pouring his prayers into Alexander's remaining ear, addressing Aubon thus: "We conjure thee, in the name of Jesus Christ our savior, and the son of the almighty God, that thou depart and no longer torment the said Alexander." Shortly thereafter, Alexander stood up and declared, "He is gone, he is gone," and the two brothers joined in hearty prayers of thanks. Aubon had finally gone, and Alexander was never again known to "be perplexed with the like terrible vexations."

This final attack confirmed an early modern theory that demonic repossession commonly followed exorcism or dispossession and that the subsequent repossession frequently constituted a worse affliction than the original possession. The Protestant dispossessor John Darrell would later warn that, once cast out, the devil would surely return; and, if the dispossessed person were as a "house empty, swept and garnished" (i.e., with a heart empty of faith, open to further evil), he would surely be repossessed. For instance, a famous story of Saint Bernard's exorcising a possessed woman told how, despite the saint's kindness and consideration toward the demon, commiserating with him and inviting him to leave the woman to rejoin his old friends (the other demons), the ungrateful possessing spirit almost immediately repossessed the woman "worse than before." Similarly, the demoniacs Katherine Wright, Thomas Darling, and William Somers were all repossessed following their dispossessions by Darrell, exhibiting the expected "worse than before" pattern.

Title page showing the jaws of Hell with Lucifer and Satan.
From the *Livre de la Deablerie*, printed by Michel Le Noir, Paris, 1568.

The account of Alexander Nyndge's affliction by the demon Aubon was subsequently written by the demoniac's brother, Edward, who had performed the dispossession. Edward opened this account by displaying his theological erudition in a long explication of the nature of Satan, who, Edward reminded us, was originally an angel, "full of power and glory." When Satan sinned and was cast from heaven, "he was utterly deprived of glory and preserved for judgment," but he lost none of the power with which he was created. To this day, said Edward, Satan retains the same power as that of other angels, who "are very mighty and strong, far above all earthly creatures in the world." Satan has "such power and authority that he is called the god of the world. His kingdom is bound and enclosed within certain limits, for he is the prince but of darkness. But yet within his said dominion (which is in ignorance of God) he exercises a mighty tyranny. Our savior compares him to a strong man, armed, who keeps his castle." Furthermore, since angels are far beyond man in understanding and wisdom, the same is true for Satan: "He has searched out and knows all the ways that may be to deceive. So that if God should not chain him up, his power and subtlety joined together would overcome and seduce the whole world." The multitudes of infernal spirits are single in purpose (to hate God and man), so they are referred to collectively as "the Devil." Edward Nyndge's view that the multitudes of infernal spirits are single in purpose (to hate God and man) and thus are collectively known as one entity (the devil) reflected the opinion of many post-Reformation English Protestants that demons serve only to enforce Satan's will, and are therefore merely manifestations or extensions of him. In fact, some early modern clerics explicitly denied that evil spirits could be differentiated from each other because such differentiation would imply order and classification rather than the chaos that is Hell.

Edward Nyndge believed that his brother's case was "worthy to be remembered both for example and warning." The interpretation of an event such as Alexander Nyndge's conflict with Aubon was essential to that event's function as a public exemplum, as were all such cases of personal misfortune, the Elizabethans prizing communal moral and theological education far above individual privacy. Was the demoniac possessed by God, Satan, or both? If he claimed to be possessed by God, was he to be perceived as a saint, as a benighted victim of the disguised Satan, or as a willful heretic spewing blasphemy? If, on the other hand, he seemed to be possessed by Satan, could the devil's word be trusted? Although the father of lies, Satan was also known to speak the truth sometimes, as attested by Scripture. If the truth, was it the whole truth, forced from his unwilling lips by the presence or name of God? Alternatively, was it a partial truth, intended to lull and mislead bystanders into unwitting heresy? If the theological assertions of the possessing spirit ran counter to the known beliefs of the demoniac or his witnesses, were those assertions to be interpreted as God's revelation of his truth or as Satan's ironic inversion of that truth? If it was agreed that the demoniac was possessed by Satan, was he a sinner being punished by God (like Saul) or a saint being tested and refined (like Job)? If, during his possession, the demoniac mimed the seven deadly sins for his audience, did he embody those sins himself, or did God judge his audience to do so? Although all agreed that such cases of spiritual affliction were exempla, they often disagreed on what each case was an exemplum of.

In concluding his summary of this case, Edward Nyndge said that his brother's case was "worthy to be remembered both for example and warning. For describing the horror and unheard of misery that fell upon him, we may be thereby drawn to descend into ourselves and to look into our souls betimes, lest heaven pour down the vials of wrath upon us." The concept of such a spiritual descent derived from a common metaphor much in use by early modern theologians. For instance, Arthur Dent thought that men must "look downward" into their souls to comprehend "experimentally" the sufferings of Job, David, and Christ. William Perkins likewise conceptualized the introspection necessary to gain a better assurance of salvation as a "descent," a metaphor implying the necessity for a soul's journey into despair before passing into joy. Perkins perceived conscience as both "a little God" and "a little hell," explaining that "holy desperation" was the necessary "hammer" with which people must break their own "stony hearts" in order to be receptive to God's mercy.

Chapter 5
Robert Brigges

Shortly before Christmas, 1573, a wealthy gentleman named Robert Brigges (pronounced "Bridges") attended a theological lecture in London. The lecture concerned the subject of unforgivable sin, and Brigges became much troubled by the suspicion that he himself was an irredeemable sinner, hated by God, and doomed to eternal damnation. Returning home despondent from the lecture, Brigges gradually became more and more convinced of his own damnation. He attempted suicide several times over the next few months by several means, including hanging, stabbing, and drowning. Becoming more hallucinatory and depressed as the days wore on, Brigges was finally attended by a physician, who diagnosed him as excessively melancholy and prescribed bleeding, purging, and an unspecified "physic." This course of treatment initially benefited Brigges, but the good effects were only temporary, and he continued to fall more deeply into despair. On April 11, 1574 (Easter Sunday), Brigges swallowed an "ordinary potion" which he had used before with no problem, but this time he vomited the medicine and swooned, remaining senseless for twelve hours.

The next morning, Brigges gradually began to lose his sight (a loss accompanied by great pain), then his hearing, and finally his feeling. The bystanders tested the loss of this last sense by pricking and pinching his flesh and touching his eyeballs with their fingers, coming to the conclusion that in his fit he differed "nothing from a dead man but that he spoke and drew breath." Then, quite surprisingly, Brigges began to expound quickly and authoritatively on the Ten Commandments. His language was so remarkable (particularly because he was known to have read very little Scripture) that a scribe was appointed to keep a record of his words, but he sometimes spoke so rapidly that his words were lost. During this speech, he paused occasionally as though to listen to an opponent's arguments, then responded by framing answers designed to confute those arguments. His speech was accompanied by violent emotional shifts as he quickly moved from weeping, to laughing, to raging. Gradually, the bystanders came to understand that, although Brigges was occasionally hearing and responding to the voices of God and Jesus, the bulk of his discourse was with Satan.

This day established a pattern that Brigges followed for seven more days, with the time of daily onset and pattern of his afflictions so regular that he became a local show, with people crowding his room each morning. These bystanders watched during the many hours of Brigges' daily battle with Satan, dispersing only when Brigges finally said the Lord's Prayer and the creed, praying to have his senses restored. Each day they observed as Brigges' sight and hearing returned gradually as he rubbed his eyes and temples, a restoration requiring at least half an hour and accompanied by extreme pain. During this week, Satan alternately tempted Brigges to commit various sins and accused him of having already committed them. Pointing out that Brigges was predestined to either salvation or damnation and that his behavior was therefore irrelevant to his soul's destination, Satan argued that he might as well follow whatever sinful course of action he chose. Satan supported this argument by citing Scripture to prove that Brigges was already damned because of his wealth. Brigges, resisting, countered that refraining from sin was a mark of the elect: "What, wouldst thou have me run that course: do I what I will, I am predestined either to be damned, or to be saved? . . . No, no, I will not tempt my Lord my God so." Nothing daunted, Satan, over the course of the week, tempted Brigges to greed, murder, blasphemy, despair, idolatry, heresy, and atheism.

These concepts register very differently in most modern minds than they did in the minds of Brigges and his contemporaries. To a great many of us, murder registers primarily as a criminal offense, a felony in law, secondarily as a moral disruption of the social order. Greed registers as a social impropriety; despair, as a psycho-medical affliction treatable with counseling assisted by Prozac. Idolatry, blasphemy, and heresy barely register at all, and indeed, many modern educated people are hard-pressed even to define these terms with any modicum of accuracy, much less to perceive them as serious offenses. Atheism, though perceived by some as socially provocative or spiritually deadening, nonetheless registers in many modern minds as a legitimate choice. To Brigges and his contemporaries, however, these attitudes and behaviors were not ethical, moral, legal, or social missteps; they were *sins,* heinous offenses against God himself, deliberate floutings of his word, willful rejections of the innocent Christ's bloody sacrifice for humankind's sake. This concept is central to our understanding of Brigges' experience.

A modern reader cannot hope to understand Brigges' affliction without acknowledging that it derived from religious conflict and therefore required a solution derived from religious reconciliation. Modern psychiatric labels, the product of today's secular medical establishment, do not adequately explain or even accurately describe the state of mind of Robert Brigges as he strove with Satan during the spring of 1574. The inadequacy of such labels stems from their inability to comprehend the centuries-old idea that man's afflictions are the result and manifestation of sin. No approach to early modern demon possession that ignores or trivializes this idea can hope to access the mental state of the sufferer with a modicum of historical understanding.

Anthropologists have long observed that in many cultures the symptoms of illness manifest themselves in a communal religious idiom. Religious societies share a nearly universal belief that affliction, especially affliction manifesting itself in mental distress, indicates the fallen spiritual condition of the afflicted person or of his community. Christian theology has always posited as a fundamental principle that sickness and sin are related because illness and death entered the world together with man's fall from grace. Evil is the cause of all afflictions, both spiritual (sin) and physical (disease). If a person is freed from the evil that afflicts him, he becomes whole again in both body and soul. Martin Luther, for instance, characterized sinners as lunatic and demon-possessed; Paracelsus believed that the madness and possession of sinners were signs of their alienation from God. During Brigges' time, many famous sermons were preached to argue the correspondence between insanity and sin. To understand the mind of Robert Brigges, we must acquaint

Lucifer beginning to reign over the souls of sinners. Illustration by John Baptist Medina for John Milton's Paradise Lost, *London, 1688.*

ourselves with—and temporarily accept—the concepts that furnished that mind. That Brigges' torment was the direct and just result of sin was perhaps the most important of those concepts.

The temptation to greed began with Satan's accusation that Brigges had sold his soul for money, with Satan displaying a signed and sealed document attesting to that sale. Brigges hotly denied the accusation, countering that Satan had forged his signature on the document. Over the course of the week, Satan intermittently continued to attempt to bribe Brigges with fine clothes, plate, bags of money, land, and a ship laden with gold, and alternated these profferings with threats of impoverishment if he did not submit.

Satan's temptation to murder invited Brigges to assassinate the queen's chief minister, William Cecil, Lord Burghley. Brigges refused, referring to Burghley as "a pillar of this land" and worthy of all the blessings that God had bestowed on him, contending that God had "made a hedge" about Burghley to protect him against Satan's merest touch. Perhaps the impetus for this particular temptation was the October 11 assassination attempt of the previous year by Peter Brychett on Sir Christopher Hatton, another of the queen's privy councilors. Clearly motivated by religious animosity, Brychett, a fervent nonconforming Protestant, perceived Hatton as "a willful Papist" whose powerful government position rendered him dangerous to the country. Since Brychett belonged to the same professional society as Brigges, they very likely knew each other, and this incident may have planted the seed of Brigges' own temptation to kill Burghley.

Satan also tempted Brigges to swear and to blaspheme God's name, to deny God's existence, to trust in Satan or in himself rather than in God, to interpret Scripture falsely, to deny Christ's divinity, humanity, and even his legitimacy, to believe God a liar, to believe that scriptural miracles were mundane magic tricks. Playing on Brigges' desperate state, Satan tempted Brigges to even greater despair, attempting to persuade him that God hated him and refused to hear his prayers, to know that God despised him as a sinner. Encouraging him to commit suicide, Satan offered him a noose and a dagger, both of which Brigges rejected.

Satan's tempting of Brigges to idolatry was an overt bid to reclaim Brigges for the Roman Catholic Church. Satan said that Brigges was damned because he trusted in faith alone rather than in good works.

The Protestant position was that God's first covenant with man, the covenant of works, had been replaced by virtue of Christ's sacrifice with the new covenant of grace. The old covenant constituted a contract for man's performance, a quid pro quo, a form of wages, thus implicitly assigning to Adam, Noah, and Abraham the status of God's servants, to be rewarded or punished according to their performance. The new covenant, on the other hand, constituted God's unconditional promise of grace, a gift to his children regardless of their behavior. This was the Protestant doctrine that Satan attacked Brigges for embracing.

Satan accused Brigges of subscribing to a "new" religion and tempted him to worship idols and to pray to saints, pointing out that many learned men, including some of Brigges' own countrymen, were Catholics. On the accusation of the novelty of his religion—a perpetual sore point with the Protestants—Brigges countered: "Thou liest falsely; it is the true and ancient religion, though by the subtle devices of Antichrist it hath been suppressed for a time." As explained by Bishop John Jewel, the most "spitefully spoken" accusation against any religion at the time was that it was new—that is, man-made, artificial, false, lacking God's authority; "as there can be no change in God himself, so ought there to be no change in his religion."

In addition to mere argument, Satan also attempted to bring Brigges around through intimidation, threatening to destroy Brigges' friends and family, to suffocate him by thrusting his fist into his mouth, to burn him or tear him to pieces. Satan also attempted to strip Brigges of his earthly spiritual comfort by attacking the popular cleric John Foxe, Brigges' spiritual ideal, accusing Foxe of adultery, betrayal, bewitchment, hypocrisy, and blasphemy. Satan's most sophisticated temptation during this week was to challenge Brigges to a debate on the question of God's existence. Satan posited the thesis that God does not exist and that everything occurs "by the course of nature"—that is, without the direction of intelligence, that earthly events are not precipitated by an act of divine will but rather follow some blind, random pattern of natural law. He then challenged Brigges to disprove this thesis and to prove the existence of God, a challenge that Brigges took up with great enthusiasm.

In response to these various temptations, Brigges countered with arguments from Scripture and logic, resisting with much spirit. He cited examples of God's mercy toward sinners as shown, for instance, in the parables of the prodigal son and the lost sheep. He prayed and sang to keep his spirits up. At one point, he heard the voice of God encouraging him to stand fast against Satan's arguments and threats.

Raised a Catholic, Brigges was experiencing a religious conversion. The early modern Protestant mind would have perceived this conversion as an act redounding to the glory of God, not to the credit of Brigges. The unregenerate sinner was powerless to perform the slightest salutary act, much less initiate the process of his own salvation. Thus, Brigges' conversion would have been perceived as a demonstration of the power of God, who had finally opened Brigges' ears and heart to grace. Such a conversion was essential to salvation, constituting a sinner's necessary transition from the state of nature into which he had been born into a state of grace. Those who never experienced this turning to God died as they had been born, with all their sins upon them, unredeemed by Christ's sacrifice, forever damned to perdition.

Given the intensely sensitive religious climate of the time, such conversions were fairly common, generally following a fairly predictable pattern. A conversion might be precipitated by a sinner's recognition of his inherent depravity, a recognition that overwhelmed him with helplessness and despair, convincing him that he was indeed the chief of sinners and that he could do nothing to escape damnation. This intense spiritual struggle mirrored Christ's agony on the cross, an agony that he had willingly assumed for man's sake. This feeling might last months or years; indeed, many initiates never progressed beyond it to a later stage of peace and acceptance.

A religious conversion was sometimes marked by great emotional upheaval, its primary emotional response being fear. Some preachers deliberately attempted to induce this fear in an effort to initiate the conversion process, reminding each congregant that he or she was a "worthless worm," a "filthy nothing," a "half-devil," a "guilty wretch . . . sleeping on the brink of hell." Groaning, trembling, shaking, swooning, shrieking, falling into trances, and weeping were often considered evidence of the operation of divine grace. This instigation of frightening self-examination was necessary, it was thought, for the sinner's hardened shell of pride and complacency to crack and splinter, thus opening his heart to grace. An individual's ostentatiously public sacrifice of the cautious and guarded social persona in favor of a showy display of individual vulnerability could serve to mobilize the

emotions of the crowd, to demonstrate the truth of the relevant doctrines and thus win converts.

Several theological principles enjoined upon Elizabethan Protestants may have contributed to a widespread social anxiety. For
instance, millenarianism was an essential component of the central
doctrine that Satan and his kingdom waged eternal war against God's
favored creature, man. Before the mid-seventeenth century, the apocalyptic view of history was not revolutionary but mainstream,
espoused by bishops, government ministers, and other pillars of the
establishment. Most early modern people possessed little faith in the
future of humanity, believing that the world would end very soon.

Another such principle was predestination, the idea that God had
determined the eternal fate of each person, who could neither know
that fate nor change it. Rather, that person must blindly accept the
probability of damnation as both God's execution of justice and his
demonstration of love. Because all people are utterly depraved and
deserve to die for Adam's sin, God's damnation of most is just, and
his mercy toward the few elect is undeserved grace. Human certainty
of individual salvation is impossible; some of the elect never feel
God's grace in their earthly lives; the illusory ease felt by some of the
damned serves merely to render them more heinous in God's sight.
Most were damned, but for a sinner to assume that he himself was
assuredly damned and consequently to despair rather than seek grace
through rigorous self-examination was a lazy and prideful act, a form
of self-indulgence that spared the sinner the arduous task of facing
his evil nature. Preachers often tempered this difficult doctrine with
assurances of salvation for the auditors of their sermons, but the basic
principle was reiterated repeatedly from every pulpit, documented in
shorthand by the newly literate congregations, and circulated widely
in manuscript to be absorbed and believed by a large audience. Robert
Brigges was part of that audience, and he clearly got the message.

Brigges' conversion manifested itself in a repudiation of his earlier
Catholicism, to which Satan tempted him to return on the grounds
that many respected people are Catholics. When Satan continued this
argument, observing that entire countries oppose Brigges on this subject, Brigges responded that truth is not necessarily the prerogative of
the majority: "Elias was alone against all the false priests . . . One
Jesus Christ against all the Jewish hypocrites . . . I care not for Italy,

France, and all the world. If all the world were set against me, I alone grounded upon Christ in his faith do assure myself to have the truth." Brigges' specific objections to Catholicism appeared in doctrinal arguments, such as his rejection of good works as a means to salvation and his refusal to pray to saints or adore icons. When Satan tempted Brigges to the former, he stoutly resisted; Christ "never said go to Peter or go to Paul, so wouldst thou have me to draw His glory from Him the Creator and to give it to the creature?" When tempted to adore icons, he protested: "I will never follow thy inventions, nor I will never go a whore-hunting under green trees. . . . I will worship one God in heaven and none else."

The pattern established during the previous week broke on the eighth day, Tuesday, April 20. On this day, Brigges' fit lasted only an hour before he regained his senses. Finally leaving his chamber, he went to church to solace himself, accompanied by a friend. While there, Brigges suddenly heard Satan whispering in his ear, telling him that he was severed from God and citing a quotation from Proverbs to prove the terrible assertion. Naturally distressed, Brigges returned to his chamber to look up the quotation and found it accurately quoted—much to his amazement since he had never read it. Resolving to have an authority expound the citation to him, Brigges made a visit to John Foxe, one of England's most eminent godly men, a well-loved preacher and evangelist, a celebrated prophet, healer, and dispenser of wisdom and charity, a cult figure approached by all sorts of people in need of alms, prayers, and spiritual healing.

During this visit, Foxe presumably assuaged Brigges' anxiety, at least temporarily. Then Foxe and Brigges went out together to visit a man named Stephens, who, like Brigges, was tortured by Satan's accusations of blasphemy and threats of dismemberment if he called upon Jesus for help. Foxe comforted and exhorted Stephens, encouraging him to defy Satan and pray to Jesus. Stephens made a little progress in achieving this goal but not much. Foxe and Brigges then departed, with the latter promising to visit Stephens again the next day and to continue to help him.

Brigges did not keep his promise to visit Stephens the following day. On that day, Wednesday, April 21, he was himself struck down again by Satan—and this time the attack was worse than ever before. Not only was he, as formerly, bereft of sight, hearing, and touch, but, in addition (and for the first time), he was bereft of speech, just like Stephens. For two hours he lay, "striving and strangling" with tears running down his cheeks, unable to utter a coherent sound. Suddenly he cried in a loud and vehement voice, "Jesus Christ, Jesus Christ, in spite of the devil, thou son of the highest, to thee be all glory, but shame and confusion to him that hath stayed my tongue from glorifying thee." After this exclamation, he gradually recovered his other senses again.

Brigges' unconscious emulation of Stephens' mutism was significant for its implications concerning the role of the Logos, of God's Word versus man's words, in Brigges' possession. Before his visit to Stephens, on several occasions Brigges had temporarily lost his sight, hearing, and touch—but he had retained his speech. This fact suggested the importance of language as man's conduit to God. His compulsive oral exegesis of Scripture while blind, deaf, and numb served as a revelatory sign to the crowds of onlookers, dazzling not only because of the speed of its delivery, sometimes too swift to be transcribed, but also because Brigges was known by his friends to have read very little Scripture, thus emphasizing that he acted as God's mouthpiece rather than in his own right. Brigges' hours-long running commentary on scriptural interpretation and problematic theological issues, repeated day after day, seemed nothing short of miraculous to his onlookers.

The word cannot function as a vehicle of revelation when it emanates from an ungodly source, however. One of Satan's blasphemies in his temptation of Brigges was to assert that Christ was not a metaphorical lamb led to the slaughter on man's behalf but a literal sheep. Although this assertion seems less sophisticated and persuasive than some of Satan's other temptations of Brigges, it is significant in its allusion to the early modern dispute over how far Scripture is to be literally interpreted. In this long-running dispute, both Protestant and Catholic theologians attacked their opponents for espousing or practicing too much literalism in the reading of scripture. For instance, Protestant ministers John Deacon and John Walker argued that scriptural texts that referred to the corporal features of incorporeal God were "metaphorically commended to our human capacities." Similarly, early modern Catholics, despite the implication of the doctrine of transubstantiation that they espoused literalism over symbolism in theological matters, often cautioned against excessively literal reliance on Scripture. Their argument derived from a mistrust of human language (especially in print and in translation) as an adequate conveyance for revelation, espousing instead reliance on the immediate (i.e., nonlinguistic) apprehension of God's presence. As one early modern Catholic writer said, "miracles are more evident proofs of a true religion than are the Scriptures, especially considering how Scriptures are so subject to false misconstruing and devilish bad interpretation."

Brigges naturally responded to Satan's sophomoric assertion that Christ was a literal sheep as would any other educated, linguistically sophisticated person: with utter contempt, reminding all that Satan's word is no good, that he is the father of lies and a liar himself. Truth is the opposite of whatever Satan says: "I said it is false because thou sayest it is true." Satan's explication of Scripture constituted an obscuring of the light of truth within the umbral depths of deceit: "Thou liest, thou liest. . . . thou dost belie the place [in Scripture], for it is not taken as thou sayest. . . . Wilt thou destroy the text?" If Satan could accomplish the destruction of the text—the Word—through lies, then man's hope for salvation through truth is dead.

Brigges thus showed that he understood the drawback of words. When a man is uninspired or faithless, his words cannot function as vehicles for revelation. Nonetheless, the capacity of the word to reflect the Word, to reveal the Logos, rendered it man's most powerful potential road to God: words, not deeds. In fact, Brigges repudiated deeds—good works—as a means to salvation: "Must I show thee my faith by my good works? I never did any, for there is none that doth good, no, not one. . . . Indeed, I have not always clothed the naked, relieved the needy, nor visited the sick, which be the works of Christianity. . . . Saint Paul sayeth that faith only doth justify and not good works." Brigges knew it to be vanity for sinful man to believe his "good works" to be salvific: "Although I never did good works, as I confess I have not, for let me do all I can, yet am I an unprofitable servant."

This elevation of faith over works, of words over deeds is presented as theologically true in Brigges' experience, as shown in the affront displayed by Satan, who repeatedly threatened to incapacitate Brigges' speech: "Thou seest, oh Lord, that he would stop my breath because I do speak of thy name. He would thrust his fist into my

Death and his demonic helpers are lurking everywhere. From Elluchasem Elimithar's Schachtafeln der Gesundheyt, illustrated by Hans Weiditz, printed by Hans Schott, Strassburg, 1533.

mouth to stop it, but let him not come near." Satan's demons menaced Brigges with bodily violence if he persisted in praising God: "Will you charge and shout at me? Do what thou darest, for I will speak and sing to the glory and praise of Jesus Christ. Shall I hold my peace? No, hold thou thy peace; I will speak. Lord Jesus, let him not stop my breath. . . . Stop, stop, down with your bills and guns, wretches, down with them." One of Satan's minions threatened to remove the instrument of Brigges' God-speech: "What, will you cut out my tongue?"

Thus, Brigges viewed his recurring bouts of deafness, blindness, and numbness as mere backdrop to his most spiritually significant sensory deprivation: dumbness. When he could not pray, could not speak words of forgiveness to his friends after the devil has tempted him to hate them, could not say "Forgive us our trespasses," then he truly exhibited his subjugation to Satan: "What, sayeth thou so, my Christ? Shall I hear and see again if I will forgive them or else never? Oh Lord, I cannot forgive them. And if I should forgive them with my tongue, I should but play the hypocrite, and my heart and reins are not hidden from thee. . . . Oh Lord Christ, fain I would forgive, but I cannot." Attempting and failing several times to forgive his friends' transgressions, Brigges was repeatedly unable to finish the Lord's Prayer, feeling that "he had a thing upon his tongue as heavy as two pounds."

Satan's attack of Wednesday, April 21, was repeated the following day, leaving Brigges bereft of speech for four hours and of his other senses for seven hours. After Brigges regained his speech, he again engaged in argument with Satan, who challenged him to explicate the Lord's Prayer. Brigges did so, beginning with the invocation and proceeding through the petitions, interspersing his exegesis with occasional counterattacks, contemptuously calling Satan a "deceitful wretch" and "an ass." Eventually, Brigges recovered his sight and hearing "after his accustomed manner."

The next day, Friday, April 23, Brigges was again deprived of all his senses, including speech, throughout the entire day and night. So tormented was he that at eight in the morning on Saturday, April 24, his professional colleagues arrived to find him catatonic and barely breathing. Nineteen hours after the onset of this particular crisis, John Foxe arrived to lead the assembled bystanders in prayer on Brigges' behalf. Foxe first exhorted the bystanders to prepare their minds for prayer by forgiving those who had offended them and repenting of their sins with a sincere intention to amend their lives. Then, the witnesses on their knees and Foxe on his feet, they prayed together for the restoration of Brigges' senses, Foxe leading the prayers with a "most vehement voice and hearty spirit." Following the first prayer, Brigges' speech was immediately restored, and he cried out, "Christ Jesus, magnified and blessed by thy name, at whose name the devil ceaseth to molest thy creature."

Following the restoration of Brigges' speech, Foxe made a second prayer for the restoration of his other senses, and Brigges' sight was likewise quickly restored as "sudden sparks of light flashed" from his eyes, which had formerly been "as dark and dim to behold as horn or wainscot [oak]." Unlike the previous restorations of Brigges' sight, this one was instantaneous and painless, and both Brigges and the assembled company considered it a miracle. Brigges' words of thanks were, "Glory, praise, and power be unto thee, oh Christ, by whose power the dumb receive their speech, the deaf their hearing, and the blind their sight."

Foxe's routing of Satan did not last long: the next morning, Sunday, April 25, Brigges was again attacked and deprived of his senses. This assault was different from the previous ones. Until this day, Satan had concentrated primarily on undermining Brigges' religious faith by shaking his trust in his spiritual allies: God, Jesus, and John Foxe. Now, having given up this approach, Satan began to "lay new engines to trap [Brigges], namely, matters of worldly affection, hatred, falsehood in friendship, love lost, and such like." In this new attempt to divorce Brigges from his earthly community, Satan suggested to Brigges the existence of a number of temporal treacheries, such as that Brigges' friends were false and wished him dead so that they might acquire his lands and goods. One of his friends, a London draper named Clark Waye, was said to have wished that Brigges would die so that he could move in on Brigges' rich widow—or, as Satan crudely said, "might serve [Brigges'] wife with Clarke's for his funeral." Another pair of false friends "uttered many secret speeches touching his miserable estate," with one of them saying, "If the physician had given [Brigges] one scruple [1/34 of an ounce] of a purgation which he minded to have done, he had sent him to God or the devil." Satan further revealed other secret speeches and injuries "suggested against his wife and children," implying a lack of loyalty and love even on the part of those closest to Brigges.

Whereas Satan's previous assaults on Brigges' religion had proved fairly unfruitful from the start, with Brigges every day exhibiting renewed vigor in his faith, this new type of attack was far more effective. Believing Satan's assertions that his friends and family hated him, Brigges "was thereby led into the extremest degree of rage and rancor against all his friends and kindred, wherein he would [have] their murder and destruction." In this state of social isolation, Brigges lay for four or five hours wishing his friends "to die a thousand deaths," declaiming so against them with such vitriol that at times the scribe deemed his words "not fit to be expressed." The crowd assembled at his bedside, grieved at his intemperance, and prayed for him to be able to forgive those who had wronged him, but he could not. Repeatedly attempting to say the Lord's Prayer, he was prevented over and over from saying, "forgive us our trespasses as we forgive those who trespass against us." Temporarily broken, Brigges at one point sighed and said, "I can go no further, for in praying to be forgiven no other wise than I forgive, I pray against myself." That is, since he could not truly forgive, he could not truly be forgiven. Nevertheless, Brigges persevered in his attempt to pronounce the troublesome petition and finally succeeded. Those assembled at his bedside again recited Foxe's prayer for the restoration of Brigges' eyes, and again Brigges instantly regained his sight.

The next day, Monday, April 26, Satan launched a devastating new temptation to Brigges' lust and pride. A beautiful female demon, the queen of hell herself, approached Brigges and offered him her love, her maidenhead, her hand in marriage, and a dower of great riches. This apparition of delight presented herself as sick with love for Brigges, singing and dancing enticingly. Initially, Brigges was so struck by her beauty and charm that his behavior was gentlemanly and deferential. He addressed her as "gentlewoman" and advised her against further association with Satan. Admiring the great attractions of this "goodly creature," Brigges exclaimed, "Jesus, Jesus, I never saw a fairer skin and breast," observing that all other women looked like "bagwash" (dirty laundry?) compared to her.

This temptation was clearly the most difficult of all for Brigges to resist, and his fight against it consumed the better part of two days. Eventually, however, Brigges was able to begin rejecting the allure of the demon queen with increasing certainty. Indeed, his initial deference finally deteriorated into such rudeness that he contemplated offering her his posterior ("base mouth") to kiss and altered his reference to her from "gentlewoman" to "strumpet bitch." This rudeness was exacerbated when Brigges saw the heretical Catholic cleric provided by Satan to perform the demonic marriage ceremony: "a poll-shaven [Catholic] priest," "a farting priest," a "parson of Satan."

When Satan first presented the lovely demon queen to Brigges, the introduction was accompanied by an invitation to Brigges to participate in a hellish revel with Satan's rabble of demons. Brigges retorted, "I will not mask with you; I know what you are well enough. Put off your masking robes and appear in your likeness." Two days later, Satan reiterated his offer to have his demons perform for Brigges' entertainment, an offer that Brigges again rejected: "No, sir, you deceived me . . . therefore I will not see thy masque, for I do not love to see a masque of devils."

Brigges' association of masques and masking with infernal deceit was common among many pious people who perceived masquerading as a form of deceit, as one early modern voice explained: "If the devil did not mask himself and transform himself into an angel of light, if the false prophets, idolaters, heretics, hypocrites, witches, and his other followers were not disguised and masqueraded in a robe of innocence, they would not attract so many people." The same language was used to denounce both social masking and the deceptions of Satan, since he was "the father of lying and hypocrisy. Now what are masques and mummings but lying and hypocrisy? For he who carries a mask, not only by changing his speech but also the whole of his bodily costume as well as gestures and ordinary actions, wants others to believe that he is quite different from what he actually is, and what is that but to lie with all his person?" Masks suggested metamorphosis, boundary violation, ambiguity, deceit, and illusion. Satan accomplished his primary mission of parodying the sacred, ironizing the holy, and mocking God through counterfeiting, dissembling, and masking.

One of Satan's many false guises was that of "the god of fortune," a benign alternative to the Calvinist God and his rigorous doctrines of predestination and justification by faith alone. On this false doctrine of fortune, Calvin had written:

It is a very bad temptation for the faithful, when things in the world are confused and it seems that God no longer engages with them but that fortune governs and rules. This has been the cause of those diabolical proverbs that everything is ruled by chance, that things happen blindly, and that God plays with men like tennis balls, that there is no reason or measure, or indeed that everything is governed by some secret necessity and that God does not bother to think of us. These are blasphemies that have always ruled. And why? Because the human mind is bewildered when we try to grasp confused things that surpass our judgment and reason.

It was in this guise of the god of fortune that Satan repeatedly proffered Brigges great wealth over the course of the three-week ordeal, tempting him not only to greed but also to the worse sin of idolatry in gratitude to the seemingly benevolent "god." During his temptation by the demon queen, Brigges finally articulated his realization of the diabolical identity of this munificent "god." Chastising the demon queen, Brigges reminded her that "the god of fortune is not above the God of heaven. So he whom ye call the god of fortune is the devil of hell, and the great god Jehovah is over and above him. . . . I cannot esteem the gifts of fortune, but of heaven. . . . Ah, thou arrant whore, didst thou not tell me that thou were of the god of fortune? And now I know thee to be a devil."

In keeping with the theme of venery introduced by the appearance of the seductive queen of hell, accompanying her into Brigges' consciousness on this day was a hunting train of demons with Satan himself at the head of a "notable kennel" of hounds, all in pursuit of their quarry, Brigges the stag. Like the dog, the hunted stag was an emblematic commonplace, immediately conveying to Brigges and his witnesses the idea of Everyman hunted by the world, the flesh, and the devil, equipped by his antlers (God's commandments) to deflect his enemies temporarily but ultimately doomed to destruction. In this sense of a man martyred by the world, the stag also typified Christ, as demonstrated in bestiaries, emblem books, and saints' legends.

Brigges finally succeeded in turning his heart to God. Staunchly commending himself to Jesus, his "watchman" and "strong tower," Brigges fearlessly agreed to "play the red deer" in this hunt. This submission demonstrates his acquiescence to God's will, his imitation of Christ, recalling Psalm 42:1: "As the hart panteth for after the water brooks, so panteth my soul after thee, O God." Thus, Christ's name became Brigges' strongest weapon, inverting the hunt and putting

Brigges in the position of the hunter himself; he put "his fist to his mouth like a horn [and] sounded forth these words: 'Jesus, Jesus, Jesus.'" Finally restored once more to his senses by prayer at the end of this day, Brigges thanked God for his mercy.

The next day, Tuesday, April 27, the newly fortified Brigges taunted Satan for arriving without the previous day's entourage of demons, dogs, and the tempting "painted woman." Satan responded by summoning his "great dragons and ugly monsters" to "gnash [Brigges'] flesh and bones." As he did the day before when he inverted Satan's hunt, Brigges borrowed the strength of Jesus' name to turn himself into a fiery-mouthed snake in pursuit of Satan's demons, uttering "'Jesus, Jesus, Jesus,' pronouncing it hissingly." The dragons of hell may gape, asserted Brigges, but Christ's wounds gape infinitely more, swallowing up all evil, guilt, and sin. Unable to abide Brigges' continual invocation of Christ, Satan departed the chamber until the next day.

The next four days (Wednesday, April 28 through Saturday, May 1), exhibited the now-familiar pattern, with Brigges deprived of sight, hearing, and touch, engaging in argument with Satan, invoking Christ as his champion, and, several hours later, recovering his senses after prayer. Finally defeated, Satan never returned to torment Brigges again after May 1. That day marked the last battle between the two, and Brigges was never again troubled by the fiend.

Chapter 6

Agnes Brigges and Rachel Pindar

Some time during March of 1574, 20-year-old Agnes Brigges, the daughter of a London weaver or tailor (no relation to Robert Brigges of the previous chapter), began to experience a vague affliction. A few months later, about June 20, she fell into a trance. Worried, she visited John Foxe's house the next week, presumably to ask his advice about her strange affliction. At Foxe's house, Agnes Brigges met Mistress Elizabeth Pindar with her daughter, 11-year-old Rachel. Mistress Pindar explained to Foxe, Agnes Brigges, and the others present that her daughter was subject to trances, that her body periodically swelled and heaved, and that she sometimes ejected unnatural objects from her mouth, such as black silk thread and feathers. These signs had convinced Mistress Pindar that her daughter was possessed by a demon. Returning home, that night Agnes Brigges began to exhibit symptoms similar to those she had heard described by Mistress Pindar. She began falling into trances more frequently than before, her face and voice altering strangely. During each trance, she emitted some foreign object from her mouth: hair, lace, bent pins, a tenterhook, and nails.

The ejection of foreign objects from the mouth was very commonly interpreted as a sign of demon possession during the early modern period. Instances in which this sign manifested itself prominently included the 1620 case of William Perry of Bilson, who vomited pins, wood, thread, rosemary, and feathers; the 1675 case of the Meredith children of Bristol, who vomited pins; and the 1679 case of Alice Burt, who vomited stones. All of these cases were later proved fraudulent, with the presumed demoniacs privately hiding the foreign objects for later expulsion in front of witnesses. One manner of accomplishing this was described in the account of the 1680 case of a 13-year-old girl who surreptitiously stuck pins into the front of her clothing at the waistline. During her fits, the girl doubled over and extracted the pins with her lips and teeth. Then straightening up, she spat the pins out as proof of the demonic presence within her.

Many who manifested this symptom, however, were not consciously simulating illness. They were suffering from what we would today label *allotriophagy* or "pathological swallowing," a phenomenon that has been documented for many centuries. Modern cases of this disorder are demonstrated through X-ray technology, which reveals that the sufferer compulsively swallows hairpins, thermometers, teaspoons, and so on. These objects are later involuntarily extruded from the body through the mouth or anus. If the objects are small and sharp, such as needles or shards of glass, they are sometimes extruded through the skin. During the early modern period, many cases were documented of copious, repeated, and violent public vomiting of blood, membrane, bone, insects, hairballs, and excrement. Such unnatural productions were commonly attributed to the workings of Satan, either through his ability to wreak havoc with the natural world or else through his ability to create illusions. Physician Johann Weyer opted for the latter explanation, contending that the ejection of objects through the mouth was an illusion created by Satan, who, he thought, caused the items to materialize in the mouth just before ejection. Weyer believed that Satan did not have the power to cause the distention required of the esophagus to pass such objects through and attempted to explain at length how the anatomy of the esophagus and trachea precluded such a possibility. Regardless of whether the vomited objects were believed to have come through the body, however, they were largely perceived as Satan's responsibility.

We do not know what Foxe's spiritual advice was to the two afflicted girls, but we do know that he was not the one who attempted to dispossess them of their demons. That office was performed by two other ministers, William Long and William Turner, about two weeks later, during mid-July. During the dispossession of Rachel Pindar, William Long did not pray to God to evict the demon but addressed the demon directly, commanding it "in the blood of Jesus Christ" to tell the assembly why it had come. "And Satan spoke," reported Long, "but we could not understand what he said, but he made a mumbling" that sounded like "Joan, Joan, let Joan alone." The other minister then addressed the demon in the same manner and for the same purpose, but the demon again refused to answer the question. Then the entire assembly knelt, prayed to God, and as a group commanded the demon to say who sent it. At this third command, the demon finally responded, saying that "Old Joan" had sent him into the body of Rachel Pindar.

Technically, possession was accomplished directly by Satan himself, with no use of a human intermediary, whereas bewitchment was accomplished on Satan's behalf by a human being—a witch—who commanded an evil spirit to afflict another person. This distinction was crucial in law: most acts of witchcraft (especially those directed at other people rather than at animals) were felonies, and, barring unusual circumstances, a person convicted of such an act was judicially executed. Conversely, acts of possession were not addressed by human law, since man's jurisdiction over Satan was, naturally, nonexistent. Cases of possession were perceived to fall within the domain of the cleric and (sometimes) the physician, but cases of bewitchment also fell within a third domain: that of the law courts. Of these three domains, this last afforded the afflicted person's community the greatest formal opportunity to participate in and influence the outcome of events. In the first two domains, the members of the community could, of course, describe the afflicted person's symptoms to the attending physician or pray with the attending minister, but their active participation in the drama was generally minimal. If a legal proceeding was brought against an accused witch, however, the participation of the members of the community was greatly increased as they acted as officers of the court, testified as witnesses, and deliberated as jury members. Moreover, for those whose social position rendered them little status, such as children, adolescents, and servants, taking on the role of witch-accuser earned some temporary prestige.

Many authorities argued for caution in the accusation of witches in cases of demon possession. Physician Johann Weyer observed that no scriptural authority existed for the idea that possession could occur through a human agent. Conversely, scriptural authority existed for the idea that evil spirits, with God's permission, could easily afflict people without the intervention of witches. Similarly, physician Richard Brinley argued that nothing was "more usual with the common people than to ascribe to witchcraft all disasters, mischances, or diseases whatever to vulgar sense." Brinley went on to list examples of naturally occuring conditions that were often ascribed to possession: catalepsy, apoplexy, phrenitis, hydrophobia, convulsions, and others. Like Weyer, Brinley pointed out that demons did not require human assistance in order to afflict people: "It is most certain that the devil often does much evil of himself (by God's permission)" without the assistance of intermediaries. Despite such cautions, the widespread belief in the existence of witches was supported by both divine and human law. "Suffer not a witch to live" (Exodus 22:18) made no sense as a scriptural mandate unless witches did exist. Similarly, long-standing statutes classifying witchcraft as a felony in law made no sense unless witches did exist. Given the considerable social support for the belief in the existence of witches, the cautions of skeptics such as Weyer and Brinley must have seemed like irrelevant quibbles to a great many people. Furthermore, any explicit denial of the existence of witches would have earned the denier the wrath of England's judiciary, who were, after all, upholding the law of the land by convicting and executing witches.

When the company assembled with Long and Turner asked the demon why "old Joan" had so afflicted Rachel Pindar, the demon said, "For her body and soul." The company rejoined, "Thou shalt not have it; Jesus Christ hath bought it with his precious blood." The demon denied this, accusing the company several times of lying. Turner observed that Satan, not Christ, was the liar. The demon then tried a new tack, saying that he had come to claim Rachel Pindar because she was a sinner—that she had sinned against the Holy Ghost, that her sins were "before her face," and that the demon would therefore have her. The assembly repeated that Satan could not have her, that Christ had bought her with his blood and had forgiven her sins because of her faith. At this, the demon expanded his target, first threatening the entire company with damnation, then saying, "All the world is mine," claiming that he had been the one to take Christ from the cross, implying that even Christ's soul belonged to him. The company continued to accuse him of lying and to demand that he say his name. After some resistance, the demon finally capitulated to the company's demand for his name, admitting that his name was Legion and that he—they—consisted of "5,000 legions" of devils, all encapsulated within the body of Rachel Pindar. Interestingly, the anonymous writer of this account, who was one of the witnesses present, continued to refer to this demon as "Satan," not "Legion," after the revelation of the latter as the demon's name. This use of the term "Satan" reflects the original generic meaning of the word as an undifferentiated adversary rather than the more modern meaning of the word as a proper name.

The company, having now limited the demon's power by discovering his purpose, master, name, and number, ordered him by the blood of Christ to depart. The demon resisted, threatening to tear the company and the demoniac into pieces. He also threatened to bring death to the famous preachers Lawrence Humphrey and John Foxe, "death very terribly." When the company continued to resist these threats and to command the demon's departure, the demon responded, "You have not written it." William Long's servant responded, "If we have not written it, the Lord God hath written it in our hearts."

This brief exchange about writing had significant implications for those gathered around Rachel Pindar's bed in 1574. Despite the educational advances of Queen Elizabeth's early reign, her society was still largely illiterate. Furthermore, reading and writing were taught and learned as separate skills, not in parallel fashion as today, with the result that many more people could read than write. Women, particularly, could only rarely sign their names, as evidenced by the account of this very case. Of the thirteen women who bore witness to the truth of the events as documented in this account, only one woman signed her name; the others made simple marks or left the spaces next to their names blank. Writing was therefore a more prestigious skill than reading, so those who could write were perceived as more socially authoritative than those who could not. In this brief exchange, we are witnessing a taunt by the demon implying that since the company's command was merely oral and therefore less weighty than a written command, the company itself did not possess the authority necessary to control the demon.

When the demon's threats failed to intimidate the assembly, the demon tried a different approach: asking for bribes. He promised he would vacate the body of Agnes Brigges only if the company would give him a cherry, or an apple, or some thread or hair, or a nail paring.

The Devil making love to a witch.

If none of these requests could be granted, he said, he would leave the body if someone in the company would merely wag his finger or say "I pray you." The demon explained that, because he had been paid to possess the body of Rachel Pindar, he should be paid to leave it: "I had of Old Joan a drop of blood to come hither, and shall I depart away with nothing?" He also threatened to remain in the body for "four score years and ten" if he received no payment. The company refused every request, saying, "Thou shalt have nothing," and William Long commanded the demon to depart "into the bottomless pit of hell." Plaintively, the demon asked Long one last time, "What wilt thou give me?" Long, predictably, answered, "Nothing."

When Christ had ordered the demons possessing the Gadarene man to leave his body, the demons asked Christ if they could enter the bodies of some swine grazing nearby instead, and Christ gave his permission. The demons accordingly entered the swine, causing them to hurl themselves into the sea and drown. Early modern Catholic exorcists sometimes cited this account as a precedent to justify their negotiation with a possessing demon in a battle of wit and strength, as long as they committed no theological error in the process. To Protestant dispossessors, however, such negotiation was itself a theological error, implying as it did that God, through his representative, somehow needed to placate, cajole, or otherwise strike a bargain with Satan. Furthermore, they also perceived such negotiation as a tactical error. To grant any request of the evil power, no matter how trivial, was perceived as sign of weakness and lack of confidence on the part of the dispossessor or exorcist. After gaining even a small concession, the demon would be sure to demand more and more, to gain in power and confidence. An example of this danger was demonstrated in a case of demon possession in Vernois in 1697, in which the demons possessing a young boy contemptuously refused a bribe of mere plums, demanding instead a more extravagant prize of broth with eggs. After getting the broth, the demons departed, whistling insouciantly. Fortunately, the boy was cured.

Finally, the faith and fortitude of Master Long and the company prevailed. Realizing that he was losing the battle, "Satan cried with a loud voice a perfect speech that all might hear, 'Hear me, hear me,' diverse times." Attempting one final stalling tactic, Satan begged that he might be allowed to stay until the next day: "Let me tarry till tomorrow that my lady comes, and I will tell you more of my mind." Refusing, as always, to accede to any request by the demon, the company said, "Thou shalt not tarry for nothing," and so the demon disappeared for good.

Presumably, near the same time but in a different house and with a smaller group of witnesses, the same two ministers dispossessed the other young woman, Agnes Brigges. During this event, Agnes Brigges's lips "moved with nonesuch moving as could pronounce the words uttered"—that is, the movement of the lips did not correspond to the sound emanating from them. The spectators perceived that the voice of the demon was "somewhat bigger" than Agnes Brigges's natural voice.

Ventriloquism, though rare, did occasionally manifest itself in cases of early modern English demon possession. The connection between possession and ventriloquism had scriptural authority: many of the original Hebrew and Aramaic words of scripture were commonly translated into English as *witch* or *conjurer,* but scholars of the time argued that more accurate translations for these words would also include *idolater, diviner* (false prophet), *astrologer, prestidigitator, enchanter* (one who utters incantations), *necromancer* (one who seeks information from the dead), *soothsayer, poisoner*—and *ventriloquist.* The word *ventriloquism* derives from the Latin words for *speak* and *belly,* demonstrating the old belief that the voice in question originated in the ventriloquist's stomach. One skeptic observed,

> This imposture of speaking in the belly hath been often practiced in these latter days, in many places, and namely in this island of England, and they that practice it do it commonly to this end, to draw many silly people to them, to stand wondering at them, that so by the concourse of people money may be given them, for they by this imposture do make the people believe that they are possessed by the devil speaking within them and tormenting them, and do by that pretense move the people to charity, to be liberal to them.

In a case of fraudulent possession that occurred the same year as that of Agnes Brigges and Rachel Pindar, a 17-year-old servant, Mildred Norrington, used ventriloquism to respond to the questions of her dispossessing ministers, creating the illusion that her possessing demon had answered the ministers from within her belly. In a later case, both the demoniac and the dispossessing minister may have used ventriloquism to create the illusion of a demon speaking with two voices at once.

During the fits of the demoniac Agnes Brigges, her eyelids moved but refused to open, and "she had a great swelling in her throat and about the jaws." The ministers' questioning of the demon revealed that the "Old Joan" who had been accused by both Agnes and Rachel of sending demons into their bodies was Joan Thornton, "dwelling upon the quay." This person had summoned the demon by reciting the Pater Noster several times, a Catholic act. The demon also reported that Old Joan kept "in her bosom next to her skin" a familiar spirit that sometimes appeared "like a dog and sometimes like a toad." The demon's vagueness regarding the shape of Old Joan's familiar spirit was not surprising in light of the commonly accepted idea that such spirits were not real animals at all but demons that assumed the shapes of dogs, cats, rabbits, toads, insects, and other small animals in order to expedite and disguise their comings and goings. Witches were often presumed to accomplish much of their malignant work through the mediation of such familiars, whose job it was to transmit the witch's evil influence to its intended victim, afflicting a farmer's horse with lameness, his wife with sterility, or his child with death. One test of guilt was to isolate the suspect and wait for a flea or a rat—the presumed familiar spirit—to appear and confirm the suspect's identity as a witch.

Agnes Brigges' demon was not as forthcoming about his name as was Rachel Pindar's demon, "Legion." When asked his name, this demon merely responded, "Ark, ark," barking like a dog, as did Alexander Nyndge's demon. At least one of the witnesses decided to test the authenticity of Agnes Brigges's demon by asking it questions in Latin and Dutch, but the demon refused to answer these questions or to speak in these languages.

Such tests had always been part of Catholic exorcism rituals, with the exorcist requiring a possessing demon to differentiate holy water from plain water, holy relics from other objects, or sacred words in foreign languages from ordinary words. Testing in this manner was more problematic for Protestants since their theology did not recognize any essential difference in sanctity among objects or words. They were therefore forced to convert the element of the sacred in the differentiation test into something else, such as differentiating between fresh and stale water. However, the loss of the element of the sacred greatly reduced the significance of such tests in the eyes of the witnesses, so the differentiation tests were largely dropped by the Protestants. In some cases, however, they retained the language tests. For instance, in the later case of William Perry, the demoniac manifested his possession by revulsion during the recitation of John 1:1 ("In the beginning was the Word . . ."). This was an important verse because it was perceived as the ultimate expression of Christ's role as man's savior, a truth that expressed "the archpillar of man's salvation." To test the authenticity of Perry's possession, the cleric in the case, the bishop of Coventry and Litchfield, recited several Greek texts to Perry, including John 1:1, to determine whether he could discern the same verse in another language. If Perry's demon were real, it would manifest the same revulsion regardless of the language in which it was recited. Perry failed to react, however, to the significant verse pronounced in Greek, so he was determined to be a fraud.

Weakening, the demon within Agnes Brigges agreed to leave the young woman's body. William Long ordered the demon to blow out the candle as a sign that he would not return. The demon did so, plaintively leaving his final words behind, "Give me a thread." Immediately upon these words, Brigges "rose up and held up her hands and said, 'He is gone; he will come no more.'"

The accounts of the two cases of Agnes Brigges and Rachel Pindar were quickly (and illegally) printed and circulated. They caused an uproar serious enough to warrant the attention of the authorities, for less than a month later, Matthew Parker, the archbishop of Canterbury, ordered an investigation into the two cases and interrogated one of the demoniacs personally. On August 11, Agnes Brigges and Rachel Pindar were taken into custody and questioned. They both confessed to fraud, and their confessions were witnessed by the archbishop, a city alderman, the city recorder, a representative of the Lord Mayor, the minister of Saint Margaret's in Lothbury (Agnes Brigges' parish), and other important citizens.

In her confession, Agnes Brigges admitted that she had been inspired to feign most of her symptoms after meeting Mistress Pindar and her daughter Rachel at John Foxe's house and hearing what Rachel's symptoms were. Thinking to herself that such symptoms would be fairly easy to simulate, she began that night voiding foreign objects from her mouth. The pins she had herself bent before inserting them into her mouth, presumably to render them less painful during her ejection of them. The lace she had stripped from her own sleeve; the hair she had pulled from her own head. The tenterhook she had concealed in a window until it was needed; the nails she had pulled from the valance of her bed. The strange grimaces and voices she had simulated: "all that she did was feigned and counterfeit and no truth therein." She had acted, she said, alone in this counterfeit: "Nobody was privy to her doings but herself."

Confession notwithstanding, we should remember that Agnes Brigges had experienced apparently genuine symptoms before she ever met Rachel Pindar. She had complained of a vague affliction months before her meeting with the other girl, and she had fallen into at least one trance. Indeed, the reason she had met Pindar and her mother in the first place was that she had visited John Foxe to consult with him about these distressing manifestations. In her case, therefore, the implication is not that she manufactured her symptoms out of whole cloth but that she exaggerated the symptoms of a true illness.

Of course, many early modern cases of demon possession contained some element of imposture. In some cases, the imposture was all that existed: a conscious intent to deceive and no actual affliction at all. In a considerable number of cases, however, the demoniac actually did seem to suffer from some real ailment, and the element of imposture consisted of an exaggeration—perhaps conscious, perhaps not—of that ailment. For instance, an epileptic adolescent, observing the sympathy and release from responsibility that accrued to her during her seizures, might begin to exaggerate and prolong her symptoms, perhaps eventually simulating them outright. Once possession had been posited, the community's sympathy for the adolescent would increase, and the adolescent would continue to be reinforced in perpetuating the behavior eliciting that sympathy. She might progress from exaggerating the symptoms of her seizures to simulating or inducing them. What began as an illness gradually slid into illness combined with fraud.

Several early modern authorities observed that apparent demon possession often consisted of an exaggeration of a genuine natural illness. Minister Richard Bernard said, "Even a counterfeit may have some natural disease upon him or her, and make advantage thereof, adding their own juggling tricks thereto. . . . Care therefore must be had to difference the counterfeiting from that which is natural, which requireth judgement." Cleric Samuel Harsnet pointed out that many demoniacs were unconscious frauds, adolescents with symptoms that were not medically serious but were sufficiently bothersome that an influential cleric, wishing to gain glory as a Catholic exorcist or Protestant dispossessor, could "work upon" the youth, eventually diagnosing possession credibly to all concerned, including the patient. One well-known case in which an exaggerated natural illness was presented as demon possession was that of Ann Gunter, a Berkshire girl, the daughter of a country gentleman. In 1605, Ann began exhibiting common symptoms of possession such as fits, swelling, foaming, blindness, deafness, and the extrusion of pins from her body. Placed under the supervision of the Bishop of Salisbury, who tested the authenticity of Ann's affliction by placing some marked pins in the girl's way, Ann was determined to be a fraud when she extruded the marked pins. The bishop sent her to be examined by other officials, including King James, to whom she confessed that she had a "natural distemper" (that her Oxford physicians had determined to be epilepsy or hysteria) that her father had encouraged her to exaggerate in order to simulate demon possession.

Rachel Pindar's confession was similar to that of Agnes Brigges. She had voided hairs from her mouth that she had pulled from her bed cover. She had several times filled her mouth so full of these hairs that the resulting accretion "would stop in her throat, so as she was fain the drink after the same." She also periodically voided feathers and threads that she had removed from her own bedding and secreted in her mouth. Like Agnes Brigges, she admitted feigning the strange facial expressions and voice alterations that characterized her "possession." Unlike Agnes Brigges, however, Rachel Pindar said she did not act alone in her fraud, claiming that her own mother was her accomplice. For instance, the ball of hairs that caused Rachel to be so thirsty and that she occasionally voided from her mouth was preserved by her mother, presumably for Rachel's future use. Her mother also encouraged her in her imaginings, she said, by inducing her to say what form the devil took when he appeared to Rachel, suggesting possibilities for Rachel to consider: like a man with a gray beard, like five cats, or perhaps like ravens and crows. She admitted that her accusation of Joan Thornton as a witch who had sent the demon into her was untrue and begged forgiveness for this slander. She ended her confession by asserting hearty repentance for her fraud and begging forgiveness of God, Joan Thornton, and the rest of the world.

Early modern English demoniacs were often children and adolescents harboring resentment against adults. The training, catechizing, and disciplining of children was founded on the assumption that a child was born inherently depraved and acquired true humanity through nurture rather than nature, that reason and social responsibility had to be forcibly inculcated into a child, that the indulgence of children's natural self-centeredness and willfulness created criminals and other social undesirables. Because to the early modern mind, anarchy was far more threatening than tyranny, parental discipline, even excessive discipline, was preferable to indulgence. Even humanists such as Erasmus believed that a child's behavior must be regulated to a very great degree because that behavior was perceived to mirror internal character. Such regulation extended to parental control over the child's face and body. Children were not allowed to furrow their brows, whistle through their noses, puff out their cheeks, press their lips together, lick or bite their lips, yawn, laugh too much or without good cause, let their hair fall onto their foreheads, scratch their heads, or stand with their weight unevenly balanced. These and other aberrant behaviors all indicated specific character flaws that had to be suppressed externally if they were to be corrected internally. For instance, coughing during conversation was considered a liar's dodge used to gain time to invent.

Thus, children's daily routines were formal and strict. They learned to rise early, pray, greet their families, groom and dress, attend to their lessons, spend their spare time reading, memorize new Bible verses every day, be quiet and courteous, punish themselves when they neglected their duties, and be humble (and not vain) in their learning. Except for reading and writing, individual activities were discouraged, not only dicing and cards but also chess and swimming. After their initial "sleep of reason," when they reached the age of moral accountability at six or seven years of age, children were deemed capable of mortal sin and thus subjected to regular and strict chores, spankings, and beatings. Constantly exhorted to be aware of their duties to their parents (such as obedience to parents' wishes in the choice of profession or spouse), children learned that those duties extended throughout their lives, even after they became adults themselves, even after their parents died. Thus, they realized that individuality must be subordinated to communal responsibility. They acquired moral and theological principles through catechism, not discussion, never being allowed to analyze these principles but simply being compelled to know them by rote.

In addition to the chores, spankings, and beatings intended to socialize and humanize a child, regular and repeated threats of eternal damnation formed the fabric of a child's early learning. "Learn to die" was among the earliest sentences taught to children, and death was a central theme of the juvenile religious literature of the early modern period. Children were taught to imagine themselves in their death-beds, coffins, and graves. The vocabulary lists of the *New England Primer* include the words *vice, soul, Babel, duty, heinous, damnify,*

Satan rebaptizing young sorcerers.

everlasting, fornication, exhortation, abomination, and *purification.* The child's alphabet in the same primer pairs each letter with a couplet related to that letter, many of these couplets reinforcing the inevitability of death and the probability of damnation: (G) "As runs the Glass, / Man's Life doth pass"; (X) "Xerxes the great did die / And so must you and I"; (Y) "Youth forward slips / Death soonest nips." Children learned that "liars shall have their part in the lake which burns with fire and brimstone," that "upon the wicked, God shall rain an horrible tempest," and that "woe shall come to the wicked, it shall be ill with him, for the reward of his hands shall be given him." The hysterical repudiations of Scripture by demoniacs as a protest against the constant round of prayers, sermons, admonitions, and catechisms in religious households reflected children's saturation in apocalyptic imagery from their earliest days. Possession legitimated normally unacceptable behavior, such as spitting at a minister or tearing up a Bible; the heresy was Satan's, not the afflicted child's.

Unlike Agnes Brigges, Rachel Pindar seemed not to have been exaggerating a natural illness; her confession indicated that her "possession" was a wholly deliberate and conscious simulation. Such simulation in a nine-year-old child was undoubtedly even more convincing because many adults naively believed a child to be incapable of imposture. That children were indeed capable of perpetrating such frauds, however, was demonstrated in a number of cases, such as that of William Perry, who in 1620 faked possession by producing demonic-looking black urine in his chamber pot. A spy discovered that Perry had added ink to the pot to produce the effect. Furthermore, he had secreted an ink-soaked piece of cotton under his foreskin in case he was called upon to produce the black urine in public.

On August 15, the Sunday following the interrogations, the confessions of Agnes Brigges and Rachel Pindar were read aloud to the huge congregation at Paul's Cross, the most important church in London, and the two girls publicly repented. They stood before the congregation and acknowledged their counterfeit, behaving penitently, asking forgiveness of God and the world, and requesting the congregation to pray for them. Their confessions were shortly thereafter published in print (by order of the archbishop) to warn the public to beware of similar deceits. The printers of the unlicensed pamphlets documenting the cases were imprisoned. And despite Agnes Brigges' attempt to protect her mother by disavowing the latter's knowledge of her deceit, Mistress Brigges was committed to prison at Westminster until the girl's penance had been accomplished. In a letter to the queen's principle minister, Lord Burghley, Archbishop Parker wrote, "I am so grieved with such dissemblers that I cannot be quiet with myself. I do intend, because these books are so spread abroad and believed, to set out a confutation of the same falsehood. The tragedy is so large that I might spend much time to trouble your honour withal."

Chapter 7
Sarah Williams

During the autumn of 1585, fifteen-year-old Sarah Williams went to serve as a maid in the house of a wealthy Catholic family, the Peckhams, who lived in Denham, Buckinghamshire. This family harbored many Catholic priests—at least a dozen, possibly more—an illegal and dangerous but fairly widespread practice. The priests assumed aliases and disguises to protect themselves and the family, but they continued to say mass, administer holy communion, and perform other priestly functions in secret for selected members of the household and for sympathetic visitors. These activities had been criminalized as treasonous capital offenses during Elizabeth's reign, and many of the priests so situated anticipated their own capture and execution, expecting to become martyrs for their faith.

Almost as soon as Sarah arrived at her new job, the other servants told her that the house was "troubled with spirits, so as every noise and thing that she heard or saw" frightened her, and she went about her household tasks in a state of constant apprehension. One of the Catholic priests harbored by the Peckhams, Father Robert Dibdale, took the frightened Sarah in hand, attempting to reassure her by teaching her how to "bless herself in Latin, and at some words to make a cross on her forehead, at others on her belly, at others, first on one shoulder and then on the other shoulder, and with the last words upon her breast." Sarah, a Protestant, was unfamiliar with the foreign words and gestures and had much difficulty learning how to perform this blessing properly. During supper one night, a great storm arose, with claps of thunder so loud and flashes of lightning so startling that the household dogs ran through the hall barking wildly. At this occurrence, Sarah "was greatly afraid, left off her supper, and grew to be sickly." Father Dibdale recommended that she bless and cross herself as he had taught her to do, but Sarah, "being very evil at ease that night after the lightning, could not easily hit upon the words."

Early church authorities had advocated the idea that the sign of the cross repelled demons. One church father had said, "It is sufficient now to set forth, as much as need be, the potency of this sign (of the cross). How fearful a thing this sign is to the devils he will know who has seen how, when adjured by Christ, they flee from the bodies which they have occupied. For just as he, when he lived among men, put to flight all devils by a word, and restored to their former state the minds of men which had been overthrown and driven distraught by the assaults of evil; so still his followers expel those same foul spirits from men both by the name of their master and the sign of his passion. There is no difficulty in proving this, for when they sacrifice to their gods, if there be one standing by who bears on his forehead the sign of the cross, their sacred rites are rendered ineffective." From the first centuries of Christianity, therefore, the sign of the cross had been formally used in all consecrations and exorcisms as a weapon against evil. Informally, it was used even more often, with common folk routinely employing it as a preventive measure to deflect evil away from their livestock, crops, houses, and children. When they yawned or sneezed, they crossed themselves to prevent demons from entering into their temporarily unprotected mouths.

After the Reformation, however, many English Protestants protested against ritual gestures, perceiving them as mindless superstition substituting for thoughtful prayer, and they quoted scripture in support of this position: "My soul hateth your new moons and your appointed feasts, they are a burden unto me, I am weary to bear them" (Isaiah 1:14). One church official referred to the making of the sign of the cross as idolatry, hypocrisy, impiety, soul murder, and devil worship: "the sign of the cross evacuates and pollutes faith." Another critic observed that signs of the cross occurred routinely in nature with no discernible effect of deflecting evil:

I see the demoniac who throws a fit at the sight of a cross which is shown to him. Oh, Master Exorcist, how good you are! Don't you know that there is no place in nature where there are no crosses, since all matter has length and width, and a cross is nothing but length matched with width. This means that the cross you hold is a cross because a width has been put across a length. So if that demoniac has a hundred thousand lengths and a hundred thousand widths which are all crosses, why show her any new ones?

Another observed that the sign of the cross was also used by conjurers, implying that there was no difference between a Catholic priest operating within the orthodoxy of his church and a rogue, lay magician operating under no authority whatsoever.

Father Dibdale interpreted Sarah's failure to bless and cross herself correctly as a sign that she was demonically influenced, and he began to urge her to convert to Roman Catholicism. He said that her inadequate Protestant baptismal ceremony had obviously failed to wash her clean of original sin, that she was living in a state of damnation, and that she must therefore undergo a Catholic baptismal ceremony (one that included an exorcism) if she wished to be free of evil. Sarah complied. She also stopped attending the Protestant church, a legal offense very commonly committed by Catholics. Baptism notwithstanding, however, Sarah still could not perform and pronounce the blessing correctly.

Father Dibdale and nine of the other household priests, operating under the assumption that Sarah's demons were more firmly entrenched than they had previously thought, embarked on a long-term program of ritual exorcisms for Sarah. These exorcisms were grueling procedures for both the priests and Sarah, being conducted for many hours a day (generally from morning until evening), several times a week, for eight months. The priests relied on an Italian manual of exorcisms coupled with a battery of traditional weapons against Satan that had been used in the Catholic church for many centuries, including binding, flogging, humiliating, fumigating, and burning the demon (and, necessarily, the demoniac who housed the demon). Because the priests were in hiding, however, the conditions under which the exorcisms were conducted were less than ideal, and a great deal of improvisation was necessary. Furthermore, these exorcisms were for the most part conducted by inexperienced young men operating with little or no supervision. These particular exorcisms, therefore, should not be assumed to represent anything like common

Catholic practice, particularly in light of the considerable disapproval of them that was later expressed by a great many other priests, especially those who were older, better trained, and more experienced than Father Dibdale and his colleagues.

In order to better control the situation during the procedures to come, Father Dibdale and the other priests began each exorcism session by tying Sarah into a chair. They then forcibly administered various sanctified liquids to Sarah by mouth. When Sarah recoiled at drinking holy water because it was salty, they interpreted her antipathy as that of the demons inside her. Similarly, when she protested at swallowing "a hallowed drink consisting of oil, sack, and rue," the priests interpreted her protests as those of her demons. Sarah later claimed that she was compelled to drink liquids of such a revolting nature and in such great quantities that for short periods of times afterwards, she was rendered speechless and her body became unnaturally cold. The priests interpreted these characteristics as symptoms of demon possession and therefore prayed for her, applying holy water to her speechless throat. When she later recovered her speech and her natural body temperature, the priests assumed that their prayers had been answered and the touch of the holy water efficacious.

In addition to administering holy liquids to Sarah by mouth, the priests also forced Sarah to breathe sanctified smoke. They burned feathers, rue, brimstone, asafetida, and "diverse such loathsome smells which they said were hallowed," so much so that even years later "the chamber did still stink of it." The priests forced Sarah's head down so near to the burning substance that the heat caused her to "cry and screech very loud and to struggle as much as possibly she could till her strength failed her." An eye-witness later testified that Sarah had been so thoroughly suffumigated that "her face was blacker than a chimney sweeper's, which heats and smells together with their potions did make her to talk and rage as if she had been mad." Once, Sarah was "so extremely afflicted with the said drinks and smoke as that her senses went from her, and she remained in a swoon." The priests perceived that the demon inside her, who had reacted so negatively to the holy smoke, had at last been temporarily subdued: "the devil grew quiet."

Just as we do today, English Elizabethans commonly administered remedies for illness through the nose and mouth. For instance, one early modern authority on human health used a medicinal suffumigation to relieve himself from the symptoms of a cold: "I took for a perfume the rinds of old rosemary and burned them and held my mouth over the fume, closing my eyes." This treatment was advocated as a remedy for "rheums [mucous discharges] falling out of a hot head." The use of such remedies against demon-induced illness, however, was a specifically Catholic procedure, deriving from exorcism manuals recently published by the Jesuit Petrus Thyraeus and the Franciscan Girolamo Menghi. The manuals authorized the use of and listed recipes for specific combinations of substances to be administered to a demoniac by mouth or nose. These substances were considered either naturally strengthening to the patient or naturally repulsive to the demon or both, and their inherent efficacy was increased by their being exorcized and blessed before use. Such substances included plants and plant products such as cinquefoil, olive branches, frankincense, myrrh, verbena, valerian, Christ's palm, betony, dried bryony root, alyssum, empty hazelnut shells, and sesame oil. They also included minerals such as jasper, carnelian, chrysolite, diamond, red coral, and jet. One such "holy potion" that was administered by mouth to a thirteen-year-old possessed German nun required the following recipe: "Take one dram of choice rhubarb, roots of elecampane, artemisia, some lesser centaury, and aquatic mint. Let these be placed together in a new pot, except for the artemisia, and boiled in white wine in honor of the three sacred names. Let the artemisia be cooked in a pint of water. Then some poor but pious man must recite the Lord's prayer and the hail Mary five times."

The practice of exorcism by scent was a venerable one. The ancient historian Josephus had documented the exorcist Eleazar's manner of curing a possessed man by forcing him to inhale the scent of the baaras root, after which Eleazar was able to extract the demon from the man's nostrils. Exorcism by means of a scent produced specifically by burning, however, also enjoyed actual scriptural authority in the book of Tobit. Although this book had been judged noncanonical during the Reformation and removed from the Protestant Old Testament, it continued to be included in the Catholic Old Testament and therefore constituted a legitimate scriptural authority for the actions of Sarah Williams' priests. In the book of Tobit, a powerful demon possesses a young woman and seven times prevents her from consummating her marriage, each time by strangling the bridegroom. The eighth bridegroom, before attempting consummation, takes the precaution of smoking the demon out of the young woman's body with fumes from a burning fish liver. This book established the efficacy of the *profumigatio horribilis,* a repulsive burning stench, that exorcists in subsequent years could produce by setting alight substances other than fish liver oil, such as rue, sulfur, and asafetida.

Elizabethan Protestants often ridiculed the practice of exorcism through the mouth and nose as the apex of Catholic superstition. One called this practice "ignorant and sottish." Another pointed out, at great length, that the burning of fetid substances in order to drive out devils made no sense in light of the common opinion about the character and habitat of those devils: "Men acquainted with the nature and disposition of devils do affirm that those forcible violent savors and stinking odors are very delicacies for devils and allectives to their noses. And that the devil would not vouchsafe to come . . . until he were wooed by these delicious perfumes." This same commentator also characterized such substances as "drugs" to impair the judgment of the patient. Another agreed, saying, "Such perfumes [as burning rue and sulfur] are the devil's dainties." Nonetheless, the priests who exorcized Sarah Williams by these means were operating within a longstanding tradition.

While Sarah was tied to her chair and being forced to drink holy potions and breathe holy smoke, her dress (which the priests thought was "full of spirits") was stripped off, leaving her in her underwear. In this state she endured the priests hunting the demons throughout her body by touch: the priests would say "that the wicked spirits had gone down into her foot" and would "begin to hunt the devil from the foot to bring him upwards" in order to drive him out through her mouth, ears, eyes, or nose. "And the manner of their hunting of him was to follow him with their hands along all the parts of her body," with Sarah complaining that they had routinely handled her belly and other parts of her torso for this purpose. One of the priests "would usually pinch her by the arms and the neck and hands, and the places thereupon remaining blue [bruised], he and the rest would say that it was the devil that had so pinched her." When Sarah complained about this pinching, the priests assumed that it was the devil speaking.

The handling of Sarah's body derived from a centuries-old principle that the laying on of hands reflected Christ's usual method of healing the sick. This laying on of hands could consist of touch alone, or it could function as the mechanism by which a holy liquid, such as sanctified oil, could be applied to the afflicted person. Anointing with holy oil as a healing act derived from the sacrament of extreme unction, which the medieval church had promoted as curative provided the patient had sufficient faith. The oil used in exorcisms was blessed in the same way as were the bread and wine for the Eucharist, with the priest praying "that sanctifying this oil, O God, thou mayest grant health to them that use and receive it, wherewith Thou didst anoint kings and priests and prophets; so also let this afford strength to them that taste thereof and health to them that use it." In the ancient world, oil had played an important cultural role, used for the consecration of people and objects, considered a universal remedy for all ills, and, in a metaphorical extension of its function as lamp fuel, a symbol of enlightenment. Oil was therefore considered by the early church to be one of the most efficacious tools that a priest could used in exorcism, and many blessings were devoted to it, such as a prayer for God to "send upon this oil, which is the type of thy richness, the fullness of thy gracious goodness, that it may release those who labour, and heal those who are sick and sanctify those who return when they draw nigh to thy faith." In the traditional anointing of the sick, several parts of the patient were touched separately with holy oil: eyes, ears, mouth, hands, feet, and sometimes genitals.

Other liquids besides oil could be used as an adjunct to curing by touch. The saliva of a saint or a priest, for instance, was deemed holy and was used as a cure for leprosy, deafness, blindness, headaches, snakebite, and other afflictions. The methods of administration included the priest's kissing the afflicted person, spitting on him, or touching him with hands wet with saliva. One legend told of a paralytic man who traveled all the way from Rome to Ireland to seek a cure from a certain saint. The saint died shortly before the afflicted man found him, so the afflicted man purportedly cured himself using spittle from the mouth of the holy corpse. One early modern commentator observed that "the ancients made a practice of spitting into the folds of their garment to counter the evil eye." The theological basis for this belief derived from Christ's curing of afflicted people in

Mark 7:32–35 and 8:22–26 by touch and saliva: "And taking him from the multitude apart he put his fingers into his ears, and spitting he touched his tongue. . . . And immediately his ears were opened, and the string of his tongue was loosed, and he spoke right." Other curative liquids that were applied by touch included water in which a saint or his relics had been washed, wine which he had blessed, blood from his body, milk from the breasts of his mother, and, of course, holy water.

Even without the application of a holy liquid, however, touch alone had for many centuries been deemed a powerful tool against evil, as long as that touch was provided by a sanctified person. For instance, English monarchs, anointed as God's representatives with consecrated oil, were thought to have this power in abundance. Ever since the reign of Edward the Confessor, they had touched (in order to cure) those of their subjects who were afflicted with epilepsy, arthritis, tuberculosis, scrofula, and other sporadically occurring diseases. These monarchs had also touched gold rings, amulets, and coins, which were then sold to the sick as cures. Although after the Reformation, some Protestants began to perceive this practice as blasphemous (since it arrogated to a mere human being Christ's divine curative power), they had to suppress their hostility so as not to appear treasonous. The practice continued to be officially sanctioned until well into the eighteenth century, despite the private skepticism of some monarchs that the practice was merely superstition. Many early modern commentators remarked on the irony of a practice that was considered proof of divine favor if done by one person but proof of evil practice if done by another. Among Catholics, however, the touch of a saint or a priest was deemed just as curative as that of the monarch. Touching was a manner of "firing out" the evil from the afflicted person, as the holy touch was believed to burn the demon unbearably and to cause it to flee the body.

Protestants, of course, enjoyed ridiculing this concept, and much Protestant satire was generated on the subject of the fiery, burning touch of the hand of a priest and the heat of his body. One skeptic punned extensively on the "ignatian" (fiery) nature of the priests and on the name of Saint Ignatius, whose image, name, and relics were thought to be particularly efficacious against demons. (An example of this saint's efficacy in this regard occurred in 1651, when a Lancashire woman who had been possessed for a long time and subjected to unsuccessful exorcisms was finally freed on the feast of Saint Ignatius by being sprinkled with water blessed in the saint's name.) This same skeptic observed that a priest's fiery nature must imply that his natural niche was not heaven, but hell: "Will not his hand be an excellent instrument for Lucifer in hell to plague, broil, and torment his infernal fiends, that hath such a fiend-tormenting power here on earth?" One of the many parodists of this idea was Shakespeare, who ironically inverted the concept in the final couplet of Sonnet 144 so that, instead of the good "firing out" the evil, the opposite occurs:

> Two loves I have of comfort and despair,
> Which like two spirits do suggest me still:
> The better angel is a man right fair,
> The worser spirit a woman colored ill.
> To win me soon to hell, my female evil,
> Tempteth my better angel from my side,
> And would corrupt my saint to be a devil,
> Wooing his purity with her foul pride.
> And whether that my angel be turned fiend,
> Suspect I may, yet not directly tell;
> But being both from me, both to each friend,
> I guess one angel in another's hell:
> Yet this shall I ne'er know, but live in doubt,
> Till my bad angel fire my good one out.

Sarah Williams' half-dressed state increased the efficacy of the application of holy objects to her body. These objects included the priests' own clothes, including their gloves and stockings, which they put onto Sarah's bare hands and legs in order to chase the demons from her limbs into her torso. Another such holy object was a priest's stole, which was used to "beat [Sarah] pitifully about the face" in an attempt to "hunt the devil out of her." Another such holy object was a relic—a thumb bone—from the recently executed Jesuit martyr, Edmund Campion, which was forcibly inserted into Sarah's mouth. Sarah, "loathing the same" because she thought it "against nature to have a bone of a man put into one's mouth," resisted. Father Dibdale and the other exorcists interpreted this resistance as that of Sarah's demons, who were afflicted and pained by the holy martyr's presence. When Sarah began her menstrual period, the priests told her that "the devil did rest in the most secret part of her body," and ordered another maidservant to apply Campion's sacred relic to Sarah's vulva," an occurrence that Sarah later said she "loathed the memory of." Presumably, it was this same maidservant who was later induced by the priests to "squirt something by [Sarah's] privy parts into her body, which made her very sick." This unusual form of exorcism was deemed a success, since the priests "gave it out that the devil departed out of her by her priviest part." The priests told Sarah that she would never be able to have children because her womb had been tainted and torn by the demon that had occupied it for so long. (She later gave birth to five children.)

The priests' traditional approaches to expelling the evil from Sarah Williams were, essentially, magical. Magic had been important for the Catholic church from its earliest days, with both clergy and lay folk considering it an inherent feature of the religion because of the many scriptural miracles performed by "magicians" such as Moses, Solomon, and Jesus: parting the Red Sea, casting out demons, turning water into wine. Of course, religious orthodoxy mandated that magic was to be practiced only by authorized agents of the church, since the practice of unauthorized magic by lay folks undermined the church's control over its parishioners. Furthermore, secular practitioners of magic often misunderstood an essential theological principle: that the purpose of prayer was to request, not demand, divine aid. The magical elements of early Christian ritual were never held to be automatically efficacious by the church, only by the uneducated.

Though they did not approve of lay folk expropriating church magic, the medieval Catholic clergy generally tolerated the practice. Secular magicians were deemed misguided or ignorant but were rarely prosecuted, so medieval secular magicians practiced their art with a fair amount of impunity. The clergy, however, generally communicated very poorly with the lay folk, who generally did not understand arcane theological concepts despite the fact that church attendance was mandated by law; that the church was the primary official mouthpiece for the government; that it controlled employment through the licensing of doctors, midwives, and schoolmasters; and that it shaped public opinion through censorship. Despite these controls, the behavior of churchgoers was often less than reverent: contemporary accounts tell us that while in church, parishioners knitted, told jokes, spat, urinated, slept, and fought. Though such behavior was, of course, punished by church officials, many of the other co-opted parishioners approved of such subversive activity. Ignorance of religious principles was rampant throughout England, especially in rural areas. Many common folk who considered themselves good Christians did not know the name of God's son, the number of the commandments, or the identity of Adam and Eve. To the medieval Catholic peasantry, religion was not about belief, knowledge, or understanding, but about a ritual way of life.

Failing to grasp the church's distinction between authorized and unauthorized magic, many lay folk adopted the church's rituals and symbols to use for the benefit of themselves or others, either for charity or for profit. These rituals and symbols inevitably changed form and meaning through their repeated use by those who never understood their real significance in the first place. It is easy to understand how a Latin prayer repeated a thousand times by someone who does not understand Latin might well undergo changes that would render it nonsensical to someone who does have a knowledge of Latin. The church's magic words, such as formal prayers and curses, were embraced and secularized by the laity with great frequency. In cultures that are largely illiterate, language often embodies very powerful magic. We see a vestige of this concept even today in the fact that court witnesses are still sworn to tell the truth through ritual language and gestures. Just as the church used ritual curses in anathematizing and excommunicating its enemies, so did the common folk. Just as the church used ritual prayers to appease and supplicate divine power, so did the common folk. Hundreds of folk prayers, alternatively called charms, survive to this day, including the child's prayer "Matthew, Mark, Luke, and John, bless the bed that I lie on." Both clergy and lay folk used prayers of intercession to avert plague, bad harvests, or foul weather. Both clergy and lay folk used prayers and rituals of divination to find the answers to important questions: How can I cure my sick child? Who stole my cow? Where can I find buried treasure?

In adapting church practices for their own use, however, the common folk often failed to understand the theological principles underlying the practices. For instance, the church sanctioned petitionary prayers only if they were used in the public interest. Nevertheless, many poor and uneducated folk, living hand-to-mouth by any means available, sometimes prayed for divine assistance in executing a successful theft or robbery. Similarly, having been taught by the church that baptism afforded divine protection to infants, many common folk attempted to provide the same protection for their cows and horses, baptizing them with holy water in ritual ceremonies. Having been taught by the church that material sacrifice was a godly act, many folk sacrificially burned livestock or other valuable property in an attempt to counteract evil.

In 1517, Martin Luther nailed his 95 theses to the door of All Saints Church in Wittenberg. A few years earlier, this act would have incited only a minor local argument, but the recent advent of the printing press now insured that Luther's act would incite a spectacular theological controversy that raged throughout Europe. The Reformation was on. And its ultimate success in Germany, Switzerland, England, and Scotland derived at least partially from the weapon that the Catholic church had handed to its opponents on a silver syllogism: if all unauthorized magic is witchcraft, and if the Catholic church is unauthorized, then Catholic magic is witchcraft. This was the political atmosphere in which Sarah Williams' exorcists were forced to operate—risking their lives—in their attempts to save her soul.

During their exorcisms of Sarah Williams, the priests frequently discussed other cases of demon possession they had seen or heard of, describing

> the manner of [the demoniacs'] fits, and what they spoke in them, also what ugly sights they saw sometimes, and at other times what joyful sights, and how when relics were applied unto them the parties would roar, how they could not abide holy water nor the sight of the sacrament, nor the anointed priests of the Catholic church, nor any good thing, but how they would greatly commend such as were heretics, how the devils would complain that when the priests touched the parties that they burnt them and put them into an extreme heat, and how sometimes they could smell the priest.

These discussions, carried on in Sarah's presence, clearly indicated how the priests expected Sarah to behave, and she, accordingly, behaved in the expected way. She "always framed her [answers] to use such words as she thought would content the priests." Sarah later admitted that, while she was "so bound in the chair, her head being giddy with the said drink and her senses troubled with the smoke, she doubted not but that she spoke many idle and foolish words which the priest would expound as they thought good."

Later, as an adult, Sarah said that

> after she once came to be under [the priests'] hands, they used the matter so with her as that she never durst do anything but what she thought did please them, so as the longer she continued with them, the more they wrought upon her, because she had learned what words did best like them . . . [and] she could tell how to feed them with visions, saying she had seen this and that when she had seen no such matter, but only spoke to content them.

The priests perceived that they were driving demons from Sarah's body with considerable frequency. Each time they perceived a temporary victory, they asked Sarah to name the demon that had just been dislodged from her body. Sarah was afraid to deny the priests the answer they sought, so she produced names: Hobberdidance, Lusty Dick, Killico, Hob, Cornercap, Puff, Purr, Frateretto, Flibberdigibbet, Haberdicut, Cocobatto, Maho, Kellicocam, Wilkin, Smolkin, Nur, Lusty Jolly Jenkin, Porterico, Pudding of Thame, Pourdieu, Bonjour, Motubizanto, Bernon, and Delicate. Years later, Sarah would admit that many of these names came into her head from stories she had learned as a child or had been told by the women of the household as they went about their work. For instance, "Pudding of Thame" was something that Sarah had heard "spoken of jestingly when she was a child." Indeed, a variation of the nursery rhyme in which Sarah heard this name was still in use during the twentieth century: "What's my name? Puddin' Thame. Ask me again, and I'll tell you the same." Similarly, "Maho," an abbreviation of "Mahomet" (Mohammed), was a common name for the devil in early modern England, with the name appearing in folk tales and jest books. Likewise, "Hob" (and its variant, "Hobberdidance") was a common name for a goblin in English folklore.

During the months of her misery, Sarah attempted to please the priests in order to avoid some measure of binding, flogging, pinching, suffumigation, forced drinking, name-calling, and other harassment that the priests believed they were inflicting on the demons inhabiting Sarah's body. Her compliance with the priests' expectations, however, did not ameliorate her treatment. Once, Sarah pleaded with one of the priests, begging him to stop the exorcisms and asserting that she had no evil spirits within her. This priest "cast his head aside, and looking fully upon her face under her hat, said, 'What, is this Sarah or the devil that speaks these words? No, no, it is not Sarah, but the devil.' And then [Sarah], perceiving that she could have no relief at his hands, fell a-weeping, which weeping also he said was the weeping of the evil spirit." The priests perceived these fainting fits as demoni-cally induced, so they prayed for her and applied holy water to her body. When she regained consciousness, again the priests assumed that her recovery resulted from God's mastery of the demon within her. The exorcisms continued.

During this time, Sarah's mother, who had heard reports of her daughter's illness and treatment, on several occasions tried to gain access to Sarah in order to judge the situation for herself. Each time she tried, however, the priests told her that Sarah was possessed by demons and that her mother must not see or speak to her until she was completely freed of evil. "With this and suchlike answers, they sent away her mother diverse times weeping." Finally, Mistress Will-iams, now angry, used "hard speech" against the priests and demanded to see her daughter. The priests rejoined, in words as angry as her own, that she herself seemed to harbor as many demons as did her daughter, and they threatened to take her in hand and treat her with the same exorcisms to which they were subjecting Sarah. Because the exorcisms and other religious activities in the house were fully supported by the household's master and mistress, Sarah's mother could not appeal to the Peckhams to assist her in gaining access to her daughter. Indeed, one of Mistress Peckham's women told Sarah's mother that the priests would shortly "deal with her as they did her daughter." Sarah's father, too, was denied access to his daughter. The parents were not to see their daughter for four years.

Sarah's sister, who was also a maidservant in the same house, many times tried to persuade Sarah to "steal away and go home and complain how she had been handled by the said priests." Once, Sarah did just that, running away from the house and towards a brook, thinking that any household pursuers would not follow her through the water. She was apprehended, however, before she reached the brook, and the priests, who "watched her so diligently at all times as they would not suffer her to go out of their sights," naturally interpreted this behavior as demonically inspired, believing that her desperate bid to reach the water was a suicide attempt, that Satan had induced her to drown herself. She was brought back to the house, and the exorcisms continued. During these months, virtually everything Sarah did or said confirmed the priests' perception that she was possessed. Any dream of hers was deemed a vision sent by Satan. Any rumbling in her belly was heard as a demon's voice. Certainly, any impatience or frustration on her part at the priests' treatment of her was perceived as the devil's repudiation of God's holiness.

During the months of Sarah's exorcisms, other adolescents in the household were also exorcised, including Sarah's sister, Fid Williams; Anne Smith, who suffered from "fits of the mother" that were not helped by medicine; Elizabeth Calthrope, who died of a broken neck after falling down the stairs while she was in the care of the priests; William Trayford, Master Peckham's manservant; Richard Mainy, educated at the English seminary at Rheims; and Nicholas Marwood, servant to Anthony Babington, who was soon to be convicted and executed for treason along with some of the priests that had been harbored by the Peckhams. The purpose of the exorcisms was, of course, political: to demonstrate the power of the Catholic church over evil, a power superior to that wielded by the Protestants.

Such a demonstration required an audience, as with all such exemplary exorcisms and dispossessions, and the audience duly attended. One estimate numbered the audience for the exorcisms at "sometimes a hundred in a week," including both Catholics and Protestants. The estimates of the number of people converted to Catholicism by watching these exorcisms ranged from a low of five hundred to a high of three or four thousand. The exorcists believed that "those who came thither and would not be reconciled [to the Catholic church] were in great danger, whereas if they would submit themselves and reconcile themselves, then the devil should have no power of them." In the presence of these large audiences, the demoniacs (speaking with the voice of the devil) routinely praised Protestants and saluted them as comrades in evil. One important

Protestant visitor was quite offended at receiving such a greeting, saying that he had come to witness the events thinking that he "should have seen some godliness, and not to have heard the devil." He judged what he saw as "abominable," and he "marveled that the house did not sink for such wickedness committed in it." After this visitor angrily departed the house, the priests were concerned that his anger might be dangerous to them, so they spent that night in a different place.

During the late spring of 1586, about eight months after Sarah Williams' exorcisms had commenced, "there began to be great speeches in the country about the priests' doings at Denham, insomuch as diverse Catholics themselves did utterly dislike them, and the priests themselves grew to be afraid." One of the Peckhams' harbored priests was arrested in May, and the house was raided in June. The remaining priests scattered and went into hiding, taking Sarah and some of the other demoniacs with them, frequently moving them to and from safe houses in the London area, financially supported with funds provided by wealthy Catholic sympathizers. This secreting of Sarah (during which time she never saw her parents) continued for nearly four years. During this time, Sarah was on several occasions summoned by justices of the peace and other officials who hoped to induce her to testify against the priests. Still maintained by and under the influence of the priests, however, she confessed nothing. Eventually, the priests who had participated in the exorcisms were nearly all apprehended and imprisoned, with many being executed for treason. Finally, Father Dibdale himself was executed, and Sarah was committed to prison for five months for her failure to attend church during the previous four years.

Sarah was finally released from prison through the influence of her new confessor, Father Richard Yaxley, who had been among the priests harbored by the Peckham family during the time of her exorcisms but who had not participated in (or approved of) the exorcisms. Father Yaxley "caused diverse [people] to make earnest suit for her; much venison was bestowed upon the scholars, and at the last she was called before a doctor, and after some few speeches delivered." Father Yaxley then gave Sarah a dowry to allow her to marry and advised her to "refrain from the company of her husband for the first three nights" following the wedding, which she did. Perhaps the book of

Ego fum Papa.

The Papist Devil, "Ego sum Papa" (I am the Pope). From a Reformation
handbill against Pope Alexander VI, Paris, late fifteenth centry.

Tobit's story about the murderous, demon-possessed bride continued to cause some apprehension in the minds of Sarah and Father Yaxley.

Father Dibdale, Father Yaxley, and some of the other priests harbored by the Peckham family during this episode were designated Venerable Martyrs by Pope Leo XIII in the late nineteenth century.

Chapter 8
Katherine Wright

For many years, Katherine Wright was routinely beaten by her stepfather, John Meekin, so badly that her body was often covered with bruises. The young woman claimed that it was because of these repeated beatings that she developed a chronic weakness characterized by insomnia and "ill-headedness." One morning in 1586, when she was about seventeen years old, she went out to fetch water from the well. While out, she imagined that she saw "a child without feet," a frightening hallucination that proved to be the first of many "diverse shapes and apparitions" that began to trouble her greatly. About this time, she also began to suffer periodic swelling in her body, occasioned (as she later discovered) "by some stopping of humors, not unknown to diverse women."

This reference to the "stopping of humors" in women alludes to a phenomenon known in early modern England as the "rising of the womb" or the "suffocation of the mother." This idea presumed that the uterus could and did travel inside the body, rising to compress the heart and lungs, rendering the woman breathless and faint. Such malfunction was caused, it was thought, by the fact that the uterus was itself a sentient organism, capable of sensory perception and voluntary motion.

This idea was very old, dating back at least to the fourth century B.C., when Aristotle articulated the notion that the uterus was "an animal eager for young . . . believed to open and suck in male seed in conception, to have voluntary motion, and to be much affected by smells."

Fifteen hundred years later, the idea that the uterus was capable of voluntary action still prevailed, as we see from a tenth-century manuscript containing an exorcism of the womb for the treatment of hysteria: "To the pain in the womb. In the name of God the father, God the son, and God the holy spirit. Lord, our God, who commands the host of angels that are standing before him in trembling awe. Amen, amen, amen. O womb, womb, cylindrical womb, red womb, white womb, fleshy womb, bleeding womb, large womb, neufredic womb, bloated womb, O demoniacal one!" This invocation was followed by several others, each beginning "I conjure thee, O womb," by various holy names. The uterus was ordered to avoid traveling to and occupying the patient's head, throat, neck, chest, stomach, spleen, kidneys, and other body parts, being mandated to "lie down quietly in the place God chose" for it. The idea of the sniffing, traveling uterus persisted well past Katherine Wright's day, and well into the eighteenth century.

The presumed primary cause of this phenomenon was the innate humoral coldness of the uterus. In married (that is, sexually active) women, this coldness was counteracted by the heat of sexual intercourse. The sentient uterus was therefore satisfied and had no cause to travel through the body in search of heat. In unmarried (that is, sexually inactive) women, however, since no heat was transmitted to the uterus via sexual intercourse, that organ was forced to travel upward to seek heat from the warmer organs inside the woman's body, such as the heart and lungs. Furthermore, the woman's failure to evacuate seed (a universally accepted idea at the time) further unbalanced her humors, exacerbating the problem. The logical prescription for an unmarried woman suffering from rising of the womb, therefore, was marriage, and many physicians prescribed it as the appropriate remedy.

Perceived not only as mobile, the uterus was also perceived as having an olfactory sense, being attracted to sweet odors and repulsed by disagreeable ones, as Aristotle had said. The rising of the uterus, therefore, could be counteracted by introducing pleasant odors into the vagina, thus attracting the uterus and inducing it to descend inside the woman's body. Addressing this concept, one remedy for a married woman afflicted with a risen uterus was for her husband "to anoint the top of his yard with a little oil of gilliflowers and oil of sweet almonds together and so to lie with her, for this assuredly brings down the matrix again." Conversely, the introduction of offensive scents into the afflicted woman's nostrils was thought to drive the uterus away, forcing it to descend. The patient's head might be held over a chamber pot full of urine and feces. She might be forced to inhale the fumes of burning tobacco, feathers, hair, or old shoes. She might be subjected to the repulsive but therapeutic odors of asafetida, ammonia, or "whatever else has a filthy and ungrateful smell." Such repulsive scents, it was thought, would drive the uterus back down to its normal place, would "recall the disorderly and deserting spirits [humors of the uterus] to their proper stations."

The physical effects of the rising of the uterus—effects peculiar, of course, to women—were dramatic and disturbing: uncontrollable laughter or weeping, thrashing, bodily rigidity, sensory unresponsiveness, violent body motions, or other antisocial behavior. Today, the word *hysterical* is a general, non-medical term used in common speech to characterize someone exhibiting such behavior. The wide range of unusual and dramatic but often unrelated behaviors historically subsumed by this term indicate no single disease. For this reason, the word *hysteria* is no longer used as a medical diagnosis. Modern terminology has replaced it with *conversion symptom,* reflecting Freud's theory that the sufferer has unconsciously altered or converted an emotional trauma into a physical illness. In the early modern era, however, hysteria was indeed a medical diagnosis—one specifically connected with the uterus. In fact, the word hysteria derives from the Greek word *hystera*, meaning uterus. Although our first knowledge of the word's use in an English medical diagnosis occurred in 1602, twenty-seven years after Katherine Wright's case, the concept that the risen uterus caused such symptoms in young women had been well established for centuries among both medical specialists and the general community. For instance, in 1600 physician Augustine Syward diagnosed a young hysteric, Margaret Francis, as suffering from "uteri suffocatio or strangulatio." Clinician Thomas Sydenham estimated that, next to fever, hysteria was the most common disease of the seventeenth century.

Not until 1618 did French physician Carolus Piso (Charles Lepois) make the first clear medical statement that "all the hysterical symptoms [that]. . . have been attributed to the uterus . . . come from the head" and are common to both men and women. In the 1680s, physiologist Thomas Willis used anatomical dissection to prove that in hysterical patients who had died, the uterus was unaffected and could therefore not be the cause of the hysteria. He also pointed out that the uterus "is so strictly tied by neighbouring parts round about, that it cannot of itself be moved, or ascend from its place." The concept of the risen uterus, however, would remain entrenched in medical thinking until the mid-eighteenth century. As late as 1755, a commonly used manual of midwifery would assert that it was a "certain truth that the womb flies from all stinking and to all sweet things."

The symptoms of hysteria were virtually the same as the symptoms of demon possession, so the two conditions were therefore frequently connected. One physician wrote, "No man . . . is ignorant what grievous symptoms the rising, bearing down, and perversion, and convulsion of the womb do excite, what horrid extravagancies of mind, what frenzies, melancholy distempers, and outrageousness the preternatural diseases of the womb do induce, as if the affected persons were enchanted"—or possessed. The English physician who used the word *hysteria* in 1602, Edward Jorden, noted case after case of young women afflicted with hysteria (diagnosed either by him or by other reputable physicians) whose symptoms closely resembled those of supposed demoniacs: anesthesia, rigidity or palsy of limbs, heart palpitations, a choking sensation, fainting, deafness and speechlessness, immoderate or inappropriate laughing or crying, and depraved appetite. The symptomatic similarity of the two conditions reinforced the widespread perception that women—particularly young women—were more commonly possessed by demons than men. In his 1603 expose of Catholic exorcism, bishop Samuel Harsnet satirically alluded to this idea when he observed that "we find not an old woman in an age to be possessed by the devil: the devils of our time in this horizon loving more tender dainty flesh" and asked rhetorically why devils "bear such a spite . . . to young girls and maids that they ordinarily do not at all vex any but such."

Upon reporting her troubles to her parents, Katherine Wright discovered an alteration in her stepfather's behavior towards her. Dispensing with his customary impatience and abuse, he now "made much of her," with the result that she "grew to be indifferently [moderately] well" and her hallucinations disappeared. Not wishing to lose her newly won parental approval, however, she began to simulate a continuation of her former affliction: "yet she did still pretend to be troubled with her former kind of fancies and apparitions, and in her fits of swelling [she] did voluntarily make herself to seem worse than indeed she was by screeching, casting her arms abroad, starting up suddenly from the place where she sat, and sometimes by falling down, as though she had swooned."

Before long, Katherine Wright's afflictions became well known around the countryside, and many people came to see her, some motivated by charity and some by curiosity. She received so many visitors that a Master Beresford called her away from her stepfather's house and installed her in his own because, as he said, "her father's house was no fit place to give entertainment to any that should come to help her."

A month later, around Easter, Master Beresford dispatched her to the town of Mansfield to lodge with a yeoman named Edward Loades. While there, she was instructed to seek the help of a 24-year-old minister named John Darrell, "a man of hope for the relieving of those which were distressed in that sort." Two days later Wright received new visitors: John Darrell, Darrell's wife, and four other people.

Darrell examined Katherine Wright and diagnosed demon possession, asserting that he could hear the voices of several demons inside the young woman's body, one of which identified itself as "Middlecub." Having confirmed the effect, Darrell next looked for the cause, asking Wright how her fits began. She responded that they had begun shortly after she had refused to give charity to an old woman named Margaret Roper. Darrell, unsurprisingly, determined that Margaret Roper must be a witch and that she must have initiated Wright's affliction by sending the demons into the young woman's body.

Two days after his arrival at Master Loades' house, Darrell launched his assault on Middlecub and his demonic cohorts with an eight-hour prayer marathon that began at four in the morning and continued until noon. Darrell's view was that prayers were the "best means to withstand Satan" and that they "must be made without wavering." He was accompanied in these prayers for the duration by his own entourage but not by the householders, who, according to Darrell, were "not so devout that they would forebear all worldly business to attend that holy exercise."

A few years later Darrell would become famous for insisting that the prayers employed in the casting out of demons had to be accompanied by fasting. In this case, however, he did not so insist, later claiming that at this early stage of his career he had not yet fully developed his opinion on the matter. As he explained for this case, "There was no fast appointed, but I for my part did fast, and I think I did move Katherine Wright to do the like." Unfortunately for Darrell's credibility on this point, Master Beresford said he dined with Darrell on the day that Darrell claimed to have fasted: "Master Darrell's was but a curtal [brief] fast."

The yoked practice of prayer and fasting had for centuries been perceived as efficacious in all kinds of spiritual endeavors. It was widely believed that the devout who both prayed and fasted enjoyed God's favor in many ways:

> And as thus the people of God in all ages have, in the day of their adversity, assembled themselves in prayer and fasting, and God hath greatly blessed the fasts which they have in public and in common kept together in their solemn and open assemblies; so, and in like manner, the servants of God have, in secret, and apart from other, fasted and prayed, and God hath likewise greatly blessed the same unto them; whither they humbled themselves before his majesty for and because of some common calamity, either present upon the church, or imminent and hanging over it, or private affliction or want of some good thing, public or private, which also is a kind of misery.

Fasting added to prayer was perceived as a means of increasing the fervency of the spirit, afflicting both mind and body in sorrow for one's sins, and reminding the sinner of his or her corporeality and frailty. All this, it was thought, would improve the efficacy of the prayer. The practice of joint prayer and fasting as an effective weapon against demons, then, derived naturally from the principle that this same practice was efficacious in any spiritual undertaking. The practice also enjoyed patristic endorsement, as from Saints Augustine, John Chrysostom, and Clement. The third-century Pseudo-Clement recommended that those wishing to relieve sufferers of demons do so "in the lowly and meek spirit of Christ, and with fasting and prayer let us exorcise."

Among nonconformist Protestants in post-Reformation England (such as John Darrell), prayer and fasting as a therapeutic remedy for spiritual afflictions, either one's own or those of others, assumed great importance. Long after Darrell's time, throughout the seventeenth century, prayer and fasting constituted a frequent private or group activity among nonconformists, particularly (though not exclusively) to address cases of spiritual distress. It was not unusual for the devout to practice this discipline weekly, pushing themselves to such extremes (such as spending three consecutive days in prayer and fasting) that they might begin to see visions, hear voices, or make prophecies. Formal and often public, prayer fasts often attracted crowds of curious spectators, particularly if the person on whose behalf the assembly had congregated demonstrated melodramatic behavior. Not merely long sessions of pious supplication, prayer fasts were a dramatization of a psychomachy, a theatrical presentation of the battle of good versus evil, as exciting as any stage melodrama. For instance, during the day of fasting and prayer held on behalf of young Hannah Crump in 1662, the distressed girl raged, bit her own flesh, tore off her clothes, spat on the presiding ministers while they were praying for her soul, and struck the members of her family when they tried to restrain her. To the assembled witnesses, such behavior seemed manifest proof of the presence and power of an intelligent, malevolent spirit within the girl. Her eventual relief through the hours-long continuous prayer fast led by the ministers was far less significant than the triumphant subduing of Satan by the power of God, and the crowd was treated to a satisfactorily cathartic and exemplary finale: "And let all the people of England know to whom this may come, that not by our own power, but by the power of God, in the name of Jesus, [was Hannah Crump] made perfectly whole."

The popularity of this practice throughout the seventeenth century owed much to Darrell's proselytizing on the matter. His writings explained that fasting and prayer were a "perpetual secret ordinance" from Christ on how to drive away the most tenacious types of devils, those that "could not be expelled by sole prayer, without fasting annexed unto it." Christ's purpose in ordaining this method of dispossession was "to put down such an ordinary means for the powerful expelling of devils to the end of the world." Darrell stressed the "ordinariness" of these means to counter his enemies' perceptions and accusations that he was setting himself up as a miracle-worker, that he was accomplishing supernatural feats, and that he perceived himself as a holy man. Christ and his disciples, said Darrell, performed miracles when they cast demons out by a mere word, but he, in all humility, practiced demon dispossession through the non-miraculous means of prayer and fasting—acts which, in themselves, had not the power to cast out demons but rather sanctified a congregation's request to God that he do so. Darrell's followers on this point were frequently even more vociferous on the holy efficacy of prayer and fasting than he, such as the North American colonial minister Cotton Mather (he who became infamous because of the Salem witch trials), who asserted, "Prayer with fasting we knew to be a course against which none but men most brutishly atheistical . . . could make exceptions."

Darrell's success in popularizing this old practice of spiritual self-abasement as the only effective weapon against demon possession was demonstrated by the grudging support given to the practice by some who were much more skeptical than he. For instance, several physicians, including Edward Jorden (who diagnosed hysteria in the 1602 case of Mary Glover), admitted that fasting and prayer were frequently effective in calming and normalizing the behavior of demoniacs, although they also asserted the effectiveness derived from natural, medically explainable reasons, since such acts "calmed the passions."

Not everyone agreed with Darrell on the holy efficacy of prayer and fasting. Many conforming ministers perceived that, despite Darrell's disclaimers of humility, he was assuming too much personal power. They pointed out that demon possession was "an extraordinary judgment" executed by the will of God (not by that of Satan, who was merely God's instrument). Such an extraordinary event could not be effectively addressed by the "ordinary" means that Darrell deemed fasting and prayer to be. They observed that his assertion that prayer and fasting together were a more powerful means to cast out devils than was prayer alone amounted to a "blasphemous taking of the Lord's holy name in vain, by so vainly abusing the holy ordinance of prayer." Prayer was to be undertaken in perfect faith; to append fasting clearly indicated a lack of faith in prayer itself. Furthermore, the established church was suspicious of prayer fasts involving large groups of dissenters meeting in private homes without the beneficial religious leadership of a government-licensed minister. In an age in which religious dissent was perceived by the government as potentially treasonable, such meetings smacked of riot, disorder, chaos, and loss of political control.

In 1604, therefore, when a high-ranking administrative body of the English church adopted a body of canon laws, one of those laws, Article 72, expressly forbade special meetings for fasting and prayer unless such meetings were authorized by a diocesan bishop. Without such episcopal license, ministers were forbidden "to attempt upon any pretense whatsoever, either of possession or obsession, by fasting and prayer to cast out any devil or devils, under pain of the imputation of imposture, or cozenage, and deposition from the ministry." To insure that Article 72 was enforced throughout the nation, bishops were instructed to ask the church officials under their supervision "Whether hath your minister taken upon him to appoint any public or private fasts, prophecies, or exercises not approved and established by law or public authority, or hath he attempted upon any pretense either of possession or obsession, by fasting and prayer to cast out devils, yea or no?" Ministers reported for this offense were subject to an increasingly stringent penalty schedule: temporary suspension from the ministry for the first offense, permanent deposition for the second, and excommunication from the church for the third.

On the morning of Katherine Wright's dispossession, however, Darrell's enthusiasm on the subject of prayer and fasting and the political consequences ensuing from it lay in the future. On this morning, Darrell's enthusiasm manifested itself in a different way. As Wright later attested, "One fashion of Master Darrell in my pretended dispossession at Mansfield was to lie upon my belly, saying that he would by so lying press the devil out of me." When Darrell was questioned by a disapproving church commission about this episode, he admitted, "I having read in the Scriptures how Elias and Saint Paul did stretch themselves along on some that were dead in their recoveries to life, . . . I did in a blind zeal (as I think) lie upon the said Katherine Wright." He added that he could not remember what part of Wright's body he lay upon, but he did not think that it had been her belly. He hastened to add that he intended no imitation of these saints' holy miracles, but, as Katherine Wright was at the time "very unruly," he merely wanted to keep her body still. He also added that his wife was present during this procedure and that another person had assisted him in his work of pressing down Katherine Wright's unruly body.

The sexual implications of this episode were by no means unusual among cases of demon possession. Demoniacs frequently manifested behavior that onlookers could (and did) construe as sexual. For instance, in 1564 two nuns in the convent of Nazareth at Cologne "were frequently thrown to the ground and their lower torso was made to thrust up and down in the way usually associated with sexual intercourse. During this time, their eyes were shut, and later they opened them with shame, panting as though they had undergone a great labor." These attacks were at first thought to have been perpetrated by a licentious demon who forced the nuns to copulate with him. Later, it was discovered that the nuns had been having sex with young men who secretly entered the convent, and their behavior in the men's absence was attributed to Satan's corruption of their minds "with an image of the same, [which] presented to the eyes of those present the ignominious spectacle of such erotic movements." An even more notorious convent episode occurred in France in 1660, when the Ursuline sisters at Auxonne manifested their demon possession through the use of dildos, both on themselves and on each other. The interpretation of this behavior as demonic reflected the common opinion that masturbation ("the silent sin") was a sign of possession, an act forced by Satan. Skeptical Protestants, hostile to the institution of cloistered religious women, pointed out that such episodes were to be expected when young women were deprived of heterosexual activity but repeatedly subjected to sexual language and imagery in articulating their relationship to Christ, whose wedding ring they wore and into whose bed they vowed to enter. It was not at all unusual for early modern people to describe ecstatic communions with the supernatural in terms borrowed from erotic love. For instance, in the final couplet of John Donne's sonnet "Batter my heart, three-person'd God," the speaker addresses God as an importuning mistress might address her masterful lover: "for I, / Except you enthrall me, never shall be free, / Nor ever chaste, except you ravish me."

Not only did demoniacs sometimes manifest sexual behavior during episodes of possession but also their ministering clerics sometimes responded in kind. The physical and psychological nature of dispossession and exorcism often lent itself quite obviously to sexual interpretation. The demoniac, very frequently a young but sexually mature woman, often lay in bed wearing only her underwear (as we saw in the case of Ann Mylner), behaving in an emotionally and sometimes physically unrestrained manner, often arching her back, rolling her eyes up, opening her mouth, and displaying other behaviors mimicking sexual arousal. Today, the Roman Catholic Rubrics on Exorcism #19 warns,

> While performing the exorcism over a woman, [the priest] ought always to have assisting him several women of good repute, who will hold on to the person when she is harassed by the evil spirit. These assistants ought if possible to be close relatives of the subject, and for the sake of decency the exorcist will avoid saying or doing anything which might prove an occasion of evil thoughts to himself or to the others.

Both Catholics exorcists and Protestant dispossessors, however, occasionally failed to observe this principle.

For instance, cleric Samuel Harsnet, a scathing critic of dispossession and exorcism, made much of the fact that in 1585, the young demoniac Sarah Williams was greatly handled from foot to neck by the "holy hot hands" of her young exorcists, who apparently spent much time touching "her leg, her knee, her thigh, and so along all parts of her body." As we know, Williams later testified that, upon discovering that she was menstruating, the priests told her that her menses was a sign of demonic presence and attempted to exorcise her by having holy relics applied to her vagina: "At one time . . . when it began to be with me after the manner of women, the priests did pretend that the devil did rest in the most secret part of my body, whereupon they devised to apply the relics unto that place." This technique eventually caused the possessing devil, Maho, to exit Sarah Williams' body through her "nameless part, the devil's portgate," which the priests had "crossed, recrossed, and surcrossed with their holy hands . . . [and] seared with application of their reverend strong relics and their other potent holy parts."

A century later, not much had changed. Robert Calef, a Boston merchant, published a highly critical account of the dispossession of seventeen-year-old Margaret Rule in 1693 by Increase and Cotton Mather, a feat they managed by stroking her breasts and belly as she lay uncovered naked to below the waist. In treating the demoniac, Cotton Mather

> brushed her on the face with his glove and rubbed her stomach (her breast not covered with the bed clothes) and bid others do so too, and said it eased her, then she revived. . . . Then again she was in a

fit, and he again rubbed her breast, etc. . . . Then he put his hand upon her breast and belly on the clothes over her, and felt a living thing, as he said, which moved the father [Increase Mather] also to feel, and some others. . . . Then the ministers withdrew. . . . [The next night] Three or four persons rubbed and brushed her with their hands. They said that the brushing did put [the demoniac's fits] away if they brushed or rubbed in the right place; therefore they brushed and rubbed in several places and said that when they did it in the right place, she could fetch her breath.

The Mathers denied that they touched the demoniac's body in any "smutty" way. The demoniac herself, however, clearly interpreted their attention as sexual: she requested that no women (including her own mother) be allowed into the room during treatment, saying that only the company of men was beneficial to her. Following the Mathers' stimulation, she twice requested that young men attend her all night, claiming that she would die without male company.

In the case of Katherine Wright, John Darrell concluded that he had successfully dispossessed the demoniac of her demons on the morning that he lay upon her body, and Wright returned to the house of her patron, Master Beresford. Within a month, however, Beresford had determined that Wright was "as evil as before" and sent her to stay with her brother, Thomas Wright, at Whittington. Both this brother and Katherine Wright's stepfather, John Meekin, confirmed that she seemed no better after Darrell's treatment than before, continuing in her fits. Consequently, three weeks later, they requested Darrell to attend on her once more, and he agreed. Darrell's impending second visit to Katherine Wright received much publicity: "There was a great bruit [rumor] that a miracle should be done there." One witness, William Sherman, said that when he went to Thomas Wright's house at the time appointed for Darrell's visit, he found "four or five hundred people gathered together at and about the house of Thomas Wright, where the maid lay." This assertion was confirmed by Master Beresford, who, accompanying Darrell to Whittington, said that he and Darrell "found a great number gathered together to see what would become of the matter."

The hundreds who crowded around to witness Katherine Wright's affliction served an important social purpose. Like any other physically or mentally afflicted person, Wright needed to express her affliction in terms that were comprehensible to her community. The common cultural assumptions shared by Wright and her society provided the method of communicating to others the nature and extent of her problems. Within this culturally accepted context, the members of her community knew that they must help her and tolerate her aberrant behavior because they understood that behavior through a mutually comprehensible religious idiom. The temporary social alienation of the possessed person was a small sacrifice on the altar of communal solidarity. This temporary social alienation, furthermore, did not decrease the demoniac's standing in the community but rather increased it, rendering her message even more authoritative and urgent. In any culture that broadly accepts the literal, physical reality of evil, skepticism is generally perceived as an abnormal and eccentric rejection of normal values. Thus, Katherine Wright's friends and neighbors would very likely have perceived Wright's behavior as normal *within the assumed framework of possession*. This perception on the part of the observers was not merely tangential but vital to the cultural acceptance and understanding of Wright's experience.

For possession to be recognized as a legitimate phenomenon, the behavior of the possessed person had to be interpreted *by witnesses* as driven by the spiritual agent. Naturally, this behavior was expressed in terms meaningful to the possessed individual, but those terms had also to be meaningful to that individual's community. The communal interpretation of the affliction facilitated communication between the afflicted person and her fellows, allowing for the eventual reabsorption of the individual by the group. The necessity to reestablish commonality was why the affliction and its symptoms were often expressed in the religious concepts and terminology shared by the community. The existence of common cultural signs and symbols by no means guaranteed the formulation of a common interpretation of those signs and symbols. That is, possession was defined not merely by the behavior of possessed person but also by the observers' various perceptions of that behavior. Although the behavior of a possessed person was often assumed to be clearly distinct from the behavior of an unpossessed person, this was not always the case. For instance, early modern "inspired" speech among Quakers was often loud, trembling, nasal, and incoherent; but modern Quakers deem "inspired" speech to sound much like normal speech. Thus, an early modern Quaker and a modern one would interpret the same sign as having very different significations. Witnesses' interpretation of the behavior signifying possession was therefore an ongoing process that drew upon the witnesses' own personalities, motives, and beliefs.

Once more examining Katherine Wright, Darrell again diagnosed possession: "As soon as I came and saw her, I affirmed to those that were present that she was again repossessed." He asserted that she succumbed to trances in which she was "altogether senseless, and that whatsoever she either did or spake, it was not she, but the devil in her that did both." Katherine Wright's brother, Thomas, doubted this assertion, believing that "she had the commandment of her own senses and knew what she spake, because at all times she understood any questions made unto her and would answer roundly and aptly to the same." Similarly, Master Beresford doubted Darrell's assessment of the situation, saying, "At the time of her second pretended dispossession, I and others did ask her in her fits some questions, which she answered sensibly."

Darrell detected the presence of no less than eight devils, a number he ascertained by counting the voices conversing inside Wright's body, and he commanded these eight devils to reveal their names. The first name offered in response was "Roosye" [Boaster], which Darrell repudiated as a false answer, observing that "that name is common to all spirits." Darrell described this demon as speaking "in a very great voice, and in a very fierce and cruel manner." William Sherman, however, thought the voice "to be no other than the maid's voice, she lying under a covering. The speeches spoken (as Master Darrell said) by the spirit were verily taken to be the speeches of Katherine Wright and spoken by her in her natural voice and none other."

Darrell continued to press the demons for their names and was finally rewarded by one spirit's admission that its name was "Middlecub," which Darrell "approved to be his true name," the same name that had been ascertained during Katherine Wright's previous dispossession at Mansfield. Darrell confirmed the role of the accused witch in the affliction of Katherine Wright by asking Middlecub "who sent him thither," and the spirit identified Margaret Roper, as Wright herself had done during her first dispossession.

At some point during these proceedings, Darrell summoned a constable to escort him and Margaret Roper to a justice of the peace,

Godfrey Foljambe, so that Darrell could lodge a formal accusation of witchcraft against Roper and request that she be detained in jail pending a trial. Roper's confession of witchcraft would have been justification enough for Foljambe to confine her, but she made no such confession. Darrell attributed her denial of his accusation to demonic interference: "I verily think that Margaret Roper would sundry times have confessed herself to have bewitched Katherine Wright, but that still at the instant when she should have delivered those words, the devil (as I think) did stay her." Foljambe reproved Darrell for the accusation and threatened to imprison him "if he so demeaned himself any more." Foljambe apparently "found no cause in any sort to touch Margaret Roper and forthwith discharged her." Again, Darrell attributed the disappointment of his hopes to the devil's interference.

Undaunted, Darrell returned with Margaret Roper to Thomas Wright's house. There he tried to persuade Katherine Wright to scratch Roper until she bled, "saying that in so doing she should be cured." This was apparently done, "all which notwithstanding, the said Katherine received no ease thereby." Nonetheless, the eight demons lodged in Wright's body did eventually leave, presumably because of the force of Darrell's prayers. For the benefit of those spectators less spiritually attuned than he, Darrell

> took upon him to discern when every of the said eight spirits departed, saying to those that were present, 'There goeth out one spirit,' and then after a while, 'There goeth out another spirit,' and so the nimble fellow proceeded until, as he pretended, eight devils were gone out of her. It may be easily conceived in what a perplexity the people were when these eight devils were thought to be flying amongst them.

Of this evacuation of devils, Darrell himself said, "Katherine Wright, showing the signs of dispossession, as rending sore [wrenching violently], crying loud, and lying for dead, I affirmed that I believed that then one of the spirits went out of her, which signs appearing in her eight several times that day and the night following, I said she was possessed of eight wicked spirits and was also dispossessed of them." Darrell's opinion was that Wright enjoyed freedom from devils for six or eight weeks after this second dispossession but that she was eventually possessed for a third time.

Others, however, disagreed with Darrell's assessment of the case. For instance, Katherine Wright's stepfather, John Meekin, said,

> Master Darrell continued making of a wonder and a din to and with her (when he pretended to cast out eight devils of her), but what good he did her thereby, I could not perceive, neither could I find that she received any ease thereby. This I certainly know, that Master Darrell spent at Whittington some three days, and that after his departure, she continued as before in the self-same manner of fits that formerly she had used.

Similarly, Katherine Wright's brother, Thomas Wright, said,

> I could never find, either by mine own judgment or by the opinion of others that were present at the time of her said dispossessions or afterwards, that the said Darrell had done any good or ease unto the said Katherine during her abode with me. Which I most certainly do believe, for that the fits which she had before Darrell's coming to her in my house and at the time of his being with her and likewise all the time after were still alike, without any change or alteration.

Katherine Wright continued to live with her parents, simulating hallucinations and fits of swelling for the next fourteen years (until she was thirty-one years old). She did so, as she said, "partly because she was by that occasion much made of, and for that she feared that if she had showed herself to have been perfectly well for any long season, her father in law [stepfather] would have fallen to his former hard usage of her."

In 1599, however, Wright was examined by a church commission investigating the dispossessions of John Darrell. To this commission she confessed that, preceding both her first and second dispossessions, Darrell had conversed privately with her for the purpose of training her how to simulate the signs of possession convincingly, an accusation that Darrell consistently denied. Wright also confessed that never at any time had she believed that she had been troubled or infested by a demon. Never, she said, had she lain senseless in a trance but merely simulated doing so at Darrell's instigation: "I confess that Master Darrell put me in mind to be in trance and to lie as though I were senseless after my violent fits, and that at the time of my pretended dispossessing at Whittington, when I should have lain as though I had been dead, I fell fast asleep, and then when I awaked, I heard Master Darrell say to them that stood by that I had been in a trance." She also confessed that she learned the names of her evil spirits from Darrell, who initially spoke the names himself so that Wright could confirm them by speaking them back to him in the voices of the devils: "Which names . . . I remembered, when Master Darrell asked the supposed devils their names, and so did answer him in the person of the devils, according to the names that I had learned of him."

Concluding her examination by the church commission, Katherine Wright promised "to leave all her former practices and to become a new woman, and to live and work orderly and quietly with her mother and father, as it becometh an honest poor woman to do. John Darrell, however, remained resolute in asserting that Wright "was repossessed within a short time after he had left her, and that so she hath continued ever since, and so remaineth at this present."

Papist indulgence peddlers in the jaws of Hell. From a satiric
Reformation handbill, Germany, late sixteenth century.

Chapter 9
Thomas Darling

On Saturday, February 27, 1596, thirteen-year-old Thomas Darling accompanied his uncle, Robert Toon, on a hare-hunting expedition into the woods outside of the town of Burton upon Trent, Staffordshire, where Thomas was staying with his aunt and uncle. While hunting, uncle and nephew became separated, and Thomas wandered about alone in the woods. Suddenly he came upon a little old woman wearing "a gray gown with a black fringe about the cape, a broad thrummed hat, and three warts on her face." Thomas recognized this old woman as one he had previously seen begging door to door, but he did not know her name. As the old woman and the boy passed each other in the woods, Thomas happened to "let an escape" (quite by accident, he later declared). The old woman, angry, said to the boy, "Gyp [cheat] with a mischief and fart with a bell, I will go to heaven and thou shalt go to hell." The two then parted company, and Thomas told no one about this meeting until much later. Still separated from his uncle, Thomas returned home alone, feeling heavy and "very sick, vomiting and casting up what he had eaten at dinner," and retiring to bed in his illness. The next morning "he had some fits, with extreme vomitings, that all which saw him judged it to be some strange ague." Thomas also began to hallucinate, seeing green angels and a malevolent green cat outside his window. These hallucinations were judged by his friends to proceed from the lightness in his head.

Naturally worried, Thomas's aunt took a urine sample to a physician to ask for a diagnosis. The physician saw no sign of any natural disease in the urine except possibly worms, but prescribed medicine anyway. This medicine had no effect, and Thomas's illness worsened, so the aunt again visited the physician with another urine sample. Again, the physician confirmed his previous determination that Thomas's affliction did not derive from any natural illness, but this time he also offered the explanation that Thomas might be bewitched. The aunt thought this theory incredible and so told it to no one, still believing Thomas's affliction to be a natural illness—perhaps epilepsy— despite the physician's failure to diagnose it as such. Thomas's illness continued, manifesting "no continual distemperature, but came by fits, with sudden staring, striving, and struggling very fiercely, and falling down with sore vomits. It also took away the use of his legs, so that he was fain to be carried up and down, save in his fits, for then he was nimble enough." Between these episodes, Thomas behaved in a manner worthy of "one of riper years, wherein he showed the fruits of his education, which was religious and godly." He enjoyed conversing on pious subjects with other good Christians, "to whom he would signify his daily expectation of death and his resolute readiness to leave the world and to be with Christ." His one regret in dying so young was that he would never be able to grow up to be a great preacher "to thunder out the threatenings of God's word against sin and all abominations."

Adolescent Thomas Darling was displaying signs of what might have been interpreted, even by Elizabethans, as religious zealotry. Rigorous early modern theological doctrines such as millenarianism and predestination could generate or exacerbate a heightened level of social emotion manifesting itself in ecstatic religious experiences. Such experiences demonstrated the subject's immediate and intimate union with God, his privileged status in being divinely authorized to transcend normal social, political, and ecclesiastical controls. Demonstrably closer to God than anyone else in the room, the subject's vehement emotionalism became a token of divine favor. Alexander Nowell, dean of St. Paul's, observed that the "fervent affections" that often accompanied afflictions such as Darling's possession were signs of God's special grace: "the dearlier that any man is beloved of God, he is commonly more burdened with adversities. . . . The holy scriptures do testify that the Spirit of God raiseth up unspeakable groan-ings, whereby our prayers are made effectual. He therefore, without doubt, with his inspiration stirreth up our minds, and whetteth and helpeth us to pray." Thus, the culturally recognizable manifestations of those afflictions—for instance, Thomas Darling's "staring, striving, and struggling"—proved the subject's spiritually favored position within his community.

As an assertion of an individual's participation in the Godhead, ecstatic religious experiences had the further effect of threatening the established order. Since the subject's relationship with God was out-side the control of the organized spiritual community, it was automat-ically suspect and required careful supervision. In post-Reformation Europe, Christian religious ecstasy was frequently deemed dangerous to church and state authorities because it elevated individual inspira-tion over the establishment's authoritative rule. Hence, religious non-conformity, even in indifferent things such as kneeling during prayer or the wearing of clerical vestments, presaged rebellion, treason, and heresy. No doubt much of the institutional objection to personal ecstatic religious experiences derived from their socially subversive character. For instance, subjects frequently described their passionate communion with God in erotic language, the communion an explic-itly sexual one and the experience described as "half death" or "little death," just as sexual orgasm often was. Furthermore, such experi-ences often occurred within radical religious groups whose lack of orthodoxy rendered them automatically suspect in the eyes of the establishment: early modern Anabaptists, Methodists, Quakers, and so on. The fact that ecstatic experiences frequently occurred in front of large groups implied the threat of disorder and riot. Crowd behavior is psychologically regulated with considerable intensity, characterized by heightened emotion and increased suggestibility; thus, the assem-bling of a crowd into close contact with greatly limited body move-ments (such as to observe the ecstatic religious experience of one member of that crowd) facilitated swiftly contagious, strong emo-tional responses such as weeping and shouting—reactions that undermined social order and authoritarian control.

Thomas Darling suffered the same bouts of illness for over a month, until well into Lent. Then, on Sunday, March 21, his illness suddenly worsened. That day he began to fall into swoons, from which he recovered only with very great effort and pain, "striving and struggling in such sort that it was enough for two or three to hold him." At one point, he suddenly fell upon his back, roaring, and, supported by his head and feet, arched his body forcefully into the air. He then fell back down, "groaning very pitifully," turned over, and began to run around the room on his hands and feet. Then, again "striving and strangling with groaning, he fell a-vomiting." Finally emerging from this exhausting episode, Thomas fell upon his knees and cried, "The Lord's name be praised." The boy made this transition so suddenly that the bystanders were quite startled, "being no less comforted by the one than they were before grieved at the latter." This was the first of many such grand fits, which followed the same general pattern as the first and which occurred several times a day.

Thomas's friends and family prayed and read scripture aloud in an attempt to alleviate the boy's suffering, but nothing availed. Finally, a local man, Jesse Bee, "a private Christian and a man of trade," was sent for (he who eventually wrote the account of this case). Bee chose his scripture carefully and began to read the sixth chapter of the gospel according to John. At the fourth verse, Thomas lapsed into a fit. Bee kept reading, and Thomas's fits "continued one in the neck of another." Whenever Bee paused in his reading, Thomas vomited, praised God, and lay quietly. Whenever Bee resumed reading, however, Thomas's fits "came thick upon him." The fact that the reading of scripture apparently induced these fits led Bee to suspect that Thomas was bewitched. Bee mentioned this suspicion to Thomas's aunt, who offered the physician's opinion as corroboration. Overhearing this conversation, Thomas mentioned, for the first time, his meeting with the old woman in the woods. Immediately among the bystanders arose a "vehement suspicion" that this old woman was eighty-year-old Elizabeth Wright, known as "the witch of Stapen Hill," or else her daughter, sixty-year-old Alice Goodridge.

A tremendous impetus for witch belief in early modern England was the Biblical injunction in Exodus 22:18: "Thou shalt not suffer a witch to live." Because English translations of the Bible were a relatively recent phenomenon, this injunction carried great weight, despite the fact that the original Hebrew translated more accurately as "poisoner" than "witch." The availability of English Bibles coupled with rising literacy rates among the common folk greatly increased the popularity of scriptural literalism as a measure of truth. To these new scriptural literalists, to deny or even doubt the objective reality of any form of supernatural being mentioned in the Bible, whether God, demon, or witch, was an implicit admission of atheism. Moreover, atheism at that time was not just a matter of social difference, as it is now, but a crime against orthodoxy punishable by death. Needless to say, the great majority of people claimed a belief in witches, and witchcraft accusations were a normal part of village life, widespread and regular.

Thomas's fits continued for two more weeks, with his trouble-some hallucination of the green cat returning. Jesse Bee said, "When in his fits he was deprived of the use of speech, he would make signs of praying, with folded hands, sometimes lifting them up and some-times striking them upon his breast. Oft times also in these fits, he would suddenly and amazedly open his eyes, staring and striking most pitifully, clapping both his hands upon his face, not being able to endure the sight of such fearful objects as he beheld. In this manner he was tormented in the day, and had reasonable good rest in the night, except through some fearful dreams, whereunto he was much subject. Being asked if he could remember what he did when he made such signs, he answered that sometimes he prayed, and sometimes the cat tossed him up and down on a string. And thus for a good space he could remember and readily make relation of his troubles."

On April 8, the Thursday before Easter, Thomas was visited by his grandmother, Mistress Walkden of Clifton, and an aunt, Mistress Saunders. Upon being told the story of Thomas's meeting with the old woman in the woods, Mistress Walkden concluded that the boy probably was indeed bewitched and that the old woman was probably Alice Goodridge. Wanting more information before publicly accusing the old woman, Mistress Walkden sent for Alice Goodridge in order to interview her privately. When the old woman was reluctantly brought into Thomas's bedchamber, Thomas fell into a fit. After he recovered, Mistress Walkden asked Alice Goodridge if she knew the boy and was told no. "Many other questions were asked but in vain, for she would not confess anything." At the persuasion of some of the bystanders, Thomas scratched the old woman on the face and hands, drawing blood. The old woman stroked the boy with her bloodied hand, saying, "Take blood enough, child, God help thee." Thomas rejoined, "Pray for thyself; thy prayer can do me no good." In an aside, Bee explained,

> touching this use of scratching the witch, though it be commonly received as an approved means to descry a witch and procure ease to the bewitched, yet seeing that neither by any natural cause or supernatural warrant of God's word it hath nay such virtue given to it, it is to be received amongst the witchcrafts, whereof there be great store used in our land, to the great dishonor of God.

At this point, Thomas's uncle and the local schoolmaster took Alice Goodridge aside to interrogate her further. After much questioning, the old woman admitted that she had been in the woods on the day in question but that she had seen a different boy, not Thomas Darling. In response to the men's questioning, she also admitted that she had not received communion in a year and that she knew she was damned. When the men forced her to speak the Lord's Prayer and the creed, she omitted "And lead us not into temptation" in the former and the names of Christ and the Holy Ghost in the latter. Requiring a suspected witch to pronounce these prayers was a commonly accepted test both in and out of court. If the suspect omitted, mispronounced, or transposed any words in the prayer, the error was commonly interpreted as a sign that the person was indeed a witch, from the logic that Satan, the witch's master, was demonstrating his annoyance with the holy language. Such suspects were often Catholics, who had learned to pronounce prayers in Latin rather than English.

Despite the old woman's failure to pass these important tests, however, the men allowed her to return home. The next day Thomas Darling suffered many violent fits, during which he clapped his hands on his face, shrieked loudly, and said that the fearful green cat "with eyes like flames of fire" was again troubling him. His pain felt like "the pricking with daggers or stinging of bees." His uncle, perceiving the boy's great suffering, decided that the witch responsible for inflicting it should be brought to justice. On April 10, therefore, he and Jesse Bee, the "private Christian" who had read the gospel of John to the ailing boy, took their case to justice of the peace Thomas Graysley. Master Graysley ordered that the constable of Stapen Hill bring Elizabeth Wright and Alice Goodridge before him to answer the accusations. (The former had already appeared before him several times on suspicion of other offenses involving witchcraft.) Appearing before the justice, the two women denied that they intended any harm to Thomas Darling, although Alice Goodridge again admitted that she met a boy (though not, she repeated, Thomas Darling) in the woods on the day that Thomas fell ill. The women were released, but Thomas Darling continued ill during the days following this interrogation. His shirt mysteriously tied itself into knots between his legs, and he suffered for hours at a time in "senseless fits, with grievous groaning and fearful screaming, crying out, 'Look where the witch standeth with three warts on her face.'" He threw himself under the bed, shouting "Flames of fire, flames of fire!" He continued to alternate vomiting and praising God. He was terrorized by visions of devils emanating from his chamber pot.

On April 14, Master Graysley and Sir Humphrey Ferrers, another justice of peace, visited the house of Robert Toon, to which they summoned Elizabeth Wright, Alice Goodridge, and the latter's husband and daughter. Master Graysley ordered Thomas Darling to read aloud the first chapter of the gospel of John. The boy did so until he reached the fourth verse, when he fell into a fit and could no longer read. Then Master Graysley ordered Elizabeth Wright to be brought into the presence of the afflicted boy, who immediately began staring, thrashing, and gnashing his teeth. The old woman knelt to pray for the boy, but his fit continued. When she finally left the room, Thomas immediately recovered.

Sir Humphrey and Master Graysley determined that Elizabeth Wright and Alice Goodridge should be stripped and searched by a group of trusted women to ascertain whether they bore "any such marks on them as are usually found on witches." On Wright, the women discovered "behind her right shoulder a thing much like the udder of an ewe that giveth suck with two teats, like unto two great warts." On Goodridge, the women discovered "upon her belly a hole of the bigness of two pence, fresh and bloody, as though some great wart had been cut off the place." The searchers partially reclothed the two suspects, leaving the damning marks exposed, and returned them to the justices of the peace. Sir Humphrey questioned Goodridge about the bloody wound in her belly, and she responded that on Easter Sunday she had been descending a ladder

Witch riding to the Sabbath. From
Ulrich Molitor's Hexen Meysterey, 1545.

while holding a knife and had slipped and fallen, accidentally
thrusting the knife into her own belly. A surgeon summoned by the
justices refused to corroborate this explanation, saying that the
wound was much more recent than Goodridge said it was and that it
"seemed to be sucken." Further examination revealed that the
clothes Goodridge was wearing at the time of the alleged incident
showed no evidence of knife cuts. Her husband and daughter, when
questioned, "were found to disagree in their tales concerning that
matter." At this point, Sir Humphrey released Elizabeth Wright but
committed Alice Goodridge to jail.

Although the legal machinery for prosecuting witches had been in
place for many centuries, it was rarely used until Henry VIII, Elizabeth
I, and James I approved stringent new legislation which publicized
the concept of witch prosecution among the common folk and

divorced it from its old associations of heresy and blasphemy. The civil court's rules of evidence, remnants of ecclesiastical procedure, made it easy for a disgruntled villager to initiate a prosecution for witchcraft against an irritating neighbor but difficult for that neighbor to defend himself—or, more usually, herself. Judges, many of whom were privately skeptical, were sometimes forced to capitulate to public opinion to maintain order.

The court commonly followed popular opinion in exercising leniency in witchcraft cases unless the result of the witchcraft was harmful. Generally, the law became involved only in cases where harm could be proved, harm accomplished through the witch's touching the victim, looking at him, cursing him, or using mechanical aids like clay figures to work magic from a distance. Unlike on the continent, the witches' sabbath, the compact with the devil, flying, and shape-shifting did not figure prominently in English witchcraft trials, whereas witches' marks, pricking, and animal familiars did. Many witchcraft trials of the time documented the important role of children as material witnesses, although contemporary accounts sometimes comment on the unreliability of children's testimony. Some of these children may well have agreed to testify to avoid becoming the accused, as witchcraft was thought to be hereditary. Tests of innocence were imposed on suspected witches, such as forcing them to touch the corpse of the murder victim—both tests being remnants of old Catholic ordeals of innocence.

Of all the various forms of evidence admissible by the court, the most damning of all was an explicit confession of witchcraft by the accused, and confessions of witchcraft were frequent. The use of mechanical torture to extract confessions from witches was not lawful in England, but suspects were frequently starved, deprived of sleep, whipped, pricked, threatened, beaten, walked for days without rest, or asked leading and trick questions. One of King Charles I's lawyers said that an accused witch had told him that she confessed because, "being defamed for a witch, she knew she would starve, for no person thereafter would either give her meat or lodging, and that all men would beat her, and hound dogs at her, and that, therefore, she desired to be out of the world." In addition, some of those accused confessed because they, in fact, believed or wished themselves to be witches. Many poor, uneducated, unskilled, unemployed people

*Wizard riding to the Sabbath. From
Ulrich Molitor's Hexen Meysterey, 1545.*

scraped a meager living by extorting it from their neighbors through
threats of witchcraft, their only source of power.

For many more days, Thomas Darling continued to struggle with
his unseen adversary, now identified as the demon "Writhe," who
commanded the boy to worship Satan as God and to consider himself
the son of Satan. In addition to tempting Thomas to idolatry and blasphemy, the demon Writhe also tempted him to greed, offering him a
palace, a crown, and a great kingdom to rule. Thomas resisted with
much spirit and pious argument, enduring terrible torments for his
refusal to comply with the demon's commands. More visitors arrived
to witness the show, the gospel of John was again read aloud to pro-
voke the demon into its most spectacular demonstrations, old Elizabeth
Wright was again brought to the house to be stripped (this time with-

out the legal authority of the justices of the peace), and the strange growth on her body was again showed to the crowd.

Among the many ministers who visited Thomas Darling during his affliction was Arthur Hildersham, one of the most famous preachers of the age. A dissenting Protestant, he worked assiduously all his life for the greater reform of the English church. Equally famous for his zeal and his relationship to the royal family (Queen Elizabeth called him "cousin Hildersham"), he was an important religious celebrity throughout much of England. His presence at Darling's bedside, therefore, lent considerable cachet to the scene, and the demoniac was very conscious of the honor bestowed upon him by this important and godly person. Thomas many times addressed Hildersham directly during his episodes of affliction, beseeching his intercession: "Master Hildersham, preach and teach; oh, fast and pray, night and day." Hildersham carefully observed the boy's fits for several days and, equally carefully, asserted no opinion about whether he thought the boy was truly possessed by a demon. He did, however, make an important observation about demon possession, one that was apparently lost on most of the other people present. This observation was that for people to pray for the eviction of a demon possessing a human body was, in fact, a sin. Such a prayer was sinful, said Hildersham, because it clearly opposed the will of God, who had seen fit to inflict a "temporal correction" on the possessed person in furtherance of both God's glory and the demoniac's salvation. The role of prayer and fasting in such a case, said Hildersham, was not for the people to ask for the demon's eviction but to ask that God open their hearts in acceptance of his will.

Hildersham's comment made an important theological point. Why God would permit such a horror as demon possession to plague humanity, ostensibly his dearest creation, was a question that exercised a great many early modern thinkers. Reasons had to exist if God, "the cause of the order of the universe—or rather that very order itself—has created nothing at random or without order," as early modern physician Johann Weyer said. God's unquestioned omnipotence indicated that Satan's tormenting of man was indeed God's will, as Saint Gregory had said: "Satan's will is always wicked, but his power is never unjust, because he has his will from himself, but his power from the Lord. What he himself wickedly desires to do, God does not allow to be done, except justly. Therefore Satan should not be feared, because he avails nothing at all, except when permitted." Nonconformist John Webster emphasized that God's permission was not merely a passive acquiescence but an active mandate to Satan to levy torments on mankind: "there is not in God a nude, passive permission, separate from the positive and active decree, order and will of his divine providence and government, but that he doth rule all things according to the power and determination of his own positive and actual will."

Opinions varied considerably on the nature of those reasons. One common opinion was that demonic affliction was a trial of faith visited on God's chosen few, those selected for his special attention. As Weyer plainly said, "the lord God is testing you, so that it may be clear whether you love him or not." Thus, as for Job, the affliction was a badge of honor, a token of God's favor, a sign of sanctity. The contrary opinion was, however, equally common: that the affliction was God's just punishment for sin, either that of the afflicted individual or that of his community. As Peter Binsfield said, "the enormous and ever increasing depravity of the age has provoked God to let demons and witches do their worst against mankind." Far from being a sign of sanctity, therefore, the affliction was a scourge of shame. Many, like King James I, perceived no intellectual dilemma in holding both of these opinions simultaneously.

Another common opinion was that God ordained possession to demonstrate his power and glory, thus baffling skeptics and heretics, bracing the belief of the faithful, and convincing doubters of his truth. John Darrell said, "God hath . . . sent evil spirits into sundry English persons to vex them in their bodies, that thereby he might confound the atheists in England and . . . bring them to a better mind." That possession did indeed bear public witness to this truth was amply demonstrated by the hundreds, sometimes thousands of witnesses to possessions and exorcisms (or dispossessions) who were later claimed to have been converted from Catholicism to Protestantism, or vice versa. In the atmosphere of post-Reformation schism, when both Protestants and Catholics perceived that atheism and heresy were on the rise, the need for such divine demonstration was clearly more urgent than it had been in previous, more faithful ages.

Thus, despite much discussion, no consensus was reached on why God allowed possession to occur. Ultimately, of course, man could never hope to know God's reasons for allowing Satan to smite and torment certain individuals beyond others. Because God transcended the scope of man's understanding, his secret workings seemed irrational to man's limited reason. God's nature and motives were forever hidden from men, who must not expect to know or understand his mind, but only his word. Whatever the human mind did not understand had been deliberately withheld from view by God, who had no obligation whatsoever to explain himself to men and whose mercy was extended to them only for his own pleasure and for unknown purposes. As Martin Luther said, to question or seek to understand God is "to desire that for the sake of the ungodly God should cease to be God; for you are desiring that His power and activity should cease." God's will was by definition right because it was his will.

Hildersham's assessment of Thomas Darling's case apparently fell on deaf ears, but not so the assessment of the next minister to examine the situation: John Darrell, who had been threatened with imprisonment a decade earlier for his role in the unsuccessful dispossession of Katherine Wright. Darrell arrived on May 27. Like Hildersham before him, Darrell closely observed Thomas Darling in his fits. Unlike Hildersham, however, Darrell unhesitatingly assured the assembled multitude that the boy was indeed possessed by an unclean spirit. Furthermore, unlike Hildersham, Darrell informed Thomas that, far from its being a sin to pray for his deliverance from this demon, it would be a sin for him *not* to do so, would constitute capitulating to the devil. Again unlike Hildersham, Darrell assured Thomas of his certain victory over Satan, saying that Christ had promised that such demons "will or shall flee" in the face of faith sanctified by prayer and fasting. Although Darrell agreed to pray and fast with the crowd in preparation for the final battle, he refused to be present during the actual dispossession, not only to avoid the appearance of vainglory but also because he deemed his own presence unnecessary in light of Thomas's firm faith. Darrell then summarized what "interruptions were likely to follow by the enemy's rage" so that the crowd would know what to expect and would "therefore faint not in the mid-way." He then departed.

Darrell's decision not to stay for the dispossession was unusual. The avoidance of vainglory was not reason enough to keep him away during the dispossessions of Katherine Wright, the Starchy children, and William Somers, all of whom Darrell closely attended during their final battles with Satan. A sympathetic hypothesis is that he may have suspected that Darling's possession was exaggerated or faked and wished to distance himself from it. An unsympathetic hypothesis is that he may still have been smarting under the judicial warning levied on him ten years earlier, when justice Godfrey Foljambe threatened to imprison Darrell if he continued the practice of dispossession. Why Darrell chose not to stay for Darling's final show is unknown.

The next day, family and friends gathered around the demoniac's bedside at eight A.M. to pray, being much interrupted by the boy's violent fits, manifestations of Satan's protests at being thus harassed and threatened. At this final stand, the two demons inhabiting Thomas Darling identified themselves through conversations with each other. Surprisingly, neither one was Writhe, the demon who had revealed himself the previous month. As the prayers progressed, a small voice emanating from the demoniac said, "Brother Glossop [Tongue], we cannot prevail; his faith is so strong, and they fast and pray, and a preacher [Darrell in absentia] prayeth as fast as they." A big, hollow voice responded (again, from inside the demoniac), "Brother Radolphus, I will go unto my master Beelzebub, and he shall double [stop] their tongues." At this, Thomas Darling pointed to the spot in the room on which Beelzebub stood with "the witch by him," both figures invisible to the witnesses. Said Thomas (in his own voice) to Beelzebub, "I charge thee in the name of the father, the son, and the Holy Ghost to tell me whether this be she that did bewitch me or no? Dost thou say it was she?" After forgiving Alice Goodridge for her role in his affliction, Thomas then addressed Beelzebub again: "I charge thee in the name of the father, the son, and the holy ghost to get thee from me and come no more at me, for it is written 'Resist the devil, and he will fly from thee.'" At this injunction, the big, booming voice of the demon Glossop addressed his brother demon, "Radolphus, Beelzebub can do no good; his head is broken off with a word."

As the demons Radolphus and Glossop continued to discuss strategy inside Thomas Darling, they became increasingly discouraged about their chances for continued occupancy of Thomas's body. They therefore turned their attention to the assembled multitude, suggesting, "Let us go out of him and enter into some of these [bystanders] here," naturally terrorizing the crowd. They eliminated one woman from consideration because of the great fervency of her prayers. They discussed changing their abode to the body of "a man of bad faith," a man they deemed one of Satan's own people. As their hope and strength waned throughout the hours of the day, the two demons cried out with greater and greater frequency, "We cannot prevail; their church increaseth." At 2 P.M., six hours after the prayer fast began, one of the two evil spirits fled, leaving the demoniac still racked with fits but less so than previously. Four hours and many fits later, the second of the two evil spirits fled, the demoniac calling the crowd to witness that it had exited his mouth in the shape of a mouse.

Recovering very slowly from his ordeal, Thomas Darling began to sit up, to eat a little, and to take his first hesitant steps after three months of being carried on men's backs. His first trip out of the house upon his recovery was to go into the town of Burton, "that it might appear what Jesus had done for him, to the praise of his glory and admiration of those that had been acquainted with his marvelous situation." He met with John Darrell, who counseled him to beware lest the unclean spirits return in even greater force than before, "assuring him that Satan would strive to repossess him." He returned to his home and school, "from whence Satan had long kept him," and to his religious exercises. This return to normal life lasted three days.

The expected repossession occurred on June 8. Demonically attacked in front of his schoolfellows, Thomas Darling again lost the use of his legs and had to be carried home to his uncle's house. For the next several hours, he fell in and out of trances, groaning, shouting, and hallucinating. He vigorously resisted demonic temptations to tear the Bible, to succumb to the advances of a beautiful, gorgeously clothed woman, and to accept bribes of gold and silver. He also repudiated demonic threats to stop his mouth, to burn him with "flames of fire," or to carry him to hell. The nature of these temptations and threats and the language used to describe them parallels very closely the temptations and threats confronted by Robert Brigges 22 years earlier, leading us to the conclusion that Thomas Darling may have read the account of Brigges' possession (which was widely circulated in manuscript among Protestant nonconformists such as Darling and John Darrell) and modeled his symptoms, either consciously or unconsciously, on those of Brigges.

Common in many cases of possession, the imitation of specific features of other cases was, of course, often suspected or known to be conscious. For instance, New England clergyman Cotton Mather reported that a girl named Margaret Rule became possessed in 1693 six months after another demoniac, Mercy Short, was delivered of her demon. Mather found the coincidence "marvelous, resembling [Mercy Short's] in almost all the circumstances of it; indeed the afflictions were so much alike that the relation I have given of the one would almost serve as the full history of the other." He dismissed the possibility that Short was consciously or unconsciously mimicking the earlier case in the manifestations of her possession: "It were a most unchristian and uncivil, yea, a most unreasonable thing, to imagine that the fits of the young woman were but mere impostures, and I believe scarce any but people of a particular dirtiness will harbor such an uncharitable censure." Many of Mather's colleagues, however, disagreed with this judgment, deeming Rule a deliberate imitator of Short's manner of possession.

The possibility exists that the cases of both Brigges and Darling were modeled on a common original, but no such case is known. The few known cases of English possession that predate Brigges' case, such as those of Anne Mylner, Edmund Kingesfielde's wife, and Alexander Nyndge, bear no similarities either to Brigges' case or to Darling's. Several very specific similarities exist, however, between the cases of Brigges and Darling. These include the demoniac's refusal to tear a holy book at the demon's behest, the proffering of bribes of money and a seductive woman to the demoniac, the demoniac's hallucination of spectral animals (Darling's green cat, Brigges' black dog), the demonstrated ineffectiveness of medicine in treating the demoniac, the godly reputation of the demoniac and his repeated assertions of faith in the face of his torment, the demon's invitation to worship idols in exchange for kingdoms, and the sympathetic visit to the demoniac by an important minister (Arthur Hildersham to Darling, John Foxe to Brigges).

Of course, explanations can be offered for the similarities that avoid the conclusion that Darling specifically imitated Brigges, either consciously or unconsciously. The spectral animals are an extremely common motif that informs the visual vocabulary of fear in every culture, as all parents can attest. The ineffectiveness of medicine in treating the case is likewise easily explained by the very great frequency, then and now, with which episodic symptoms fail to respond to medical treatment. The godly sufferer's assertion of faith and refusal to worship idols in exchange for kingdoms are modeled on Christ's response to Satan's temptation. The visits of sympathetic ministers are quite within the purview of godly shepherds concerned for their strayed sheep. In short, chronological precedence is not necessarily the same as causality.

Such similarities, however, also manifest themselves between Brigges' case and many other later cases of possession. In the cases of Agnes Brigges and Rachel Pindar, which followed Robert Brigges' case by a few months, Satan threatened to tear the godly apart, just as he did in the case of Robert Brigges. In these same cases, the image of Christ's buying the souls of sinners with his blood was prominent, just as it was in Brigges' case. These two young demoniacs mentioned John Foxe in their ravings, just as Brigges did. In the case of Richard Dugdale in 1690, the demoniac suffered from sporadic blindness, just as Brigges did. A horrible spectral dog persecuted demoniacs Helen Fairfax, Edmond Elliot, and William Somers, just as it did Brigges. Joyce Dovey's possession was initiated at the hearing of a sermon, and she made repeated attempts to commit suicide, just as in Brigges' case. Given this list of parallels between the case of Brigges and later cases, the possibility seems strong that Brigges' case was the seminal model for many subsequent cases of English Protestant demon possession, including that of Thomas Darling.

Thomas Darling was finally saved from Satan when a voice inside him said, "He fell a little, and I caught him." Waking from his trance, Thomas said to his witnesses, "Behold, I see a lamb; hark what the lamb sayeth: 'Thou didst fall and he caught thee; fear not, the lord is thy buckler and defender.'" After lying quietly for a while, Thomas then said, "I see a milk-white dove, and the dove sayeth, 'Fear not; you shall have better news.'" This dove continued to speak words of comfort to Thomas, reassuring him that Satan was powerless to control him and that anyone who accused Thomas of dissembling his possession was the devil's tool and would "fry in hell torments." Resisting with his utmost strength and faith Satan's last-ditch attempts to tempt and torment him into abandoning his trust in God, Thomas Darling finally "opened his eyes, and . . . finding the dove's words true and himself very well, both in mind and body, and so (thanks be to God) he hath remained ever since."

Such was the state of things in 1597, the year in which Jesse Bee's account of Thomas Darling's possession and dispossession was published. Alice Goodridge, accused by Thomas Darling of bewitching him, died in jail awaiting trial. John Darrell went on to dispossess other demoniacs. The following year, 1598, Thomas Darling, his grandfather, and two witnesses were summoned to London by a court commission to testify against John Darrell. According to Darrell, the men were badgered in court and viciously cross-examined, and Thomas Darling, now fifteen years old, was imprisoned for seven weeks, threatened, beaten, intimidated, and starved. Not surprisingly, he finally signed a confession of fraud, implicating Darrell, and he was rewarded with his freedom. Then, probably encouraged by Darrell, he wrote a letter repudiating the confession. Darrel asserted that Darling had been forced to sign a blank page and his "confession" filled in later. Four years later, Thomas Darling, now a nineteen-year-old university student, was convicted by the Star Chamber, the highest court in the land, of libeling the vice chancellor of Oxford University and some of the queen's privy counselors by accusing them of being Catholic sympathizers. As his sentence required, Darling was publicly whipped before both his ears were sliced off.

Chapter 10
The Starchy Seven

In early modern England, accusations of bewitchment and demon
possession frequently occurred in border areas where social control was tenuous. One such area was Lancashire, which was
reputed to have more witches and believers in witches than any other
county in England. Just as significant as Lancashire's high population
of witches, however, was its high population of Catholics—and the
two populations overlapped considerably. During the Elizabethan and
Stuart periods, Lancashire was the most Catholic county in England.
The government's concerted attempts to suppress Catholicism failed
in Lancashire, which persisted in maintaining secret societies, disguised Jesuit priests, occult Catholics, and recusants. The county was
poor, sparsely populated, agriculturally barren, and politically conser-
vative. It contained an amount of land so huge as to be administra-
tively unmanageable. For instance, a single parish in Lancashire,
Whalley, contained forty-seven townships and over one hundred
thousand acres. These factors, combined with Lancashire's great distance from London, insured that many official posts went vacant year
after year for lack of eligible Protestants willing to immure themselves
in such a desolate place. Other official posts were filled by closet
Catholics unwilling to prosecute their fellow believers.

At the beginning of February 1594, in Cleworth, Lancashire, nine-
year-old Anne Starchy began to be "dumpish and heavy," with a
"fearful starting and pulling together of her body." The next week,
Anne's brother, ten-year-old John, began having fits of compulsive

shouting on his way to school. Both children rapidly grew worse, exhibiting these and other symptoms with increasing frequency. The children's mother, who came from a family of Catholics, induced her husband, a wealthy gentleman named Nicholas Starchy, to ask a Catholic priest to help her children, but the priest refused. Nicholas Starchy then asked a local "cunning man," Edmund Hartley, if he would be willing to help the two children in return for "large proffers" of remuneration, and Hartley agreed to help. Using "certain Popish charms and herbs," Hartley was able to quiet the children and return them to some semblance of normalcy. The children continued reasonably well for the next eighteen months, during which time Hartley visited them often.

An understanding of the role of cunning folk in early modern English society is essential to an understanding of Edmund Hartley's role in the Starchy case. Against the largely unquestioned existence of witches and other agents of the devil, the common people of early modern England had been disarmed by the Reformation. In the face of evil, they were no longer allowed to take holy communion, cross themselves, wear amulets containing consecrated herbs or holy relics, petition the saints, make pilgrimages to shrines, repeat ritual prayers, or be touched by a holy person. Neither could they rely on the church for help, because the church had no magic left, only prayer—and not even prayer with which they could fight the evil, but only prayer to be able to accept God's will. After the Reformation, therefore, many of the common folk transferred their loyalty from the clergy to lay magicians, called "wise folk" or "cunning folk."

In post-Reformation England, cunning folk served many of the same functions that pre-Reformation clergy had served: they prayed for the sick, determined the identities of thieves, ascertained the whereabouts of stolen goods, petitioned God for good weather and good harvests. Those who consulted cunning folk did not think of themselves as doing anything nefarious; they were simply asking a professional for assistance, as we would ask a doctor or a pharmacist. The service provided by the cunning person was the delivery of a charm to benefit the client. The charms sometimes took a material form—herbs and stones were popular—but were more often a set of words, either written or spoken. Most common people saw no distinction between a charm and a prayer.

They did, however, see a distinction between a witch and a cunning person: the former worked magic for evil, the latter for good. In the eyes of the common folk, therefore, the magic of the cunning person derived from God. For instance, the seventeenth-century Lancashire cunning man Henry Baggilie used prayer to take the illnesses of others into himself. Another cunning man, Thomas Hope, claimed that his power derived from his having been washed in holy water in Rome as a small boy. Many cunning folk used standard prayers, even Protestant ones, for healing. Used in this way, then, magic was considered a holy search for knowledge through divine revelation. The cunning folk healed sickness through gentle and soothing means, such as the laying on of hands, the pronouncing of ritual prayers, and the administration of herbal infusions. Their services were usually inexpensive and sometimes even free. Orthodox medicine, on the other hand, was costly, brutal, and dangerous, relying heavily on bloodletting, amputation, cauterization, and the use of violent purgatives. In most cases of mild illness, healing by a cunning person undoubtedly proved more desirable and efficacious than healing by a licensed physician.

Although it mattered to lay folk whether magic was used for good or evil, this distinction was lost on the Protestant establishment. The new official position was that *any* use of magic, regardless of purpose, worked against God. Holy water, sacramental bread and wine, incense, consecrated oil, priestly vestments, and other material trappings of the old Catholic church were now tools of necromancy, not religion. Ordination, exorcism, and consecration were blasphemous attempts by man to usurp God's power. The transubstantiation of bread and wine into flesh and blood was a parlor trick to fool the gullible. Similarly, to the Protestant reformers, prayer consisted of "words of the heart" as opposed to "words of the mouth." A true prayer was a heartfelt request to God phrased in the supplicant's own words. On the other hand, a prayer which was memorized and recited by rote for a set number of repetitions, especially one in Latin or some other unintelligible language, was not a true prayer but an incantation, a spell, a charm—a witch's weapon to force the devil's will on men. In the eyes of the reformers, therefore, practitioners of rituals and speakers of oral charms were neither holy priests nor morally neutral secular magicians, but witches.

Naturally, the reformed church's official stance against magic failed to sway the common folk, who could easily perceive the blatant conflict of interest inherent in such a position. Thus, although the new church succeeded in ousting traditional Catholic rituals and trappings from official policy and practice, it failed to obliterate them from common society. Instead, these rituals and trappings went underground, became secularized, demoted to the level of superstition, which they occupy even today, as when we automatically say "God bless you" after someone sneezes, a vestigial form of exorcism. More surprisingly, the reformed church's official stance against magic failed to convince many rural clergy, who found themselves forced to continue magical practices in order to maintain any hold whatsoever on their dwindling and increasingly skeptical congregations. Many post-Reformation clerics in county parishes practiced healing, charming, incantatory prayer, and other officially unauthorized acts to help, and keep, their congregations, and in fact continued to do so well into the nineteenth century. There exist many recorded instances of Protestant clergy using local cunning folk to find stolen church property.

In addition to rural parish clergy, other professionals often patronized or served as cunning men. One-third of all cunning men in Essex whose professions are known were surgeons or physicians. Mathematicians and astrologers also often functioned as cunning men. Civil court officials frequently consulted local cunning men or women to aid them in prosecutions, just as some police departments attempt to use psychics today. Ironically, this practice was considered particularly efficacious in the prosecution of witches. Also ironically, the cunning folk used as respected experts by the civil court in this fashion were the same people who were prosecuted as witches by the ecclesiastical court.

Thus, we see how belief in magic was reinforced throughout all levels of society despite the best efforts of the reformed church. Moreover, as with many other historical phenomena, we see an economic driver behind the belief: the perpetuation of lay magic benefited communities, especially rural communities, by providing employment. It is estimated that the number of cunning men and women in seventeenth-century England approximately equaled the number of parochial clergy, at least one per village.

We need to remember, however, that this secularized form of magic had its origins in old Catholic practice, a fact of which the government was well aware. To the Protestant establishment, both the Catholic priest and the nondenominational lay magician were conjurers and witches. Even the recitation of the Lord's Prayer during the mid-seventeenth century was sometimes interpreted by nonconformists as incantatory sorcery. Matters were not helped by the fact that many dispossessed Catholic priests cultivated impostures involving exorcism, visions, prophecy, and so on to supplement their waning positions and incomes. Essentially, much of the unauthorized magic widely practiced in sixteenth- and seventeenth-century England was an occult form of Catholicism—as we are plainly told was the case with Edmund Hartley, whose assistance to the Starchy family consisted of the administration of "certain Popish charms and herbs."

In June of 1596, Hartley told Nicholas Starchy that he was going to leave the country. At this news, young John Starchy began having nose bleeds. Each time one of these nosebleeds occurred, Hartley was sent for and used his skill to staunch the flow of blood, declaring to Nicholas Starchy that no one else could do so. He continued to threaten to emigrate and not tell Nicholas Starchy his whereabouts. Starchy, afraid for his son's health in Hartley's absence, offered Hartley bed, board, and an annual pension if he would stay. Hartley demanded more, requesting his own house and grounds, which Starchy refused. Hartley fumed at this refusal, threatening to "make such a shout as never was [heard] at Cleworth" (a threat that eventually came true, although Hartley did not hear it). He did, however, move in with the Starchy family that summer. On November 17, both John and Anne Starchy resumed their former fits, and Nicholas Starchy naturally asked Hartley to help them. Hartley required Starchy's assistance to do so, and the two men went into the woods together. There Hartley "made a circle about a yard and a half wide, dividing it into four parts, making a cross at every division." When he had finished this construction, he ordered Starchy to "go and tread out the circle."

The act of ceremonially creating a circle, often by drawing it on the ground with chalk or a stick, constituted part of the act of summoning spirits, who were minions or manifestations of Satan obliged to perform the bidding of the person who summoned them. This act was a serious legal offense, having been criminalized during the reign of Henry VIII as a statutory felony punishable by death, and it continued to be a capital crime in England for nearly two centuries, including during Elizabeth's entire reign. Despite the possible severity of the consequences, however, the summoning of spirits was practiced with some frequency among all classes of people. University students, natural philosophers, and other intellectuals generally participated in this activity in an attempt to gain knowledge of the universe. Since the ultimate natural philosopher was Satan, who knew all of nature's secrets, the intellectuals thought to command the demon to reveal these secrets to the world of men. Many less intellectual people, however, attempted to summon spirits to help them find buried treasure. The search for buried treasure, a kind of national pastime during the early modern era, was a potentially lucrative activity in a bankless society whose wealth was embodied in gold, silver, and jewels rather than in paper and plastic. Elizabethans really did bury their treasure, and others discovered such treasure with enough frequency to perpetuate the activity despite the potential penalties of summoning spirits to assist. A case from 1510 illustrates the ceremonial creation of a circle in order to conjure spirits to assist in the discovery of treasure. Nine Yorkshire acquaintances, including two knights, two priests, and a teacher, heard a rumor that a chest full of gold coins was buried in a certain village, and they jointly determined to find it by summoning spirits and forcing them to reveal the exact location of the chest. Among other activities designed to attract spirits, the nine men created three circles on the ground, each thirty feet in diameter, "with many genuflections and orisons." They then stood inside the circles for protection while they attempted to summon spirits named Belphares and Obirion. Unfortunately, the spirits never appeared, some of the magical paraphernalia was lost, the men became separated from each other in the dark, and the whole project expired as "dissention rose among the principals" while they all blamed each other for their failure.

We are not told the reason for Edmund Hartley's drawing of the circle in the woods while Nicholas Starchy looked on, but the context implies that his purpose was something more malevolent than to ask spirits for knowledge of the universe or to help him find buried treasure. Perhaps his purpose was more akin to that of Margery Stanton of Wimbish, who, in 1579, drew a circle on the ground and stabbed it full of holes, ostensibly causing her neighbor to fall ill. Similarly, in 1653 Anne Bodenham of Salisbury created a circle with which she was supposed to have summoned the spirits Beelzebub, Lucifer, Satan, and Tormenter. Mistress Bodenham exchanged some of her blood for a piece of silver from the spirits, thus sealing a contract, and the spirits accordingly poisoned a gentlewoman against whom Mistress Bodenham held a grudge. The account of the Starchy case makes it clear that Hartley perceived that he had many enemies and that he was routinely vengeful, so his purpose may well have been to harm someone else. At any rate, Nicholas Starchy was repulsed by Hartley's "wretched dealing" in the making of the circle and resolved to procure assistance elsewhere.

Starchy therefore took a urine sample from his son to a physician in Manchester, but the physician found no sign of natural illness. Starchy then consulted John Dee, the warden of the Collegiate Chapter in Manchester. Dee was much more than a mere local official. He had for many decades been England's best-known polymath and was widely reputed to be one of the wisest men in the kingdom, highly skilled in mathematics, geometry, cartography, navigation, and the occult arts (he knew all about conjuring circles), and formerly the owner of the greatest library in England. Dee's household nursemaid had been demonically possessed a few years previously, so he had practical as well as theoretical knowledge of demon possession. Dee's intervention in that case had failed, however, and the woman had committed suicide. Later, in an unrelated incident, Dee had himself been prosecuted as a conjurer and was impoverished in the process, losing his great library. Not surprisingly, then, Dee "utterly refused [to help Starchy], saying he would not meddle, and advised Starchy to seek the help of 'some godly preachers, with whom he should consult concerning a public or private fast.'" Dee furthermore summoned Hartley before him and reprimanded him. John and Anne Starchy manifested no symptoms for several weeks. On New Year's Day, 1597, the children, with Hartley as their chaperone, set off to visit a relative in Manchester. While in the city, Anne and John decided to visit Dee, who had asked to see them. Hartley, still smarting under Dee's reprimand of the previous month, forbade the children this visit, so they chose to go without him. Hartley, angry, told them that it would have "been better for them not to have changed an old friend for a new"

Sorcerer exchanging the Gospels for a book of black magic.
From R. P. Guaccius' Compendium Maleficarum, Milan, 1626.

and made other "menacing speeches" before abandoning them in a rage to find their way home alone.

Three days later, John Starchy was suddenly struck with a sharp pain in the neck and cried out that Satan had broken his neck. That night, in bed, "he leaped out on the sudden with a terrible outcry that amazed all the family. Then was he tossed and tumbled a long time, was very fierce like a mad man or a mad dog, snatched at and bit everyone that he laid hold on with his teeth, not sparing his mother, smiting the next [person], and hurling bedstaves, pillows, or whatsoever at them and into the fire." He behaved in this manner every day for the next two months. At the same time, John's sister, Anne, also began to be tormented again, as were three other young girls in the household (ages ten through fourteen), who were wards of Nicholas Starchy. The five children all began to bark and howl like dogs, baying in unison, continuing for fifteen minutes at a time. After each howling fit passed, they "fell a-tumbling, and, after that, became speechless, senseless, and as dead." At times they sang, laughed, and danced wildly, ignoring all attempts by the adults to govern them: "if others called to them, they heard them not, answered not, and yet talked one to another." They told Mistress Starchy that the spirit driving their behavior appeared to them as "an angel like a dove" and required them to "follow him to heaven, which way soever he would lead them, though it were through never so little a hole, for he told them he could draw them through," and they accordingly poked holes in the walls to expedite their exit. They ran from the adults in the household and from the neighbors, calling them "devils with horns," and hiding under the beds. The observers noticed that the children's fits overtook them only when they went about "godly exercise," never while they were at play. John Starchy also began compulsively washing his hands: "whensoever he washed, he would have new water; if it were the same wherewith he washed before (for he could tell), he refused it."

The Starchy children were just five among the many early modern demoniacs who were observed "falling senseless" or "lying as dead." Bystanders often tested the genuineness of the apparent senselessness by pinching or sticking pins into the demoniac's skin. If the demoniac did not respond, the possession was often deemed genuine, despite the fact that some educated and observant early modern people did not necessarily perceive this condition as supernaturally induced. For instance, ministers John Deacon and John Walker said, "Some [men] having received many dangerous gunshots in wars, yet (being wholly taken up with resolution and purpose to fight) they felt (for the present) no pain at all." Deacon and Walker added that it would not be logical for the devil to dull the pain of those he afflicted; "no, he would rather augment and increase the feeling of pain that their torment might be so much more intolerable to them." Most Elizabethans, however, did not know that this condition ever occurred naturally. The condition they described as "senselessness" is what we now would term *analgesia*, insensibility to pain. The condition then characterized as "lying as dead" is what we now would call *anesthesia*, insensibility to pain coupled with a loss of consciousness. Both conditions occur naturally in the human body, induced by the brain's release of opioids known as endorphins ("morphine within") and enkephalins ("in the head"). The release of these chemicals can be increased by vigorous exercise, hearty laughter, physical contact with others, and music—stimuli all reportedly present in the case of the Starchy children, who spent months dancing, singing, playing, and laughing at their parents. Since endorphins and enkephalins were isolated and named only in the 1970s, however, the bystanders in the Starchy case may be forgiven for not invoking this phenomenon as an explanation for the children's behavior.

During this same time, Satan targeted his sixth victim in the Starchy household: thirty-three-year old Margaret Byrom, a poor relation of Mistress Starchy who was visiting the family. Her affliction commenced following an embrace with Hartley. When the two parted,

> she endeavored to arise but was so benumbed and giddy that she could not stand, yet being lifted up, she strove to go, but being unable, fell down and was senseless and very unruly. . . . [She] wist [knew] not what she said, nor knew nor saw any of them save Hartley only, whom she both knew and said she saw, albeit her eyes were shut close that she could see nothing; at him she railed and angerly smote.

After Byrom's fit abated, Hartley tried to comfort her, pretending "to bear a loving affection towards her, and it was thought that he kissed her."

At this point, Hartley's kisses had already earned a sinister reputation in the household: "Now they judged in the house that whomsoever he kissed, on them he breathed the devil. He often kissed John for love (as he said); he kissed the little wenches in jest; he promised Margaret Hardiman [the fourteen-year-old ward] a thrave of kisses; he wrestled with one Joan Smith, a maid servant in the house, to kiss her, but failed of his purpose." Hartley's attempt to kiss Margaret Byrom, however, had an unanticipated effect: "When he came to comfort Margaret, she could not abide his company." She accused him of bewitching her, saying that he was "ever in [her] eyes, absent and present." Her fears proved well founded: a week later, she was violently thrown about the kitchen by an unseen force, first tossed towards the fire and then under the table. Her belly felt as though it contained something like a "rolled up calf," which periodically rose up towards her heart with its head and nose full of nails. After distending her belly and tossing her about, it exited through her mouth with a cold breath, causing her to bark and howl like a dog. Finally, it "plumped down into her body, like a cold, long whetstone," chilling her so that her teeth chattered and her body quaked with cold. When she tried to warm herself, she was forcibly "picked backward."

Satan's seventh victim in the household was another mature woman: a thirty-year-old maidservant named Jane Ashton. A year earlier, she had secretly entered Hartley's private chamber and had looked through his possessions. At that time, she had been stabbed with a sharp pain in the throat, as though a pin or hook was sticking her, and she had coughed up blood for two days. Now, a year later, she too began to bark and howl, just as the other six demoniacs were doing. As with Margaret Byrom, Hartley was known to have courted and kissed Jane Ashton and had even promised her marriage.

The situation of seven demoniacs in one household was unusual but not unprecedented. European demon possession during the last half of the sixteenth century commonly manifested itself in groups rather than individuals. For instance, in 1554 in Rome, eighty-two women who had recently converted from Judaism to Catholicism were possessed by demons that claimed that they were sent by Jews to reclaim the women for Judaism. Another occurrence of mass demon possession occurred in 1566, in which thirty Dutch children were possessed, and the ministrations of several exorcists were unsuccessful. In 1593, 150 German adults and children were possessed at the same time. Notable in this last case is the fact that zealous public preaching against the devil commenced in that year and that government-mandated public prayers exacerbated the problem. The worst cases of mass demon possession occurred in convents throughout France, as noted in the previous chapter.

Cases such as these that involved dozens, scores, or hundreds of individuals are difficult to assess as fraudulent. Such an assessment would amount to a conspiracy theory attributing formidable powers of organization, strategy, and communication to the individuals in the affected group—individuals who, for the most part, were relatively uneducated, immature, and socially powerless. Rather, we must assess these cases of mass possession within a larger historical context of psychic epidemics, collective psychoses, mass delusions, and group psychopathology. Such psychic epidemics have historically occurred as a reaction to disturbances of social life, characterizing periods of great political or intellectual upheaval, such as those following revolutions (either suppressed or successful) or military actions (either victories or defeats). Psychic epidemics occurred generally in areas where life was hard and uncertain, where the people were poor and uneducated, and where reason had less social value than passionate emotion. Many historians have commented on the pervading sense of pessimism and melancholy that pervaded Europe following the Reformation, the widespread feeling of impending doom and apocalypse aggravated by religious schism and socioeconomic transformation. Psychic epidemics were reactions to stressful situations: attempts to control such situations, to communicate frustration about them, to compensate for them, or to validate opposition to them. These episodes were perpetuated through a sort of psychic contagion that was particularly likely to occur among groups of individuals living highly regulated, close-knit lives together, such as the residents of a small village (Salem, Massachusetts) or a household (the Starchy home).

At the end of January, still very ill, Margaret Byrom left the Starchy house in Cleworth to return to her own home in Salford. Hartley accompanied her, and she continued to suffer sporadic violent fits after arriving at her own house. She alternated compulsively between fasting and gorging, "slossing up her meat like a greedy dog or hog," shaming her mother and disgusting her friends. On February 10, she was cruelly attacked by an invisible agent, this spirit racking her body mercilessly and causing her breath to stink and smoke so badly that her neighbors could not stand to come near her. She became stiff, breathless, and senseless; and the spirit made "a loud noise in her belly, like that in the belly of a great trotting horse." After the stench had somewhat dissipated, sympathizers gathered around her bed to pray, including Hartley, but something about Hartley's prayers aroused the suspicions of a clergyman (John Dee's curate, in fact) named Matthew Palmer. Palmer challenged Hartley to say the Lord's Prayer, but Hartley proved unable to do so. Palmer then haled Hartley before two justices of the peace. These officials took Hartley into custody and prepared to examine the potential witnesses against him: the seven demoniacs, who were notified of this impending judicial questioning.

Two nights before Margaret Byrom was to be questioned by the justices, "the devil in the likeness of Hartley" appeared to her, ordered her to be careful what she told the justices, and promised her silver and gold if she would be circumspect in her testimony. This vision appeared again the next night with the same message. When the justices arrived the next day to conduct the examination, bringing with them the accused man, Margaret Byrom was rendered speechless and could not testify against him. Instead, she was repeatedly cast down to the ground, envisioning a "great black dog with a monstrous tail, a long chain, and open mouth, coming apace towards her." The attack of this fierce spectral dog was followed by attacks from a "big black cat" and, less menacingly, "a big mouse." These visions were accompanied by pain, contortions, temporary blindness, weeping, heavy-headedness, a swelling belly, alternating bouts of fasting and gorging, and bodily rigidity. All these symptoms continued to plague Byrom for weeks following the justices' examination of her. Next to be examined were the five children of the Starchy household. Like Margaret Byrom, they too were unable to respond to judicial questioning on the subject of Edmund Hartley's influence over them. Instead, they sank down onto the floor, unable to speak a word except for their assertion that Hartley would not allow them to testify against him. At this moment, the maid servant Jane Ashton began to bark and howl, and one of the children said, "Ah, Edmund, dost thou trouble her now, when she should testify against thee?"

In March of 1597, despite his refusal to confess, Hartley was convicted at the Lancaster assizes. Since the seven demoniacs had not been able to testify against him, the most damning evidence was Nicholas Starchy's testimony that he had witnessed Hartley make a circle on the day that the two of them had gone into the woods together. Sentenced to death for the felony of conjuring spirits, Hartley was taken to the gallows and strung up, but the noose broke. Apparently taking this as a sign from God that he should confess his crime before death, Hartley then admitted that he created the circle. The second time he was strung up, the rope did not break, and Edmund Hartley departed this world.

Hartley's death, however, did not cure the seven demoniacs, who continued to be afflicted. For instance, on the day after Hartley's execution, Margaret Byrom was demonically attacked at church during morning prayer, being rendered senseless and immobile. Now even more desperate than before to find help for the demoniacs, Nicholas

Starchy "procured first one preacher, then another to see them, but they knew not well what to say to the affliction." Finally, through John Dee's butler, Starchy heard about Thomas Darling's possession of the previous year and about Darling's relief from that affliction through the help of John Darrell. Three urgent letters were dispatched to John Darrell—from Starchy, John Dee, and a justice of the peace—requesting Darrell's assistance. After consulting and praying with his fellow ministers, Darrell complied.

Darrell arrived at the Starchy home in Cleworth on March 16, 1997, accompanied by another minister, George More, pastor of a parish in Derbyshire. Margaret Byrom, who had been residing at her own home in Salford over the past several weeks, also arrived for the occasion. At dinner that night, the five children behaved strangely, being tossed and thrown onto the ground by an invisible force and proving by their swollen and rumbling bodies that they "had some quick [living] thing within each of them." They disturbed the adults by making jokes about Hartley's recent execution and disputed with Darrell over whether or not the devil could be hanged. Then Jane Ashton, the maidservant, began barking, howling, and displaying her own swollen belly. The seven demoniacs were installed in a single chamber for inspection by Darrell and More and proceeded to demonstrate an array of evil behaviors. They "gave themselves up to scoffing and blasphemy, calling the holy Bible . . . 'bible babble, bible babble,' and thus they did aloud and often. All or most of them joined together in a strange and supernatural loud whooping, that the house and ground did sound therewith again, by reason whereof [the ministers] were driven . . . out of the chamber and kept out for that day." (This was the "shout as never was [heard] at Cleworth" that Hartley had predicted but did not live to hear.) That evening, the ministers exhorted and prayed with the family in order to sanctify their next day's work, and the loud whooping ceased.

The next morning, the seven demoniacs were ushered into a large parlor to lie on couches in the presence of Darrell, More, another minister named Nicholas Dickens, and about thirty other witnesses. The bystanders spent the entire day in fasting, prayer, and Scripture reading. The demoniacs spent the day thrashing their bodies about, crying aloud in a "strange and supernatural manner," lying as though dead, and crying to God for mercy. Jane Ashton was "full of pain, and it seemed to her as though her heart would have burst; she strained up much phlegmy and bloody matter." John Starchy "was so miserably rent that abundance of blood gushed out both at his nose and mouth," and he gnashed his teeth fearfully. The others periodically vomited "something like phlegm and thick spittle." They all "used much light behavior and vain gestures, sundry also filthy scurrilous speeches . . . also they spake blasphemy, calling the word preached "bible babble; [Darrell] will not have done prating, prittle prattle." Finally, some time after five in the afternoon, Margaret Byrom cried out, lay breathless and motionless for half an hour, and then sat up "most joyfully, magnifying God, with such a cheerful countenance and voice" that the assembled crowd all rejoiced with her. Her demon had fled. Shortly thereafter, John Starchy was also delivered of his demon, and, one by one, the rest soon followed. After they had had a while to rest and recover from their terrible experiences, the demoniacs were asked to describe the shapes in which their demons had exited their bodies. Margaret Byrom said that her spirit, in the shape of a crow, had worked its way up through her belly and throat and out her mouth, leaving much pain and "a filthy smell" throughout her body, and had then vanished in a flash of fire out the window. John Starchy described his spirit as departing in the shape of a hunchbacked man, "very ill favored." Anne Starchy's demon exited her body in the shape of a "foul ugly man with a white beard." Another demon fled in the form of a hedgehog, threatening and wheedling until the last second before its final expulsion. Content with the day's work, everyone retired to bed.

Near morning, however, Jane Ashton began to shout so loudly that "the whole house did ring of her again." Ministers Darrell, More, and Dickens hurried to her room, eager "to enter the second time into the field," for they well knew that Satan had not yet been wholly defeated. Ashton was brought into the parlor so the ministers and fifty witnesses (twenty more than the previous day) could pray for her and observe her torments as her evil spirit forced to her to vomit, shake, and weep. Many hours later, she was delivered of a demon "ugly like a toad." In response to questioning by the ministers, Ashton confessed that this demon had never left her body the day before and that she had merely pretended to be dispossessed. The demon, she said, had promised her some relief if she would conceal his continuing occupation of her body, but he had lied. Master Dickens reprimanded her, "[Never] believe the devil again; beware of lying, he teacheth to lie, and you are caught for lying." As expected, for a few days and nights after the dispossessions, "the unclean spirits returned ever and anon" to attempt repossession of their former victims. The latter were occasionally thrown to the ground or deprived of bodily movement for some space of time, and they were forced to withstand powerful threats and wheedling promises of gold, silver, and velvet. They managed to resist, however, and three years later still continued unmolested by Satan and enjoying God's mercy, all except one. Jane Ashton later became a Catholic, "for which opportunity and advantage the devil watching and no doubt compassing, he then recovered her." She continued to have fits even after going to live with a Catholic uncle and being exorcized by priests.

Four decades later, in 1634, John Starchy, now a respectable fifty-year-old justice of the peace, heard testimony relating to a ten-year-old boy's accusations of sixteen people as witches. Justice Starchy was instrumental in bringing the accused to trial, where they were all convicted and incarcerated pending execution. Four of those convicted were exonerated and released by order of the king, but many of the remainder died in prison. The boy who had testified to Justice John Starchy against the sixteen people later confessed that his entire story had been fabricated.

Chapter 11
William Somers

In 1591 William Somers, a fourteen-year-old musician's apprentice, traveled from his master's home in Bellyn, in northwest England, to a market town named Bromsgrove. At Bromsgrove William found a hat with no apparent owner, a hat with a metal band that Somers at first thought to be gold but later discovered was copper. Pleased with his find, Somers was soon taken aback when an old woman unknown to him demanded that he hand over the hat to her. He reluctantly did so, but he adamantly refused to give up the metal hatband. The old woman departed with threats, and that night Somers saw a "strange light in the chamber where he lay, which cast him into a great fear, and thus he continued frighted for a time."

Shortly thereafter, Somers' master, Anthony Brackenberie, moved his lodgings from Bellyn to Holme, near Newark upon Trent, in the county of Nottingham. One day, going upon his master's business into Newark, Somers was suddenly thrown by an invisible force into a ditch about eight yards from the highway on which he had been walking. Stunned, he lay in the ditch for a while before being able to get up and resume his journey. After he had traveled just a few more steps, however, he was again picked up by a powerful unseen force and hurled into a thorn bush about sixty yards away from the road. Again stunned, he lay in the thorn bush for an even longer time than he had lain in the ditch. When he was finally able to resume his walk to Newark, he had lost about four hours of the time that he had scheduled for the journey. Some time later, upon his return journey from Newark to Holme, when Somers approached the place on the road from which he had been so unceremoniously snatched and hurled into the ditch and the thorn bush, he became ill and began to experience sporadic fits that continued after his return home. His master, not believing his apprentice's story about why he had lost so much time and why he was behaving in this strange new manner, thought that Somers was counterfeiting his affliction, and began to whip him regularly for the "continual trouble" he was causing. Somers apparently felt no pain from the whip and "was more strangely handled every day" by the invisible force.

After about three weeks of witnessing Somers' fits and the pointlessness of punishment, Master Brackenberie finally decided that Somers' affliction derived from "some strange visitation and hand of God." Accordingly, he made arrangements to send Somers home to his widowed mother in Nottingham. Shortly after arriving at his mother's house, Somers' affliction eased, and his behavior returned to normal. Somers explained his recovery by saying that the evil spirit that had afflicted him had promised him a respite of six years, at the end of which time he would again be tormented. In the meantime, however, Somers still needed a trade. Shortly after his return to Nottingham, therefore, he was bound as an apprentice to Thomas Porter of Nottingham, who, like Somers' former master, was a musician. Somers ran away from this master at least twice.

Throughout the seventeenth century, the fifth commandment mandating the honoring of one's parents was interpreted to apply to obedience to any authority: wife to husband, subject to monarch, congregation to minister, or servant to master. Masters acted in loco parentis to their servants and apprentices, governing the progress of their careers, supervising their religious training and practice, forcing or disapproving their marriages. Thus, early modern service was viewed by many masters and servants as not merely an economically or socially dependent status but also as a psychologically dependent one, reducing adults to the psychological level of children. This view is exemplified by the case of a forty-year-old manservant whose master, upon finding out about the servant's sweetheart, broke off the match and dismissed the man, thus depriving him of both woman and living. Conversely, another manservant and the woman whom he had impregnated were forced to marry against their will, the man later absconding and being imprisoned. Like children, servants were expected to submit to corporal discipline, the appropriate limits of which varied considerably from family to family, with beatings, rapes, and forcible dismissals common and difficult to appeal. Servants who fled were tracked and branded; those who retaliated in kind to a master's blows were prosecuted for petty treason. Succumbing to demonic possession was one of the few ways to alleviate, even if only temporarily, an intolerable service.

Five years later, on March 20, 1596, the now nineteen-year-old Somers was dispatched to the house of his mistress's sister, Mary Milwood, in Walton, Derbyshire. While traveling on this errand, Somers encountered an old woman at Blackwell Moor, at a deep coal pit next to the road. This old woman questioned Somers about his dwelling and his errand. Presumably, he answered and the two parted company. About a mile and a half further down the road, however, Somers met the same old woman again, who this time passed him without speaking. The next day, as he was returning home to Nottingham, Somers met the old woman at the coal pit. This time, she demanded that he give her a penny. He told her he had no money. She countered by telling him that she knew that Mary Milwood had given him three pence and again demanded a penny, adding that she would throw him into the coal pit and break his neck if he did not comply with her demand. Now afraid, Somers admitted that he had a thruppence coin, which he exchanged with the old woman for her tuppence, so that she gained the penny she had demanded. This transaction completed, the old woman then offered Somers a piece of buttered bread from her bag, which he refused. She again threatened to throw Somers into the coal pit and break his neck if he would not eat the bread she offered him. Naturally, he took and ate the bread, which, to his surprise, "was as sweet as any honey." Then the old woman asked him if he knew a person named Katherine Wright. When Somers said he knew no such person, the old woman said, "She is my neighbor, and she and I will come to Nottingham one of these days and see how thou dost." At this point, a cat leaped into the old woman's arms and she embraced it before leaving Somers.

The next year saw the expiration of the six-year period of respite that William Somers claimed the evil spirit had promised him. At the beginning of October, 1597, Somers, now twenty years old and still apprenticed to Thomas Porter, began to

use such strange and idle gestures in laughing, dancing, and such-like light behavior that he was suspected to be mad. Sundry times he refused all kinds of meat [food] for a long space together, insomuch as he did seem thereby to pine away. Sometimes he shook as if he had had an ague. There was heard a strange noise or flapping from within his body. He was often seen to gather himself into a round heap under his bed clothes, and being so gathered, to bounce up a good height from the bed. [He] also beat his head and other parts of his body against the ground and bedstead in such an earnest manner and so violently that the beholders did fear that thereby he would have spoiled himself, if they had not by strong hands restrained him, and yet thereby he received no hurt at all. In most of his fits, he did swell in his body [and sometimes] seemed to be twice as big as his natural body. Often also was he seen to have a certain variable swelling or lump, to a great big-ness, swiftly running up and down between the flesh and skin through all parts of his body. Many times when that swelling [occurred], these or the like words were heard out of his mouth: 'I will go out at his eyes or ears or toes,' at which speeches the said swelling evidently appearing in such parts did immediately remove and vanish away. This swelling did not only run from eye to eye, from cheek to cheek, and up and down along in the body, but being now in the one leg, presently it would be in the other, and so of the arms in the like manner. And in whichever arm or leg it stayed, the same member was inflexible and exceedingly heavy, as if it had been so much iron.

In addition to these manifestations, Somers exhibited other types of "strange handling." Suddenly

he would be cast headlong upon the ground, or fall down, draw-ing his lips awry, gnashing with his teeth, wallowing and foaming. In sundry of his fits, he did utter so strange and fearful a screech-ing as cannot be uttered by man's power. He was of such strength as sometimes four or five men, though they had much advantage of him by binding him to a chair, yet they could not rule him. And in showing that strength, he was not perceived to pant or blow, no more than if he had not strained his strength nor struggled at all.

He laughed and wept violently for no apparent reason. He repeatedly cast himself into the fire and attempted to stab and hang himself.

Somers' language, impudent and shameless, was as disturbing as his behavior: "His speeches were usually vain, delivered in a very scoffing manner, and many times filthy and unclean." (We will never know the interesting content of these speeches because they were "very unfit once to be named.") He furthermore blasphemed and swore, "using one blood oath after another, sometimes saying 'I am God,' and sometimes saying, 'There is no God.'" When reciting the Lord's Prayer, he refused to pronounce the "not" in "Lead us not into temptation." He interrupted and badgered the pious bystanders who attempted to pray for him. He occasionally spoke phrases or answered questions in Latin or Greek, languages presumed to be unknown to him. "Many strange speeches were uttered by him, not in his own name, but as spoken by an evil spirit possessing him," such as that this spirit had been sent by "his dame," that the spirit's name was "Lucy" (Lucifer), that he was the prince of darkness, and that he had once lived in heaven. In response to questions from the bystanders, Lucy admitted that he had been sent to possess the body of William Somers by a woman who lived in Worcestershire and that this woman's malevolence stemmed from "a hat and hatband."

William Somers' case came to the attention of the mayor of Nottingham, who importuned John Darrell to come and help Somers as he had previously helped Katherine Wright, Thomas Darling, and the seven Starchy demoniacs. When Darrell arrived in Nottingham on November 5, 1597, a neighbor reported to him that Somers was deathly ill, his face and hands black and cold, his body breathless. Upon reaching Thomas Porter's house, however, Darrell discovered Somers "very lively and in one of his accustomed fits," with many bystanders looking on. After assessing the situation for a while, Darrell confirmed that Somers was indeed possessed by a devil.

That evening, in front of an appreciative audience of about sixty people, Somers "acted many sins by signs and gestures," such as brawling, swearing, picking pockets and cutting purses, pride, hypocrisy, spiritual "sluggishness," drunkenness, gluttony, dancing, gambling, and murder. The sin of whoredom he illustrated by attempting to sodomize a dog. He conducted this entire pantomime, which lasted about an hour, with his eyes and mouth shut, blind, and silent. Only when he mimed a sinner coming to the gallows as a result of these crimes did he momentarily laugh for joy and clap his hands on his thighs in triumph. The sins "were in such lively and orient colors painted out" that many in the crowd thought that the skill necessary for such a performance had to derive from a supernatural source. When the pantomime was over, a voice inside Somers said, "I must be gone." Darrell perceived this performance to be God's judgment on the wicked citizens of Nottingham.

The next day, Sunday, Darrell exhorted the demoniac, his master's family, his parents, and the many other witnesses to prepare themselves with fasting and prayer throughout the long night ahead before they attempted the difficult work of dispossession on the following day. Meanwhile, Somers' demon tormented him cruelly, forcing his tongue backwards down into his throat so far that when the onlookers peered into his throat with a candle, "they could see no tongue nor part of it." Despite the misplaced tongue, however, the demoniac managed to utter the words "For corn, for corn," a phrase interpreted by the bystanders as a criticism of men's "insatiable desire of gain" (through raising the price of grain). Darrell, wishing to make known the fact that he had "no special gift" in dispossessing demons greater than that of any other person, requested three other ministers to assist him in the next day's holy work.

On the morning of November 7, a crowd of 150 people assembled. Somers, fighting and screaming, was brought in by several strong men and laid on a couch. Darrell and the other three ministers began reading aloud some pertinent texts from scripture. For the next several hours, Somers "was continually vexed and tormented by Satan," his body swelling and being tossed up and down, his face disfigured, his mouth awry and gaping, his neck distorted, his tongue distended, his teeth gnashing, his eyes staring, his voice roaring and screeching. He foamed at the mouth "like a horse or boar, roping [the foam] down to his breast, notwithstanding there was one purposely standing by with a cloth ever and anon to wipe it away." He occasionally tried to choke himself with his hands; he occasionally shouted "Corn!" in a reference his previous day's criticism of men's greed. When Darrell tried to encourage the demoniac by saying, "All things are possible to he who believes," Somers responded, "Thou liest."

That evening, just as Darrell was expostulating on the words, "Then the spirit cried, rent him sore, and came out, and he was as one dead," Somers' spirit amazingly cried, rent him sore, and came out, leaving the demoniac as one dead. The crowd was astonished and cried out with one voice, "Lord, have mercy upon him," rejoicing in Somers' deliverance. That night, however, "a thing like a rat" patted Somers on the mouth and crept down his body to his "privy parts," where it apparently entered into his body. Thus did the evil spirit repossess Somers "many times and in sundry ways" following Darrell's dispossession of him.

Nonetheless, Darrell's treatment was initially deemed a great success, and Darrell was invited by some of those who had witnessed the dispossession to be their preacher at Saint Mary's Church in Nottingham, Darrell's first offer of continuing employment in a church. He accepted the appointment but soon disappointed his congregation by insisting on preaching, Sunday after Sunday, on only one topic: demonic possession. Some of his new parishioners complained to Master Aldridge (the vicar) that "they could hear of nothing in his sermons but of the devil." Furthermore, one consequence of the sporadic occupation of Somers' body by spirits was to imbue him with the apparent ability to detect witches, an ability in which Darrell had great confidence. As Somers named witches and had convulsions when those he accused were brought to him for confrontation, Darrell had the accused witches arrested—thirteen people in all. His goal, he said, was to "discover all the witches in England." His congregation's complaints, however, had damaged his credibility, and he was able to garner local support sufficient to make the charges stick in only two cases. One of these cases was that of Alice Freeman, who happened to be related to an important local official, a Master Freeman, who was an alderman and justice of the peace. Alice Freeman was soon exonerated of the charges against her, but Darrell had made an enemy of a powerful man and had furthermore disappointed the congregation that had appointed him preacher at Saint Mary's church.

The vast numbers of legal prosecutions for witchcraft initiated by common folks against their own neighbors during the early modern era prove the existence of extremely serious social tension, the source of which was in part economic. For instance, when Henry VIII dissolved the monasteries, thousands of acres of England's most

The Devil carrying a witch off to Hell.

valuable land passed from the church to the aristocracy. However, whereas the church had maintained much common land for the benefit of the poor, the aristocracy built fences and walls enclosing their new estates. By the end of the sixteenth century, the common land had been much reduced. Farmers whose families had for centuries relied on common land on which to graze their herds could no longer maintain their animals without paying grazing fees. If a farmer could not pay, his livelihood vanished and his family fell into beggary.

In addition to enclosing common land, the aristocratic estate holders imposed heavy new fees on their tenants. For instance, the court rolls of one town in sixteenth-century Lancashire show that heirs could inherit their fathers' land leases upon payment of one year's rent. However, in 1608 this fee increased from one year's rent to twelve. Again, the result was effective eviction for those who could not pay the exorbitant fee. The division between rich and poor widened considerably: prolonged inflation, an increased population, an expanding market, and rising prices meant that land-owners prospered while the landless suffered. In Lancashire's Pendle Forest, for instance, land that had previously supported two tenant farmers now supported up to thirteen. In the absence of the Catholic Church, one of whose primary aims was the maintenance of the poor, thousands of formerly respectable families were reduced from sufficiency to subsistence or below.

With land at such a premium among those who were lucky enough to still have some, boundary disputes became a routine part of village life. Land boundaries were denoted largely by streams, fields, fences, hedges, drains, and other agricultural markers, all of which were more or less ephemeral: streams and drains can be rerouted or filled in, fields can be extended, fences and hedges can be torn down. The welter of official boundaries confused matters further, since any particular site might be marked with different boundaries denoting any combination of civil parish, ecclesiastical parish, township ("vill"), baronial estate, chapelry, quarter, tithing, borough, city, county, hundred, wapentake, ward, shire, riding, diocese ("see"), archdeaconry, and deanery. The frequent boundary disputes, often carried on through generations, were memorialized in dozens of place names like Callans Wood in Worcestershire, Threapwood near Wrexham, and Flitnell in Northamptonshire, these names all deriving from words for "challenge" or "dispute."

These economic pressures encouraged the disintegration of the traditional social unity of village life. Communal celebrations and activities, formerly performed many times a year to reinforce social solidarity, fell into disuse with the increase in class stratification: the aristocrats and gentry, more intellectually and physically removed from the peasantry than ever before, were no longer willing to foot the bill for what they perceived as a drunken peasant rout. The decay of old manorial customs also increased the tension between the givers and the receivers of charity. No longer did a widow automatically inherit her late husband's holdings. If no one was willing to take her in, she begged or starved. No longer was the gleaning of scrap grain considered a perquisite of hired reapers; it could now be prosecuted as theft.

These severe economic pressures hurt not only the newly enlarged beggar class, but also the neighbors on whom the beggars relied for charity: villagers, tenant farmers, and small landholders. Though not beggars, these people lived constantly on the verge of beggary. One third to one-half of the country's population at this time lived at subsistence level. The daily economic clash was thus not between rich and poor, but between poor and poorer.

Nevertheless, the village community, hardly affluent itself, was not inclined to give, and the new Protestant church was less inclined to make it give than the old Catholic church had been. Whereas the old church had advocated charity, the new church advocated the extirpation of sin. The newly emerging Protestant work ethic, which said that God helped those who helped themselves, clearly implied a causal relationship between sin and misfortune. Beggars were demonstrably sinful since God had afflicted them with poverty. According to the new church, then, charity actually encouraged evil to flourish. The old traditions of neighborliness and social accommodation were dying, giving way to a new and growing sense of privacy and individual responsibility. The witchcraft prosecutions of this time helped perpetuate the disintegration of the communal system that had characterized English life for centuries.

Despite the teachings of the reformed church, however, the common folk were not yet comfortable with this position. For centuries, neighborliness and hospitality had functioned as vital bonding agents in England's small, rural, highly interpersonal communities. The average villager could not refuse charity without feeling guilt, and this fact is probably responsible for most of the witchcraft accusations. Stereotype has it that most of those accused of witchcraft were poor old women, but economic or educational level, age, and sex were actually far less significant in determining who was accused than was willingness to turn the other cheek. Several historians have pointed out that the only personality trait common to all accused witches seems to have been self-assertion in the face of social injustice. Time after time, historical records show that accusations of witchcraft were often preceded by a breach of neighborliness committed, not by the accused, but by the accuser. A villager refused to give charity or to pay promised wages to a neighbor; the neighbor publicly complained; the villager accused the complaining neighbor of witchcraft to justify the breach of neighborliness. In psychological terms, the accuser transferred the guilt to its source, the accused witch.

English courts condemned about five hundred men and women to death for witchcraft during the last half of the sixteenth century and the first half of the seventeenth. This is far fewer than died during the same period for the same reason in Scotland, which condemned two to three times as many as England, and on the continent, for which the estimate is about forty to fifty thousand. Despite England's relatively modest conviction rate for witchcraft, however, it was a crime of major importance in some counties.

About eighty percent of the convicted witches were women. Why this rate was so high has been a topic of much speculation among historians. One believes that women are always perceived as a source of disorder in any patriarchal society, with the specific focus of that disorder being women's control over their own reproduction, especially with regard to birth control and abortion. True, pre-industrial women, who were largely self-reliant as far as medical care was concerned, exercised considerably more such control than their postindustrial counterparts do. Other reasons cited for women's high rate of conviction for witchcraft are their intimate connection with small social groups, their resistance to social change, and their psychological dependence. Of course, we must not lose sight of the simplest possible explanation: in general, it was the poor and powerless people who were convicted, and the poor and powerless were far more likely to be women than men.

In January of 1598, at the instigation of the irate Master Freeman, William Somers was charged with bewitching to death a man named Sterland. The charge was brought by the dead man's widow and neighbors, who alleged that Somers had stepped on Sterland's foot during a crowded market day in Nottingham, causing Sterland to sicken and die a few days later, his foot mysteriously blackened. Master Freeman, in his capacity as justice of the peace, took custody of Somers and presented him to the appropriate magistrates, who ordered him jailed pending trial. In his own defense, attempting to deny that he had ever had any traffic with spirits, Somers asserted that he had faked his possession, that his entire six-year display of supernatural fits had been fraudulent. The magistrates for the case accordingly removed Somers from jail and committed him instead to a house of correction called Saint John's, pending further investigation into his case. At Saint John's, Somers was threatened with whipping and pinching with "knipknaps" (pincers) unless he repeated his admission of fraud in an official confession. Furthermore, an alderman named Jackson, a colleague of Master Freeman, reputedly promised

Somers ten pounds plus an establishment in any trade he chose if he would make such a confession. After three days of these threats and bribes, Somers, not too surprisingly, confessed. He also stopped manifesting any signs of possession.

John Darrell's position on this new development was that Somers' confession of fraud was a lie induced by Satan to conceal the fact that Somers was still possessed—that he still belonged to the devil. That Somers had finally quit showing symptoms of possession proved that Satan wanted to conceal this fact. Darrell was outraged; his reputation and livelihood were at stake. He therefore gathered together some sympathizers who supported his request to the archbishop of York that an official church commission be created specifically to investigate the case of William Somers. The request was granted, and a commission was formed. The members of this commission included the high sheriff of the county of Nottingham, the mayor of the town of Nottingham, the archdeacon of Derbyshire, one knight, three esquires, four ministers, and other respectable local officials. On March 20, 1598, this commission examined seventeen people who had witnessed some manifestation of Somers' possession. Every one of these witnesses testified that what they had seen was something "neither nature nor art can compass"—that is, that Somers could not have faked his possession. Also examined were Somers' custodians at Saint John's, who admitted to having threatened Somers into confessing his fraud.

Then William Somers himself was called before the commission to testify. Upon his appearance in the room, Somers, who had for over a month manifested no symptoms of possession, was suddenly and violently dashed to the floor. When the commissioners tested his sensibility by thrusting pins deep into his hands and legs, he did not react, nor did blood issue from the wounds. He also displayed other signs of evil influence so affecting that even the greatest skeptic on the commission, the archdeacon of Derbyshire, who had previously been convinced that Somers was counterfeiting, now pronounced Somers' affliction as proceeding from "the finger of God." The commissioners were satisfied and returned their verdict to the archbishop of York: William Somers had not counterfeited his possession.

Somers himself confirmed this verdict, asserting that his previous confession of fraud had itself been fraudulent. When asked why he had belied himself and God's truth in such a heinous manner, Somers told the following story:

> Being at Saint John's, there came unto me a thing like a dog that said unto me, if I would consent unto him and say that I was a counterfeit, he would give me a bag of gold. If I would not, he would make me be hanged, or else he would tear me in pieces. If I would, I should do anything that I would take in hand, and he would come to me like a mouse and help me. And then came to me a thing like an ass that said that if I would not say that I was a counterfeit, he would cast me into a well, and so went away.

Somers also confirmed that his keepers' whipping, pinchings, threats of hanging, and promises of money and employment were part of his motivation for his confession of fraud. He quoted these keepers as saying that "I had better say I was a counterfeit and live like a man than to have nothing, for if I should say I was a counterfeit and go into the clergy's hand, I should have nothing."

Somers, freed from Saint John's following the commission's examination, now went to lodge at the house of Edmund Garland, one of Darrell's sympathizers. While in this house, Somers "was daily in grievous manner tormented by the devil, often cast into the fire but not burnt . . . was of extraordinary strength and supernatural knowledge, wherewith was made manifest that he was repossessed." After ten days of this behavior, the mayor of the town of Nottingham, the town clerk, Master Freeman, and some of the other aldermen relieved Garland of responsibility for the demoniac and "got Somers into their own possession again," presumably to prevent Darrell and his sympathizers from staging a public dispossession in the church, an event that would have undermined public confidence in the secular establishment that they represented and provoked social disorder. As soon as Somers was again in the custody of the secular officials, he ceased displaying symptoms of possession, "as if he had been a counterfeit indeed," observed Darrell, "and nothing less than a devil in him." He also reaffirmed his initial confession of fraud, explaining that he had produced his preternatural foam by secreting a piece of black lead in his mouth. A week later, the Nottingham assizes commenced. Somers was called before the court and confessed that he had counterfeited his possession. The judge therefore ordered Somers to simulate his symptoms for the court to prove that he could manifest them at will, which he did.

As Somers switched his story back and forth, the town of Nottingham was torn apart with doubt, fear, and confusion. The pulpits "rang of nothing but devils and witches," and the residents were afraid to walk the streets. Factions arose, hotly contending with each other for possession of the truth, and, when words failed, rocks were thrown. The situation had outgrown the possibility of local control and now warranted attention on a national level. Accordingly, the archbishop of Canterbury, the most powerful cleric in the land, summoned John Darrell to London to be imprisoned pending examination by a church commission, the members of which included the archbishop himself, the bishop of London, the two lord chief justices of England, and several other important officials. William Somers was also summoned, as were two of Darrell's other demoniacs, Katherine Wright and Thomas Darling. Under questioning, Somers, Wright, and Darling all confessed to simulating demon possession, and all accused Darrell of connivance in their fraud. We will never be able to assess these accusations with certainty—these three demoniacs, as we know, were extremely unreliable witnesses—but the court used these accusations as the basis for its verdict: Darrell was unanimously "condemned for a counterfeit," was "deposed from the ministry," and returned to prison to await sentencing. Two years later, still not sentenced, he was released to return to his home in northern England and, briefly, to preaching—but never again to the dispossession of demons.

Chapter 12
Mary Glover

In April 1602, old Elizabeth Jackson, a charwoman living in London, used a "certain fashion of subtle and importunate begging" to ask her neighbor, fourteen-year-old Mary Glover, for some clothing for her own daughter. Mary refused the request, angering Mistress Jackson. When Mary's parents, "religious persons of good credit and estimation among their neighbors," discovered the quarrel between their daughter and the old woman, they sent Mary to apologize. Mistress Jackson received the conciliatory Mary into her house on Friday, April 30, but she then locked the door and refused to let the girl out. She then "railed at her, with many threats and cursings, wishing an evil death to light upon her," hurling curses and abuse on Mary for an hour before releasing her with a final curse: "My daughter shall have clothes when thou art dead and rotten." Upon leaving Mistress Jackson's house, Mary immediately fell ill, her "countenance and color much altered," and she languished in a neutral state for three days.

The following Monday afternoon, Mary Glover was sitting in her father's shop eating a posset (a hot, spiced mixture of milk and ale, thickened with bread or egg). Suddenly, Elizabeth Jackson entered the shop and demanded to speak to Mary's mother. When Mary informed Mistress Jackson that her mother was not available, the old woman answered her very rudely and departed. Mary then tried to finish eating her posset but discovered that she "was not now able to let down one drop more of it, her throat seeming unto her locked up."

Speechless, she was taken home and put to bed, where she suffered terribly for the next eighteen days. Several times each day, her throat swelled so extremely that it seemed deformed to the onlookers, and she could neither speak nor eat. During this entire time, her only sustenance was what little broth could be forced down her throat with a spoon. The physician who was attending her diagnosed squinancy (quinsy/acute tonsillitis) and prescribed various remedies, none of which helped. The only relief Mary experienced during this time occurred whenever one of the bystanders periodically thrust a finger into her throat to open it, "whereby something seemed to move downward," temporarily alleviating her painful strangulation.

Mary's parents assumed that their daughter was dying and ordered the parish church bells tolled for her. Old Elizabeth Jackson, hearing the knell, was reported to rejoice, "I thank my God he hath heard my prayer and stopped the mouth and tied the tongue of one of my enemies." Mistress Glover, hearing this report, confronted Mistress Jackson, who denied speaking so harshly of the afflicted girl. To prove her sympathy, Mistress Jackson sent Mary Glover an orange, "in token of kindness, and the maid took it so kindly that she kept it in her hand, smelling it often the most part of that day." Unfortunately, this gift proved harmful to the girl, whose hand (the one that had held the orange), arm, and side were subsequently anesthetized and paralyzed.

On the nineteenth day, Mary Glover's throat opened, and she could again swallow freely. New symptoms, however, began to manifest themselves, such as a swollen belly and recurring fits of dumbness and blindness. When these new symptoms began to appear, Mary's physician ordered a course of treatment for the rising of the womb. When this treatment failed, however, he withdrew from the case, asserting that Mary Glover's affliction had no natural cause and was therefore not within the purview of an earthly physician. Another physician took over the case, treating Mary for melancholy over the course of the next several months, largely unsuccessfully, and several other physicians were consulted from time to time.

During this time, Mary recovered enough health to leave her sickbed sometimes and attend to her daily routine. One day in mid-June, as she was again sitting in her father's shop eating some bread, Elizabeth Jackson passed by and looked at Mary, saying nothing. The bite of bread that Mary had been chewing immediately fell from her mouth, and she tumbled off her stool onto the floor in "a grievous fit." From this moment until the day of her deliverance six months later, she could never eat a bite without being thrown into a fit. Another time, upon seeing Elizabeth Jackson look at her while they were both in church, Mary again fell into a series of fits, which increased

> both in strength and strangeness daily . . . insomuch as now she was turned round as a hoop, with her head backwards to her hips, and in that position rolled and tumbled with such violence and swiftness as that their pains in keeping her from receiving hurt against the bedstead and posts caused two or three women to sweat, she being all over cold and stiff as a frozen thing.

During these contortions, Mary's mouth often gaped wide, emitting "a great venemous and stinking blast," a breath so foul that when it touched the women attending on Mary—her mother, her sister, and a neighbor—their skin swelled and blistered, and they became nauseated.

One day, when Mary and her mother were going about their business in London, they met Elizabeth Jackson in the street. Mary's old enemy once again cast her evil eye on the girl, and Mary was hastily taken home to commence a series of fits with new characteristics. While she sat up in bed, for instance, her arms and hands mimed actions such as fencing, shooting a bow, playing a harp, or dancing (with only the upper part of her body). Her body thrashed violently in reaction to her bystanders' pronouncing of the sixth petition of the Lord's Prayer, "Deliver us from evil." Her body slowly attenuated, her neck and arms stretching out to appear much longer and thinner than usual, before returning to normal with the same slowness. She exhibited a great range of other strange behaviors, many of which seemed to the bystanders to be impossible to counterfeit. Frequently, especially during or following prayer, her lips clamped tightly shut, her eyes rolled up inside her head, her hands compulsively contracted into fists, and her body thrashed and contorted violently, rendering her "a terror to all beholders."

Despite the punishments inflicted on her body whenever Mary tried to pray, she persisted in doing so as often as she was able, to the great astonishment and admiration of her witnesses. Lifting up her right hand and her eyes to heaven, the girl, "with the signs of a devout mind and fervent spirit, would utter these words: 'O Lord, I give thee thanks that who hast delivered me this time and many more; I beseech thee, good Lord, deliver me forever." On other occasions, she prayed, "Lord, teach me a good use of this thy affliction, yet not as I will, but thy will be done." She prayed fervently and "to good purpose, and with a great variety of spirit, as for the pardon of her sins, the manifestation of the truth, the glory of God, and the satisfaction of his church." She also prayed for "patience and deliverance in God's good time" and for "the curbing of Satan, if he were an instrument or otherwise, for curing the imperfections of her body." She thanked God for all her previous deliverances and for convincing the world that she was not counterfeiting her fits. She disclaimed her own merits and submitted herself wholly to God, who had promised that all things shall be for the best. These prayers were often immediately followed by violent and agonizing fits that incapacitated Mary for many hours. Despite knowing the probable consequences of her pleas and thanks to God, however, Mary persisted in praying.

The fits described thus far were categorized by one of Mary's physicians as her "ordinary" fits, occurring several times daily, whenever Mary tried to eat, whenever she lay down in bed, and at other times. One of the witnesses of Mary Glover's sufferings estimated that she suffered violent ordinary fits at least a hundred and twenty times and painful ordinary fits at least six hundred times before finding permanent relief. In addition to these ordinary fits, however, Mary also suffered from "extraordinary" fits, which she experienced only when she was in the presence of Elizabeth Jackson. During these extraordinary fits, Mary manifested many of the same symptoms that she did in her ordinary fits, such as sensory deprivation and bodily rigidity, but she also manifested symptoms that implicated Elizabeth Jackson as the source of the evil that was afflicting her. For instance, when Mistress Jackson touched or looked at Mary, or even merely entered the room in which Mary was, Mary's body might "wallow over unto her," her arms and legs straining towards the old woman. Even more damning, Mary might, in her trance, emit a whispered voice through her nose: "The mouth being fast shut and her lips closed, there came a voice through her nostrils that sounded very like 'Hang her, hang her.' The repetition whereof never ceased so long as that Elizabeth Jackson was to be found within the compass of that roof; and she no sooner departed the house but the voice ceased." The emanation of this eerie voice through Mary's nostrils occurred many times and was heard by many horrified listeners.

The first instance of one of these extraordinary fits occurred upon the occasion of both Mary Glover and Elizabeth Jackson being summoned to meet with a local magistrate concerning Mary's accusation that Mistress Jackson had bewitched the girl. Mary had agreed willingly to this confrontation, predicting that it would yield proof of the old woman's infliction of evil on the girl, as indeed happened: "The maid was brought in, who, before she had spoken six words, fell down into this fit . . . and at this time it fell out that first that voice, 'Hang her, hang her,' sounded, all the while Elizabeth Jackson remained in the house with her." After this first occurrence of Mary Glover's extraordinary fit in the presence of Elizabeth Jackson, further experiments were made in other locations and in front of other witnesses, all with the same results. A knight, a lady, several clerics, and several physicians all witnessed similar occurrences that were interpreted as accusations of the "wicked mediatrix of [Mary's] woeful affliction." In all these cases, Elizabeth Jackson's responses—trembling, panting, and showing other signs of fear—were interpreted as "notes of a ruined conscience" that condemned Jackson by her own behavior.

On October 18, 1602, the recorder of London (the city's chief legal officer), John Crooke, summoned Mary Glover and Elizabeth Jackson to appear before him at his chamber at the Inner Temple, one of the four inns of court that constituted England's law school and that housed the most powerful and educated men in the country outside the royal court. Determined to subject Mary Glover's accusations to empirical examination, Crooke set up a test. He had Elizabeth Jackson exchange clothes with another woman who resembled her: "aged, homely, gross-bodied, and of low stature, very comparable to Elizabeth Jackson." He then had both women muffle their faces and, separately, walk into the room in which Mary Glover was waiting. When the imposter dressed in Elizabeth Jackson's clothes entered the room, Mary did not respond. Nevertheless, when the disguised Elizabeth Jackson entered the room, Mary was thrown into one of her extraordinary fits, complete with the whispering voice emanating from her nostrils. While Mary was still suffering in this fit, Crooke tested her further. He heated a pin in a candle flame and thrust it near her eye to see if she would flinch. She did not. He held burning paper so close to the palm of her hand that the bystanders could all see the blisters rising on her skin, but still she did not respond. Turning his attention to Elizabeth Jackson, Crooke ordered the old woman to say the Lord's Prayer. She predictably skipped the sixth petition ("Deliver us from evil"), so she was compelled to repeat the prayer again. This time, when the old woman pronounced the troublesome petition, "the body of the maid rebounded in the middle," as it had previously done whenever this phrase was pronounced in Mary Glover's presence. Crooke ordered Elizabeth Jackson to be taken from his chambers and committed to prison pending trial.

On December 1, 1602, Elizabeth Jackson was brought to court to be tried for witchcraft and was seated among the other prisoners in the dock. Mary Glover, called to testify against the accused, stood with her face to the judge and her back to the dock, apparently unaware of Jackson's presence in the room. Suddenly, Mary "felt a commanding power seize upon her, and therefore . . . cried, 'Where is she? Where is she that troubleth me?'" She then sank onto the floor, senseless, writhing, her face distorted, and the voice from her nostrils saying, "Hang her, hang her." The courtroom erupted in disorder, and Mary Glover was carried by three strong men to a nearby chamber and laid on a bed. Some hours later, the judge, the recorder, and several justices of the peace inspected the unconscious girl in her chamber, repeated the recorder's earlier tests with heated pins and fire, forced Elizabeth Jackson to be brought into the room and to lay her hand on the girl, and ordered Elizabeth Jackson to repeat the Lord's prayer and the creed. All of these tests yielded the usual results: Mary did not react to the heat, but she did recoil from the touch of the old woman; and Mistress Jackson failed to pronounce her prayers properly, so back to prison she went.

The court officials retired to discuss the evidence, which weighed considerably against Elizabeth Jackson. Besides Mary Glover, another alleged victim had testified against Elizabeth Jackson. Witch's marks had been found on the old woman's body. Two physicians testified that the girl's afflictions could not have stemmed from natural causes. Moreover, although two other physicians testified that this could have been the case, they hedged their testimony about with so many qualifiers that their words were not persuasive. They furthermore admitted that they did not know how to cure the girl. The judge, impatient with what he perceived as professional shilly-shallying, concluded, "Then in my conscience, [her disease] is not natural, for if you tell me neither a natural cause of it nor a natural remedy, I will tell you that it is not natural."

The early modern English criminal court's rules of evidence were very different from what we deem legal and appropriate today. Hearsay was perfectly admissible, as was testimony by children. For accusations of witchcraft, the legal system assumed a progressive three-tiered system of categorizing evidence. For the first tier, legal justification existed for a magistrate's examination of the accused if the latter had a notorious reputation as a witch, cursed or threatened or harbored known malice towards a victim and that victim subsequently suffered misfortune or fell ill, was related by blood or friendship to a known witch, failed to sink when immersed in water, or displayed an excessive interest in the illness or misfortune of a neighbor. For the second tier, that of "strong presumption," if the accusation came from a cunning person or a victim on his or her deathbed, then this evidence was deemed weighty enough to contribute to conviction if it was corroborated by other evidence. For the third tier, that of "sufficient proof," any one of the following constituted sufficient evidence to convict the accused of witchcraft without the necessity for corroborating evidence: an accusation by a known witch, an unnatural mark on the body of the accused, at least two witnesses attesting to the accused's pact with Satan or to the accused's relationship with a familiar spirit, suspicious pictures or images in the house of the accused, the giving of a gift from the accused to a victim followed by the victim's illness or misfortune, or the explicit confession of the accused. We know that Elizabeth Jackson repeatedly and publicly cursed, threatened, and harbored known malice towards Mary Glover, that she displayed excessive (and inappropriately jubilant) interest in the girl's illness, that she bore unnatural marks on her body, and that she gave a gift (the orange) to the girl before the affliction worsened. Her conviction, therefore, followed logically upon the rules of evidence widely observed by the legal system of her time.

After the court reconvened and the judge made his final address to the jury, the latter deliberated only briefly before returning a verdict

Weighing of souls by the Archangel Michael. Xylographic page from
Ars Moriendi, printed by Johann Weissenburger, Landshut, 1514.

of guilty. Elizabeth Jackson was sentenced to a year's imprisonment and to stand in the pillory four times during the course of that year in order to publicly confess her crime, the maximum sentence allowed by the law for an act of witchcraft that did not kill a person. After the convicted witch was led away, Mary Glover's extraordinary fits gradually ceased, and the voice from her nostrils was silenced forever: "the supreme commander of men and angels, good and bad, did shine upon her with his favorable countenance." Unfortunately, however, her ordinary fits were

> augmented, both in length and strength, above measure, so as there appeared some just fear of her life, the fit extending (at length) to about twelve hours' time, in which she had, at the least, six great courses of pangs, every one of these consisting of one hundred or one hundred and twenty short returns, every return containing five or six or more grievous pangs, mixed with a most strange and irresistible beating and rebounding of her right leg and body.

Some of the witnesses perceived that Satan's new stratagem to kill Mary was to trick the bystanders into accidentally strangling Mary as they desperately tried to hold her down in her violent thrashing fits. Many now refused to touch her during these fits for fear of harming her further.

The fact that Mary Glover continued to suffer despite the conviction and incarceration of Elizabeth Jackson implied that the girl was still in Satan's thrall and that "no corporal physic" would do her good. John Crooke, London's recorder, criticized the city's ministers, saying that they should be "ashamed to see a child of God in the claws of Satan without any hope of deliverance" while men of the cloth stood idly by. Mary Glover's parents also implored some ministers of their acquaintance for assistance. On Wednesday, December 15, 1602, therefore, six ministers met at the Glover house to plan a session of fasting and prayer on Mary's behalf, discussing and determining the order of events and the assignment of duties to each of the six. One, a skilled preacher, was assigned the task of preparing and exhorting the family members and others who would participate in the day's solemn work. He began this exercise at six in the evening, and led Mary and her family and friends in prayer for over an hour.

The next morning, about 24 people, including the six ministers, met at the distant house of a friend "for the more quiet and security to perform that good work of prayer, fasting, and supplication." Mary Glover entered the room holding her Bible and sat quietly on a bench near the fire. Beginning at about eight o'clock that morning, the crowd fasted and prayed for Mary's deliverance from Satan's power, determined not to cease in their efforts until the girl was free from evil. Most of these people would remain in this room, without rest or food, for the next eleven hours. A divinity student who was in the crowd said that, during all this time, "not one quarter of an hour was free from employment in some action of the ministers," who took turns preaching, reading from the Bible, leading the crowd in prayer and meditation, and exhorting the crowd to approach this holy work with humility. The minister who spoke first, "pressing the same point upon the parents and the poor maid by name, urged them to rip up the secrets of their hearts touching their lives forespent; the poor soul, the daughter, began to weep, yet moderating herself, she endured all his speech, even to the end of his sermon." At the end of this first sermon, Mary admitted that she had begun to feel pain throughout her body.

Throughout subsequent sermons that day, Mary continued to weaken, growing pale, beginning to weep, losing her voice, and wringing her hands. The prayers and fasting continuing for several more hours, at about two o'clock in the afternoon, Mary fell into a fit, first struck with blindness and dumbness, and then struck with swelling in her belly and throat, then paralyzed on her left side. Shortly thereafter, however, she recovered sufficiently to pray, her voice initially so low and soft that no one could understand her words but gradually gaining strength and volume. The witnesses were overjoyed at this happy sign, and one young law student who attended burst into tears of joy and rushed out of the room "with blubbering cheeks." Greatly encouraged by Mary's ability to pray, the bystanders redoubled their efforts. The ministers continued to take turns preaching for several more hours, and Mary continued to alternate between falling into fits and recovering from those fits sufficiently to pray.

At about six o'clock in the evening, darkness fell, "and now was come the hardest of all the day's labors, both in respect of the party's sufferings, the preachers' prayers with vehemence therein, and the people's perturbation." So exhausting had been the previous ten hours' efforts that the oldest of the six ministers began to flag, his voice becoming faint. Mary Glover had "entered into her sharpest conflict with Satan," her tongue black and doubled inward, her face viciously distorted, her expression fierce and threatening, her mouth gaping and frothing, her body writhing and thrashing as she barked like a dog. Discipline faltered, and the bystanders fell into disarray and confusion in their attempts to restrain the demoniac. The ministers were forced to abandon their planned prayers amidst the confusion and noise and to attempt basic crowd control. Mary Glover's father "roared right out with abundance of tears in the disquietness of his mind and anguish of his heart." When one of the ministers rebuked Satan (inside Mary Glover), Mary "turned her face towards him (though her eyes were shut) and did belch out spittle at him disdainfully, as also at others that knelt on each side of her." One of the men who was restraining Mary at this point said "that he had much ado to forbear spitting again in his foul face. I say *his* (quoth he) for that methought I saw [Satan's] ugly countenance in her then deformed visage."

One of the six ministers present, Lewis Hughes, the young vicar of an important London parish, perceived that the fierce "pride and rage of Satan" that he was witnessing in the possession of Mary Glover was a sign than the demon's defeat was close at hand. Hughes therefore now redoubled his efforts, restraining Mary Glover forcefully, and "lifted up his voice upon the sudden and prayed loud and vehemently . . . he urged the Lord now to show his power and to give check to Satan and command him to be gone." Suddenly, smiling and weeping at the same time, he cried, "He flies! He flies!" Mary Glover responded by grimacing and spitting into his face. For several dramatic moments, the minister and the demoniac strove together, he repeating, "He flies!" and she "casting out foam upwards into his face." Only one of the other ministers had the presence of mind to continue praying during this struggle for Mary's soul, but his prayers did the trick: Mary suddenly fell down as though dead, her body motionless and stiff, her eyes and mouth closed, her head lolling, her color lifeless. What happened next was "observed and afterwards constantly affirmed" by a few—but not many—of the witnesses: "there was a thing creeping under one of her eyelids, of the bigness of a pea." It was now seven o'clock, and those who had been with Mary since the beginning of her dispossession had been praying and fasting for eleven hours.

After Mary continued in her deathlike trance for a while, "suddenly in a moment, life came into her whole body, her mouth and eyes opened, and then lifting up her hands and stretching them wide asunder as high as she could reach, the first word she uttered was, 'He is come, he is come . . . the comforter is come! O Lord, thou hast delivered me!'" These words struck her father with great force, for, as he explained, "This was the cry of her grandfather going to be burned."

Everyone in the room at that moment would have interpreted these words as highly significant. Mary's grandfather, Robert Glover, was a celebrated Protestant martyr who had been burned at the stake as a heretic in 1555 during the Catholic reign of Mary Tudor. Glover's martyrdom had culminated an aspiration that he had possessed all his life, even as a youth, as was copiously documented by John Foxe, the famous Protestant martyrologist and a family friend of the Glovers. Robert Glover displayed what psychologists now call "the classic martyr syndrome," tormenting himself with insecurities brought on by the family's favoritism towards his brother John. Although Robert was bigger, stronger, better educated, and more articulate than his brother was, John remained the parents' favorite son. Robert determined, therefore, that if he could not surpass his brother in life, he would do so in death. Much evidence from letters and other personal documents indicates that Robert's main goal in life was to avoid an "unprofitable" death. As many other persecuted Protestants of his time believed, he thought that the light generated by his martyr's fire would act as a beacon to heaven, insuring him a seat closer to God than that of his brother. In his death speech, he declared himself "numbered among the saints." Nearly half a century later, Mary Glover's echoing of her grandfather's words at the moment of her release from evil would have immediately conveyed to everyone in the room the idea that Robert Glover's heroic sanctity had been passed down to his granddaughter, now proved to be a Protestant saint worthy of her family heritage.

Although few early modern demoniacs could claim a heritage as proud as Mary Glover's was in their aspirations to Protestant sainthood, other cases of demon possession did sometimes display this characteristic. For instance, we have already seen that the case of Thomas Darling a few years earlier presented a version of this phenomenon. Like Mary Glover, Thomas Darling resisted the evil possessing his body with vigorous theological arguments, appearing to carry on both parts of a dialogue between good and evil, a dialogue clearly modeled on Christ's temptation by Satan. We know that Darling aspired to be a preacher in order "to thunder out the threatenings of God's word against sin and all abominations" and that he admired and often directly addressed the famous Puritan minister Arthur Hildersham, who visited the boy in his illness.

The later case of demon possession of Mercy Short illustrated even more clearly the concept of the demoniac as a Protestant saint. In her sufferings, the girl made speeches that showed her "marvelous constancy" to God and to her officiating minister (Cotton Mather) when her possessing demon slandered them. Her theological sophistication impressed everyone who listened to her spirited arguments against the demon that possessed her. For instance, at one point, she challenged the demon to prove its claim that it was Christ by incarnating as a man and allowing itself to be crucified. She also implored the demon to exercise its free will by repenting and begging God's forgiveness for its sin of pride and disobedience. When the demon castigated her for being fatherless, Mercy Short replied, "No, I been't fatherless; I have God for my father." The demoniac continued to engage in considerable theological debate with this demon for many weeks, a debate that clearly displayed her staunch faith, wit, and intelligence against the forces of evil.

When Mary Glover spoke the words that communicated her hard-won freedom from evil at last, cries of victory broke out all through the room, and Mary fell on her knees to make a joyful prayer of thanksgiving to God for her deliverance. The ministers and others joined her, also on their knees, making their own prayers of thanksgiving on her behalf. One of Mary's relatives approached her with joyful tears on his cheeks and said, "Welcome, Mary, thou art now again one of us."

This remark implied that Satan's departure marked the beginning of Mary's reintegration into her community. Formerly alienated from God and from other people, Mary now returned to the fold, again unified with her earthly community, newly conjoined with God's

Protestant kingdom. As Scripture said, the return of the prodigal sinner to the flock occasioned more rejoicing than the steadfast faith of one who was never tempted. That is, separation from one's community must occur before reintegration could be celebrated. Such separation was central to many religious rituals, such as Christian communion and baptism, which required a phase of division from one's community before the phases of transition (to a new state of being) and reincorporation could occur. The dramatization of this lesson was a major function of early modern possession and dispossession, the first of which served to identify a disaffected individual and isolate him from the community to preserve its safety and the second to reabsorb that individual back into the community after his decontamination and the expulsion of the demon. This type of spiritual battle illustrated the essentially antagonistic tensions of Christian theology, stretched between opposing poles of light and darkness, good and evil, life and death, salvation and damnation, God and Satan. In possession and dispossession, these antagonistic forces were incarnated both externally (in the officiating minister and in Satan) and internally (within the demoniac).

Immediately after the dispossession, the six participating ministers discussed and decided how to best to document their experience for posterity without attracting unwanted official attention to their actions. The witnesses were admonished not to publicize what they had seen and heard. They were also told that, "if any of them should fall into the hands of any to be examined, they would then be as careful as might be to keep the poor ministers out of danger, who losing hereby their liberty of preaching should lose all the means they had of their maintenance." The ministers and witnesses crept out of the house secretly, two by two, under cover of darkness. Unfortunately, though, Lewis Hughes, the young minister who was restraining the demoniac at the actual moment when Satan apparently fled her body, decided to report the incident to John Crooke, the recorder of London, whom he perceived to be an ally.

Crooke advised Hughes to make his report directly to the city's highest clerical authority: Richard Bancroft, the bishop of London. Hughes did so, but the bishop received his report with great displeasure. Bancroft was furious at the manner in which this case had torn London apart for eight months. The citizens had several times mobbed the buildings in which Mary Glover had displayed her spectacular symptoms, creating public disorder and spawning at least one instance of a purse being cut by a thief while the purse's owner watched the show. Many of these citizens had been increasingly convinced that Mary was simulating her possession and that Elizabeth Jackson was innocent, and they had disrupted Jackson's trial with cries of "Counterfeit!" when Mary Glover displayed her symptoms. The College of Physicians, the leading medical authority in the country, had been violently divided on the subject of whether Mary's affliction was natural or supernatural, and this professional schism had caused the college to be publicly humiliated by the judge during Jackson's trial. Furthermore, the ministers and others who had gathered secretly to fast and pray for Mary Glover had done so without the authority of the church, participating in an illegal conventicle. Far from receiving Hughes' report as a joyful testament to God's power, therefore, the bishop called Hughes a "rascal and varlet," suspended him from the ministry (thus depriving him of his livelihood), and imprisoned him. The bishop dismissed the others who had participated in the dispossession as "a rout, rabble, and swarm of giddy, idle, lunatic, illuminate, holy spectators of both sexes, and especially a sisternity of nimps, mops, and idle holy women that did grace the devil with their idle holy presence."

Queen Elizabeth I died on March 24, 1603, less than four months after the deliverance of Mary Glover. Lewis Hughes was still in prison. When he was released shortly after the queen's death, Hughes immigrated to Bermuda, where he established a Presbyterian Church government, and spent the rest of his life railing against the bishops of the English church.

THE
SCOVRGE
OF
DRVNKENNES.

By *William Hornby* Gent.

LONDON,
Printed by G. E l d, for *Thomas Baylie*, and are to be folde
at his Shop, in the Middle-Row in Holborne,
neere vnto *Staple-Inne*, 1618.

The Devil of tobacco "drinking." From William Hornby's *The Scourge of Drunkenness*,
an anti-smoking pamphlet printed by G. Eld for Thomas Baylie, London, 1618.

Chapter 13

Conclusion

Ｔhe cases presented in this book spanned the last thirty-eight years of Elizabeth's forty-five-year reign. Comparing the social and official responses to the earlier and later cases, we notice some striking differences. John Lane and John Foxe, the dispossessors in the early cases of Anne Mylner and Robert Brigges, were perceived and treated as models of piety whose roles as God's champions against Satan deserved the utmost respect, and the historical record notes no contemporary skepticism about or criticism of their behavior in these cases. Conversely, John Darrell and Lewis Hughes, the dispossessors in the last five cases, were expelled from the ministry and imprisoned for their efforts. This alteration in the attitude of the public and the government toward demon dispossession was not lost on those who performed the act. Whereas Anne Mylner's deliverance was celebrated in public sermons preached from important pulpits to hundreds of appreciative listeners, Mary Glover's deliverance was concluded by her dispossessors swearing each other to secrecy and sneaking out of the house under cover of darkness. Growing church opposition to dispossession, new medical explanations for behaviors formerly interpreted as manifestations of possession, and the exposure of fraud after fraud had all contributed to this shift from credulity to skepticism. The important people who had interpreted demon possession as a manifestation of God's special attention had diminished in number, become less vocal, and lost many of their powerful champions, such as John Foxe (who had died in 1587). On the other hand, the number of important people who interpreted demon possession as a self-aggrandizing cheat had increased, become more vocal, and acquired powerful new champions.

One of the most significant of these opponents of dispossession was John Whitgift, who had been elected archbishop of Canterbury in 1583. This election had opened a new era of persecution for nonconforming Protestants, whom Whitgift considered the church's greatest enemies. Before Whitgift's election, the official attitude had been that the casting out of demons was a dissident act because it was performed by Catholics. After Whitgift's election, however, the official attitude enlarged to encompass as dissidents any person, Catholic or not, who purported to cast out demons. Whitgift was determined to oppose what he perceived as the dangerous social and political consequences of dispossession, including the generation of public fear and disorder and the undermining of church and government authority. He reactivated the ecclesiastical courts and mandated the use of an oath that forced the clergy to conform on pain of imprisonment. Whitgift and his chaplain, Richard Bancroft, hit the nonconformists with so many blows that they began to turn away from reform and toward separatism during the 1580s and '90s, despite the execution of some of the separatist leaders. A series of anonymous satiric attacks on the church, the Martin Marprelate tracts of 1588–89, though popular with the public, ironically harmed the cause by their shocking vitriol and violence, provoking many former sympathizers to turn against the nonconformists. Though some individual nonconformists soldiered on in the (false) hope that Elizabeth's heir apparent, James VI of Scotland, would institute presbyterianism in England when he succeeded to the English throne, the cause was essentially lost in England by the early 1590s. The controversies of Elizabeth's final years were therefore not concerned with church structure as much as with theology. Moreover, according to the official theology of the Church of England, the age of miracles was over. Anyone who purported to perform miracles, including the casting out of demons, therefore flouted church doctrine and was treated as a heretic.

By the time of the new king's ascension to the throne as James I of England, Whitgift and Bancroft had already been fighting against exorcisms and dispossessions for many years and had amassed an army of allies, including several influential government ministers.

Some of these took advantage of the passing of the scepter to lobby for changes in government policy that reflected the increasing skepticism of the church. For instance, three of the new king's most powerful advisers—Robert Cecil, Earl of Salisbury (secretary of state); Henry Howard, Earl of Northampton (privy councillor); and Thomas Howard, Earl of Suffolk (lord chamberlain)—all vigorously supported Bancroft's position. The notorious case of Mary Glover, concluded less than four months before James's accession, had precipitated a serious conflict of authority between the courts and the church that could be resolved only by the monarch.

Because the queen was near death at the time and therefore incapacitated, royal authority resided with Cecil, who insured the immediate publication of two books attacking belief in possession and dispossession. One of these, Edward Jorden's *A Brief Discourse of the Suffocation of Mother,* was written by the physician who had been publicly embarrassed during the trial of Elizabeth Jackson because his testimony had not convinced the judge that Mary's Glover's affliction was a natural illness. This book, possibly sponsored by Bancroft, was far more convincing than Jorden's court testimony had been. Another of these books, Samuel Harsnet's *Declaration of Egregious Popish Impostures,* definitely sponsored by Bancroft, paralleled the Catholic exorcisms of Sarah Williams with John Darrell's series of dispossessions, presenting both of them as frauds and their practitioners as heretics. During the new king's procession south from Scotland preceding his coronation, Cecil, Whitgift, and Bancroft spent much time apprising the new monarch on affairs of state, handing over copies of these books in the process. Shortly after his accession, James I, who had long possessed an intellectual interest in demonology, began to display a marked shift to skepticism on the subject. Indeed, his anti-smoking diatribe of the following year, *A Counterblast to Tobacco,* explicitly satirizes those who pretended to cast out demons: "[If tobacco] could by the smoke thereof chase out devils . . . it would serve for a precious relic, both for the superstitious priests and the insolent puritans, to cast out devils withal."

When Whitgift died the year following James's accession, Bancroft succeeded him as archbishop of Canterbury, continuing the church's work of discrediting possession and dispossession. That same year, the new archbishop accomplished a major administrative coup: the church's adoption of the *Constitutions and Canons Ecclesi-astical, Treated Upon by the Bishop of London, President of the Convocation for the Province of Canterbury.* This coup was not won without a fight. The House of Commons opposed the adoption of these canons as con-trary to statute, arguing that, under a law adopted during the reign of Henry VIII, it was the prerogative of the common law judges to decide the jurisdictional limits of the ecclesiastical judges. Nonconformists also objected, correctly perceiving that the canons were intended to oust their ministers from positions of influence within the church. Despite this powerful opposition, however, the new canon laws received James's royal confirmation on September 6, 1604. This body of laws, incorporating the previous forty-five years' worth of injunctions, inter-pretations, advertisements, orders, and articles into one coherent codifi-cation, greatly increased the church's disciplinary power and its potential for the achievement of conformity. In short, it was the church's most successful move to date against the nonconformists, and by its means were several dozen of the latter's ministers soon deprived of their clerical livings.

Some of the provisions of the new canons effectively prohibited dispossessions by rendering unlawful the circumstances under which they were conducted. For instance, one provision forbade private meetings of ministers or others "to consult upon any matter or course . . . which may any way tend to the impeaching or depraving of the doc-trine of the Church of England, or of the book of Common Prayer, or of any part of the government and discipline now established in the Church of England under pain of excommunication." Another provision read, "No minister or ministers shall, without the license and direction of the bishop of the diocese first obtained and had under his hand and seal, appoint or keep any solemn fasts, either publicly or in any private houses, other than such as by law are, or by public authority shall be appointed." The most explicit prohibition occurred in canon seventy-two. Under this article, ministers were forbidden, without license by their bishops, "to attempt upon any pretence whatsoever, either of possession or obsession, by fasting and prayer to cast out any devil or devils, under pain of the imputation of imposture, or cozenage, and deposition from the ministry." The penalties for violating this provision included suspension from the ministry for a first offense, deposition from the ministry for a second, and excommunication from the church for a third. This provision provided the church with its first specific, enforceable, legal prohibition against the practice of dispossessing demons.

Within a year following the adoption of the new canon laws, Thomas Harrison, an adolescent boy of Northwich, began to exhibit symptoms of demon possession. The boy made bestial noises and exhibited bestial behavior: "he would sometimes howl like a dog, mew like a cat, roar like a bear, froth and foam like a boar." He also reported that the voice of Jesus had whispered in his ear, telling him that he was possessed by three devils. His family and friends (whom a later commentator identifies as predominantly nonconformists) appealed to the bishop of Chester, Richard Vaughan, to issue the license mandated by canon seventy-two in order to allow some local ministers to hold a private prayer meeting on behalf of the boy. Initially, the bishop denied the request—several times. After he himself witnessed the boy's fits, however, he concluded that the boy was genuinely afflicted (though not, he thought, possessed), and issued a license to the local ministers "to use their discretion by private prayer and fasting, for the ease and comfort of the afflicted." The language of the license clearly indicated the bishop's own doubt about whether a demon was involved: "Because it is by some held that the child is really possessed of an unclean spirit, for that there appeareth to us no certainty, nor yet any great probability thereof, we think it also convenient and require the preachers aforesaid to forbear all forms of exorcism, which always imply and presuppose a real and actual possession." The bishop's skepticism furthermore manifested itself in several conditions outlined in the license for conducting the prayer meeting. The names of the four ministers authorized to pray for the boy were listed, and "none other" was permitted to attend on the boy. The boy's parents were forbidden to allow any visitors to the house during the meeting except for the four named ministers. Public prayer in church would be allowed on the boy's behalf, but any fasting was to be done privately, and no meeting could be called for that purpose. This stringently conditional license, the first issued under the new canon laws, was also the last for a very long time—perhaps as long as three centuries.

The increasing official intolerance of possession and dispossession was paralleled by an increasing public skepticism about the same phenomena, skepticism revealed in the popular literature and entertainment. Playwrights, naturally, frequently alluded to well-known cases of possession and dispossession or exorcism, always using these cases as satiric targets. One of William Shakespeare's theatrical attacks on possession intersected directly with the life of one of the demoniacs documented in this book: Robert Brigges, the wealthy gentleman whom the famous John Foxe had tried unsuccessfully to dispossess in 1574. Following Satan's final departure from his mind, Brigges, a law student, resumed his studies. A little more than a year following his encounter with Satan, he became a lawyer and began a practicing career that lasted nearly thirty years. During those three decades, Brigges maintained a chamber and ate his meals communally with other lawyers at the Middle Temple, one of the four Inns of Court that constituted England's law school. He also attended the feasts and revels that memorialized the inn's most important days. Such a day was Candlemas, February 2, one of the few pre-Reformation church feasts to survive Henry VIII's purge of the religious calendar. The inns of court celebrated Candlemas as one of their year's most significant events—sometimes celebrated in a grander style than Christmas—and always sponsored a great feast and revel for the occasion. We can assume, therefore, that on Candlemas Night, 1602, Robert Brigges was sitting in the Middle Temple's great hall with his fellows, honored by the presence of his monarch, partaking of an extravagant feast, and enjoying the evening's entertainment. The focus of this entertainment was a royal command performance of the Lord Chamberlain's players enacting a comedy written by the company's playwright: *Twelfth Night.*

One of only two documented productions of a Shakespeare play at the Inns of Court, this performance might have been the result of a family commission. Thomas Greene of Warwickshire was a member of the Middle Temple whose legal career eventually embraced several positions in Stratford: solicitor, barrister, steward, and town clerk. He was also Shakespeare's cousin. Close to Shakespeare throughout his adult life, Greene visited him at his London house, shared his Stratford house, and named his children William and Anne. Greene was called to the bar in 1602, a celebratory occasion for which a play might have been commissioned—a play written by Greene's cousin, Shakespeare, and performed at Greene's inn of court, the Middle Temple, by Shakespeare's acting company, the Lord Chamberlain's Men.

   Sitting in the Middle Temple's great hall on the night of February 2, 1602, Brigges and everyone else in the play's well-informed audience would have been highly aware of the significant shifts in public opinion and government policy since Brigges' possession by Satan twenty-eight years earlier. Controversy on the subject of possession and dispossession had surged to the forefront of public consciousness in the mid-1580s with the Catholic exorcisms of Sarah Williams and others. These exorcisms had been witnessed by huge crowds and precipitated the conversion to Catholicism of at least 500 people, thus earning the government's full attention. This attention was further focused by the fact that one of the demoniacs was a servant to the courtier and spy Anthony Babington. Moreover, one of the exorcists, John Ballard, was a primary conspirator in Babington's plot to engineer the assassination of Elizabeth, the invasion of England by Spain, and the coronation of the Catholic Mary Stuart as queen of England. The government dispensed with most of the plotters and exorcists through imprisonment and death in 1586, but the controversy over the exorcisms and their political implications continued. Indeed, it accelerated when John Darrell took it upon himself to retaliate against Weston's exorcisms by staging his own series of competing Protestant dispossessions.

   The Catholic exorcisms in Denham and the Darrell dispossessions represented the most scandalous examples of what skeptics had began to call "devil hunting" and "devil puffing," but, as we know, they were not by any means the only such cases. For instance, from 1589 to 1593, five daughters and seven maidservants of the Throckmorton family exhibited symptoms of demonic possession, their behavior resulting in the condemnation of three people to death for witchcraft. In 1591, three nonconforming zealots purporting to be both possessed and gifted with the ability to dispossess demons were incarcerated for blasphemy, one being executed and another starving himself to death in prison. These and many other cases caused both the public and the government to become increasingly impatient with the issue. The atmosphere of public opinion in which *Twelfth Night* first played, therefore, had changed considerably in the twenty-eight years since the possession of Robert Brigges. In this play's satire on religious zealotry (through its attack on Malvolio), one of the satiric targets was the belief in possession and dispossession.

Reform minister officiating at the marriage of the fool and the she-devil.
From Thomas Murner's anti-Lutheran pamphlet Von dem grossen
Lutherischen Narren, about 1518.

Thus, during the performance of *Twelfth Night* in the Middle Temple's great hall on February 2, 1602, when Maria said to Olivia, "He [Malvolio] is sure possessed, madam" (III.iv.8), the audience would have heard the word "possessed" as indicating self-serving imposture, dishonesty in the usage of others, and affected, artificial behavior. When Toby wondered if "all the devils of hell be drawn in little [i.e., compressed into Malvolio's body], and Legion himself possessed him [Malvolio]" (III.iv.78–80), the audience would have immediately recognized the word "Legion." The connection would have been not only to Christ's exorcism as told in Luke 8:26 but also to the case of the fraudulent demoniac Agnes Brigges, whose body was reported to have contained "5,000 legions" of devils, all of whom spoke as one voice when questioned as to their names, responding "Legion, Legion." A few lines later, when Toby exclaimed, "What, man, 'tis not for gravity to play at cherry-pit with Satan" (III.iv.108–09), the audience would have noted a reference to the same case. Satan had tried to negotiate with the dispossessing ministers, wheedling, "Give me a cherry and I will go," to which the uncompromising ministers responded, "Thou shalt have nothing." When Feste asked Malvolio the horns-of-a-dilemma question, "But tell me true, are you not mad indeed? or do you but counterfeit?" (IV.ii.110–11), the audience would have recognized the irony of putting this query to one who, unlike England's contemporary demoniacs, fell into neither category. When they heard Malvolio's reference to "the lady of the Strachy" (II.5.37) and Feste's admonishment to Malvolio, "Endeavor thyself to sleep and leave thy vain bible babble" (IV.2.94), a quotation of the nonsense phrase rendered infamous by the Starchy children in their mockery of the Bible, everyone in the audience would have known the reference.

The explicit falseness of the theatrical representation of possession on this night emphasized the ironic gap that had widened between the phenomenon and its audience. One of the leading skeptical voices, that of bishop Samuel Harsnet, would in the following year insistently use theatrical metaphors to expose the falseness of the Jesuit exorcisms of Sarah Williams and others. Harsnet would refer to the priests as "the actors in this holy comedy," to the exorcisms as "this play of sacred miracles," to the demoniacs as "play-fellows," and to the priests' vestments as costumes "out of the holy wardrobe from Rome." The presentation of a phenomenon on the stage implicitly conveys the idea of that phenomenon's artificiality, a point made in *Twelfth Night* itself: "If this were played upon a stage now, I could condemn it as an improbable fiction" (III.iv.119–20). Neither Robert Brigges nor many of the witnesses of his possession in 1574 nor many modern readers would put Brigges in the same category with the satiric targets of *Twelfth Night:* the confessed fraud Agnes Brigges, the hysterical Starchy children, and the welter of other faux demoniacs that had wearied the country. Brigges, however, as he sat in the Middle Temple's great hall on the night of February 2, 1602, must have been uncomfortably aware that many in the play's audience would have done exactly that: dismissed the most profound spiritual experience of his life as a theatrical humbug.

At the passing of the crown from Elizabeth I to James I in 1603, therefore, we see that both the government and the public were considerably less tolerant of possession and dispossession than they had been four decades earlier. Nonetheless, cases of possession continued to occur, as did attempts to cast out the devils presumed to be involved in those cases. Catholics continued to perform secret exorcisms for those in need, attempting to cast demons out of Grace Sowerbutts in 1612, William Perry in 1620, a Chester woman in 1663, and a Wigan man in 1691. Protestant nonconformists continued to perform dispossessions (unlicensed by the church), attempting to cast demons out of Richard Rothwell and John Fox in 1612, Roger Sterrop in 1629, the children of George Muschamp in 1650, Hannah Crump in 1661, James Barrow in 1664, Robert Churchman in 1682, and Richard Dugdale in 1690. Many of the nonconformists who participated in this activity during the seventeenth century were Quakers, at the time a relatively new group that perceived miracle working as a necessary credential to establish its credibility with new converts. For example, George Fox, a founder of the movement, was approached around 1650 by a woman who had been possessed by a demon for thirty-two years. He said, "The poor woman would make such a noise in roaring and sometimes lying along upon her belly upon the ground and with her spirit and roaring and voice, and would set all Friends [Quakers] in a heat and sweat . . . And there were many Friends almost overcome by her with the stink that came out of her, roaring and tumbling on the ground." Fox presumably dispossessed her during a prayer meeting, an episode that received much publicity: "And then the world's professors, priests and teachers never could call us any more false prophets, deceivers, or witches after, but it did a great deal of good in the country among people in relation to the truth, and to the stopping the mouths of the world and their slanderous aspersions." Such incidents were, of course, interpreted by sympathizers as evidence of saintliness and by opponents as evidence of diabolism. Opponents generally perceived Quakers as neo-Catholics, the latest development in the continuing process of the Catholic subversion of the country. Many preachers and government officials made explicit references to the Catholic sources of Quaker diabolism, focusing particular attention upon the role of the Jesuits in spreading such "doctrines of devils."

However, the seventeenth century also witnessed the advent of a new type of demon-router: one who made little or no pretense to divine authority. For instance, the dispossessors of Anne Gunter in

1605 and Henry Smith's nephew in 1616 were not only women but also the very witches who were accused of sending their familiars to torment the victims. Similarly, the dispossession of Katherine Malpas in 1621 was attempted by one Francklin of Ratcliffe, a sorcerer who was paid twenty shillings for his services. Margaret Hooper was dispossessed in 1641 by her husband (a yeoman) and her son. In 1664, Robert Pyle's possessing demon was sucked out of his body by his two young children, who were held to his mouth by his wife. In 1665, Mary Hale's possessing spirits, who refused to be cast out by a conjuror named Woodhouse, recommended instead the services of a rival, a conjuror named Redman. In 1689, the daughter of a man named Alexander was dispossessed by an astrologer, who conjured the demon to depart in the names of Tetragrammaton and the Trinity, accompanying his conjurations with distillations of marigold, rosemary, and angelica, all gathered at the most efficacious planetary hours. Clearly, the dispossession of Satan no longer fell within the exclusive purview of the true church, whichever one that was: it was now also an individual prerogative, increasingly secular.

The increasing secularization of demon dispossession was an extension of the increasing secularization of English society as a whole. Although some people today argue that the explanation for this shift towards the secular was that the use of supernatural explanations gradually diminished because of scientific progress, most modern historians dismiss this explanation as a naïve assumption that science is somehow less driven by cultural preconceptions than, say, religion or law. A more analytical explanation is that the political significance of supernatural explanations simply faded away as secular ideologies arose, ideologies such as the pursuit of liberty, the sanctity of property, and other ideas focusing on the individual's rights within the state rather than that individual's responsibilities to the state. Before this shift, a person manifesting signs of obvious mental or physical distress was widely considered a public exemplum, a sign from God to that person's society. As such, the distressed person's problems were everyone's business. As a result of the controversy over the legitimacy of spiritual healing, however, secular (medical) forms of treatment became established as the only course of action acceptable to the orthodox elite, and the distressed person's problems gradually came to be viewed as personal rather than sociopolitical.

We see an example of this move towards the secularization of treatment in the centuries-old practice of driving out demons by touch. Two of the most distinguished fathers of the early Christian church, Origen and Saint Ambrose, had believed that the laying on of hands was efficacious in exorcism. As we know from the case of Sarah Williams, this practice had evolved from a priest's anointing of a dying person with holy oil during extreme unction, an act that the early church believed to be curative provided the patient had sufficient faith. In England, this priestly function had attached to the king during the reign of Edward the Confessor and was formalized a few centuries later by Henry VII in a ritual ceremony "for the healing of them that be diseased with the King's Evil" (scrofula, a form of glandular tuberculosis). This ceremony derived from an old manuscript exorcism and required, among other acts, the monarch to touch the afflicted person while prayers of exorcism were read over him. The efficacy of the monarch's touch was guaranteed by his function as God's anointed representative on earth, a point emphasized by the ceremony itself, which clearly demonstrated that the king's touching was a holy act modeled on Christ's healing of sick. Because of the monarch's unique role, this miracle was granted to no other person in the kingdom. In fact, others who purported to cure by touch were sometimes executed as traitors, pretenders to the throne.

During 1649–1660, however, England had no monarch, and the ceremony to treat the King's Evil necessarily lapsed. To fill this therapeutic gap, several "strokers" appeared (people who purported to heal scrofula and other afflictions by touch and prayer). The most famous of these was Valentine Greatrakes, an unemployed Irish war veteran in need of funds. Greatrakes touched to cure, not only scrofula, but also ague, epilepsy, fever, and miscellaneous aches and pains. An English physician attempted to explain Greatrakes' success by observing that his body was "composed of particular ferments, the effluvia of which he introduced into the bodies of his patients by stroking them." These "effluvia" theoretically regenerated the blood and drove the disease out through the body's orifices. Greatrakes himself had a simpler explanation: he said he was driving out devils. His approach indeed did use the exorcistic principle of driving the pain (the demon) through the body until it was forced to exit through an orifice. He treated a woman with a chronic headache by rubbing her head and driving the pain into her breasts and stomach, then rubbing those parts of her body until "she was immediately put into a tedious fit of belching, which continued the space of an hour or upwards, and that being over, she expressed her self to find more ease than she had done of 20 years before, and that she was then void of all pain, to her unspeakable joy and comfort." On another occasion, a man's "exquisite and continual pains, by the gentle touch and easy friction of Mr. Greatrakes' hand, were allured out of his arm and shoulder to the extreme joints and ends of his fingers." When Charles II recovered his father's throne in 1660, he invited his rival to stroke at a public exhibition. Greatrakes failed under the eye of the king, and his career died immediately.

The brief career of Valentine Greatrakes demonstrates the incipient secularization of the diagnosis and treatment of illness in general and of demon possession in particular. Greatrakes presented himself as a substitute for the monarch in one limited function. The fact that he was not anointed like the monarch or like a priest, however, meant that he was not holy. His service therefore seemed to derive its effectiveness from his natural, personal power rather than from his function as the conduit of God's will. Thus, we see the beginnings of a perceptual shift that came to characterize English intellectual culture and, later, most of English popular culture: what formerly looked like demon possession gradually came to look like something else.

Several historians have attempted to translate early modern demon possession into medical terminology to render the phenomenon more acceptable to the modern mind. We have already noted several of these translations, such as epilepsy in the case of Anne Mylner, postpartum depression in the case of Edmund Kingesfield's wife, pathological swallowing in the case of Agnes Brigges, and conversion (hysteria) in the case of Katherine Wright. The symptoms manifested in other cases point variously to conditions that may now be diagnosed as autism, ergot poisoning, Tourette's syndrome, sclerosis, Huntington's chorea, dyslexia, psoriasis, herpes, paranoia, schizophrenia, Parkinson's disease, compulsion neurosis, mania, senile dementia, diabetic coma, or clinical depression, among others. This multiplicity of diagnoses emphasizes the differences in the cases while ignoring an important similarity: early modern English demon possession was a *religious* phenomenon. It occurred in a religious cultural atmosphere. It afflicted religious individuals beset by religious guilt. Each case was perceived and conceptualized within a religious context and diagnosed using religious terminology. To attribute Anne Mylner's whole problem to epilepsy, therefore, would be misleading and reductionist. We cannot simply ignore the elements of sin, temptation, and self-punishment that characterized her case and all the other cases presented in this book, even those in which the demoniac was a fraud. Because possession was a religious phenomenon, it cannot be adequately explained in modern secular psychomedical terminology.

Anthropology has, on the whole, been more successful than medicine in acknowledging the essential religious component of demon possession in its analysis of the phenomenon. We have already seen some features of modern anthropological analysis in the cases presented in this book, such as Mary Glover's reintegration into her community following her ritual separation from that community. This procedure of separation and reintegration, though it assumes a variety of religious and secular forms (such as temporary imprisonment for a crime), serves the essential purpose of corporate self-defense in any society, which must identify a disaffected individual and isolate him or her in order to preserve its own safety. If that individual can be reclaimed as a social citizen, then he or she can be reabsorbed into the culture. Another feature of anthropological analysis is the assumption that the disaffection of the individual stems from a feeling of social powerlessness or helplessness, as we saw in the cases of Edmund Kingesfielde's wife, Agnes Brigges and Rachel Pindar, and William Somers. Anthropology theoretically analyzes a culture's behavior in terms of that culture's beliefs, not the beliefs of those outside the culture, and in this regard, it proves a discipline superior to medicine in addressing more comprehensively the characteristics of demon possession rather than just some small number of those characteristics. Ultimately, however, its conclusion that demon possession exists entirely by virtue of self-referential cultural definition reduces the phenomenon just as surely as medicine does. In both cases, the afflicted person becomes the source of his own problem, a problem that is either impersonal and random (the medical explanation) or insignificant and incomprehensible to the world outside the afflicted person's immediate culture (the anthropological explanation). When Satan receded from view, taking with him the concept that a person's problems were caused by an intelligent, powerful, personal, and willful evil, human suffering lost a great deal of its heroic moral significance.

That significance returned when, in the early twentieth century, the Church of England, for the first time in three hundred years, refocused its attention on exorcism, now no longer calling it "dispossession" but rather a "ministry of healing." In the 1920s, an Anglican priest named Donald Omand began exorcising, presumably under the authorization of the required episcopal license. Omand believed "that evil can permeate mankind and all creation; can force itself into things," and so his exorcisms addressed a wide variety of people, animals, places, and objects. He is supposed to have once cured a herd of sick cattle when a veterinarian failed to do so. He also exorcised circus animals, circus tents, figurines, dangerous spots in roads where accidents occurred, and a toilet. Reiterating the early modern theological concept that moral neutrality was impossible (as discussed in the chapter on Anne Mylner), Omand said that everything in the world "must be possessed . . . by goodness or badness, by God or Beelzebub." Omand's fifty-year career culminated in the 1970 publication of a book whose explicit purpose was to publicize the fact that some Anglican priests can and do perform exorcisms. This book was chatty, personal, and nontechnical, carefully steering clear of any theological or doctrinal abstraction, clearly intended for a wide public audience. The book's foreword by the Bishop of Portsmouth commended Omand's work as a "great help to many who are concerned with and worried by the supernatural world."

The publication of Omand's book coincided with a huge upsurge of public interest in exorcism in the 1960s and 1970s, an interest which the Church of England sought to accommodate, perhaps because interest in non-Christian religions and philosophies such as Transcendental Meditation, Buddhism, Wicca, and so on had caused the church to look to its own survival by offering the services demanded by current and potential congregants. In the late 1960s, the Bishop of Exeter convened a church commission to restore exorcism "to its proper place." This place was defined as exorcism's "positive aspect as an extension of the frontiers of Christ's Kingdom and a demonstration of the power of the Resurrection to overcome evil and replace it with good" rather than its "purely negative action of expelling an evil force or cleansing an evil environment." The commission prepared an exorcism training program for clergy and offered it to any diocese. In 1972, the commission published an exorcism manual, edited by an Anglican Benedictine monk, Dom Robert Petitpierre. The purpose of the manual was to "explain the underlying theology, and to offer some practical help by providing specimen prayers and forms of service." It also included guidelines and forms of prayer for the exorcism of places, people, holy water, and salt and for the laying on of hands.

At around the same time, Father Christopher Neil-Smith, an Anglican priest, received a standing license from the Bishop of London authorizing him to exorcise freely according to his own judgment. Father Neil-Smith consequently went on to perform approximately 2,200 exorcisms between 1970 and 1974, his clients including lawyers, architects, engineers, television producers, art critics, and others who clearly did not fall into the "socially powerless" category. (By contrast, Monsignor Luigi Novarese, Rome's official Catholic exorcist, who was operating at the same time as Father Neil-Smith, exorcised only about sixty people during his entire 27-year career.) In 1975, the archbishop of Canterbury defended the church's increasing emphasis on exorcism by saying, "the liberation from bondage to evil into the fullness of life—that is the work of the Church. It's a difficult task and the forces of evil are very great. I do not see exorcism as something set off against and in opposition to medicine. . . . [T]here is no doubt that there are many cases of men and women within the grip of the powers of evil [who] need the aid of the Christian church working in collaboration with the forces of medicine to deliver the person so oppressed."

The twentieth-century resurgence of possession and exorcism under the auspices of the Church of England attests to a need among many people to ascribe moral significance to human suffering. This need cannot be met by medical explanations, which generally assign the sufferer the role of random victim of chance. By allowing the sufferer to externalize, demean, judge, and evict the source of the suffering, demon possession aggrandizes the sufferer and bestows hope—no mean feat given the ubiquity of human distress.

Sources

CHAPTER 1

For pre-Christian and early Christian exorcism, see E. O. James, *Christian Myth and Ritual: A Historical Study* (London: John Murray, 1933), 197–98; Roger Baker, *Binding the Devil: Exorcism Past and Present* (London: Sheldon, 1974), 17, 21, 41, 63; Nicholas P. Spanos and Jack Gottlieb, "Demonic Possession, Mesmerism, and Hysteria: A Social Psychological Perspective on Their Historical Interactions," *Journal of Abnormal Psychology* 88 (1977): 532; C. F. D. Moule, ed., *Miracles* (London: A. R. Mowbray, 1965), 156, 160, 216–17; Susan Garrett, *The Demise of the Devil: Magic and the Demonic in Luke's Writing* (Minneapolis: Fortress, 1989), 45–46; Reginald Maxwell Woolley, *Exorcism and the Healing of the Sick* (London: Society for Promoting Christian Knowledge, 1932), 19–21, 27; D. P. Walker, *Unclean Spirits: Possession and Exorcism in France and England in the Late Sixteenth and Early Seventeenth Centuries* (Philadelphia: University of Pennsylvania Press, 1981), 4, 21; Saint Elmo Nauman, ed., *Exorcism Through the Ages* (New York: Philosophical Library, 1974), 75; and Saint Athanasius, *The Life of St. Anthony the Great* (1850; reprinted Willis, California: Eastern Orthodox Books, 1976), 40, 59, 67, 76–77. The discussion of the post-Reformation religious schism in England is adapted from Kathleen R. Sands, *An Elizabethan Lawyer's Possession by the Devil: The Story of Robert Brigges* (Westport, Connecticut: Praeger, 2002), 10–12. For the theological basis of exorcism, see I. M. Lewis, *Ecstatic Religion: An Anthropological Study of Spirit Possession and Shamanism* (Baltimore: Penguin, 1971), 23, 186; Gananath Obeyesekere, "The Idiom of Demonic Possession: A Case Study," *Social Science and Medicine* 4 (1970), 108; and Stuart Clark, *Thinking With Demons: The Idea of Witchcraft in Early Modern England* (Oxford: Clarendon Press, 1997), 391. For the sociopolitical benefits of exorcism, see Peter Brown, *The Cult of the Saints: Its Rise and*

Function in Latin Christianity (Chicago: University of Chicago Press, 1981), 106–07, 110–12; and Clark, *Thinking with Demons,* 413. For the medical contributions to belief in demon possession, see Johann Weyer, *De Praestigiis Daemonum (On the Wiles of Devils,* 1593), published as *Witches, Devils, and Doctors in the Renaissance,* edited by George Mora (Binghamton, New York: Medieval and Renaissance Texts and Studies, 1991), 414, 420; Gregory Zilboorg, *The Medical Man and the Witch During the Renaissance* (New York: Cooper Square, 1935), 180; Edward Jorden, *A Brief Discourse of the Suffocation of Mother* (1603), reprinted in Michael MacDonald, ed., *Witchcraft and Hysteria in Elizabethan London: Edward Jorden and the Mary Glover Case* (London: Tavistock/Routledge, 1991), 25; Garfield Tourney, "The Physician and Witchcraft in Restoration England," *Medical History* 16 (1972): 153; George Gifford, *A Dialogue Concerning Witches and Witchcrafts* (1593), reprinted in Peter Haining, ed., *The Witchcraft Papers* (Secaucus, New Jersey: University Books, 1974), 110; Steven Kaplan, ed., *Understanding Popular Culture: Europe From the Middle Ages to the Nineteenth Century* (Berlin: Moulton, 1984), 132; Michael MacDonald, *Mystical Bedlam: Madness, Anxiety, and Healing in 17th-Century England* (Cambridge: Cambridge University Press, 1981), 190–93; Clark, *Thinking With Demons,* 164.

CHAPTER 2

The primary source for Anne Mylner's case is John Fisher, *The Copy of a Letter Describing the Wonderful Work of God in Delivering a Maiden within the City of Chester from an Horrible Kind of Torment* (London, 1564). Fisher, a gentleman, signed his name to this account as one of the witnesses to Mylner's dispossession. The discussion of demons' use of orifices to access the human body is adapted from Kathleen R. Sands, "The Doctrine of Transubstantiation and the English Protestant Dispossession of Demons," *History* 85, (July 2000), 450–52. For fasting, see Rudolph M. Bell, *Holy Anorexia* (Chicago: University of Chicago Press, 1985), 117–19; Caroline Walker Bynum, *Holy Feast and Holy Fast: The Religious Significance of Food to Medieval Women* (Berkeley: University of California Press, 1987), 2–3, 31–35, 38; Johann Weyer, *De Praestigiis Daemonum (On the Wiles of Devils* 1593); published as *Witches, Devils, & Doctors in the Renaissance,* edited by George Mora, (Binghamton, NY: Medieval and Renaissance Texts and Studies, 1991), 455–56; Ronald A. Knox, *Enthusiasm: A Chapter in the History of Religion* (New York: Oxford University Press, 1950), 151; George Fox, *Book of Miracles* (c. 1640), edited by Henry J. Cadbury (Cambridge: University Press, 1948), 32–34; and I. M. Lewis, *Ecstatic Religion: An Anthropological Study of Spirit Possession and Shamanism* (Baltimore: Penguin, 1971), 38. For convulsions and epilepsy, see Ronald Seth, *Children Against Witches* (New York: Taplinger, 1969), 143; Richard Bovet, *Pandaemonium* (1684), edited by Montague Summers (Aldington, Kent: Hand and Flower Press, 1957), 103; C.

L'Estrange Ewen, *Witchcraft and Demonianism: A Concise Account Derived from Sworn Depositions and Confessions Obtained in the Courts of England and Wales* (London: Heath Cranton, 1933), 380–81; and Owsei Temkin, *The Falling Sickness: A History of Epilepsy from the Greeks to the Beginnings of Modern Neurology* (Baltimore: Johns Hopkins Press, 1971), 3, 7, 85–90. For parallels between possession and pregnancy and between childbirth and exorcism, see Audrey Eccles, *Obstetrics and Gynecology in Tudor and Stuart England* (Kent, Ohio: Kent State University Press, 1982), 45, 55, 59, 61, 70–71; Weyer, *De Praestigiis Daemonum*, 311, 414, 420, 442, 445; Ilza Veith, *Hysteria: The History of a Disease* (Chicago: University of Chicago Press, 1965), 63; and Keith Thomas, *Religion and the Decline of Magic* (New York: Charles Scribner's Sons, 1971), 182. For the magical efficacy of invoking holy names, see Roger Baker, *Binding the Devil: Exorcism Past and Present* (London: Sheldon, 1974), 20, 23, 42; Christopher Wordsworth, "Two Yorkshire Charms or Amulets," *Yorkshire Archeological Journal* 17 (1903), 403–04, 406–07; Traugott K. Oesterreich, *Possession: Demoniacal and Other Among Primitive Races, in Antiquity, the Middle Ages, and Modern Times* (1921), reprinted as *Possession and Exorcism Among Primitive Races, in Antiquity, the Middle Ages, and Modern Times*, translated by D. Ibberson (New York: Causeway, 1974), 167; Saint Elmo Nauman, ed., *Exorcism Through the Ages* (New York: Philosophical Library, 1974), 202; Samuel Harsnet, *A Declaration of Egregious Popish Impostures* (London, 1603), 56–57; John Gaule, *The Mag-Astro-Mancer, or the Magicall-Astrologicall-Diviner Posed and Puzzled* (London, 1652), 228; George Gifford, *A Discourse of the Subtle Practices of Devils* (1587), reprinted Amsterdam: Walter J. Johnson, 1977), E4v-E4r; Lewis Hughes, *Certain Grievances, or The Popish Errors and Ungodliness of the Service Book Plainly Laid Open* (London, 1642), 12; James Mason, *The Anatomy of Sorcery, Wherein the Wicked Impiety of Charmers, Enchanters, and Such Like is Discovered and Confuted* (London, 1612), 25–26, 76. For Christ's wounds, see Eamon Duffy, *The Stripping of the Altars: Traditional Religion in England c.1400–c.1580* (New Haven: Yale University Press, 1992) 242, 244–46, 251; and Kathleen R. Sands, "Word and Sign in Elizabethan Conflicts With the Devil," *Albion* 31 (1999), 245.

CHAPTER 3

The primary source for Mistress Kingesfielde's case is an anonymous manuscript in the collections of the British Library, Harley MS 590, folio 69. The discussion of emblems is adapted from Kathleen R. Sands, "Word and Sign in Elizabethan Conflicts with the Devil," *Albion* 31 (1999): 238–39, 246. On the stench of evil, see Saint Athanasius, *The Life of St. Anthony the Great* (1850; reprinted Willis, California: Eastern Orthodox Books, 1976), 40, 67, 79; Nicholas Remy, *Demonolatry* (1595), translated by E. A. Ashwin (London: John Rodker, 1930), 38; Jean Bodin, *On the Demon-Mania of Witches* (1580), translated by Randy A. Scott (Toronto: Centre for Reformation and Renaissance

Studies, 1995), 169; and John Darrell, *A True Narration of the Strange and Grievous Vexation by the Devil of Seven Persons in Lancashire and William Somers of Nottingham* (1600), reprinted in *A Collection of Scarce and Valuable Tracts*, vol. 3, edited by Walter Scott (London: T. Cadell et al., 1810), 175. The discussions of demon possession in women and of melancholy and suicide are adapted from Kathleen R. Sands, *An Elizabethan Lawyer's Possession by the Devil: The Story of Robert Brigges* (Westport, Connecticut: Praeger, 2002), 29–32, 74. On the demoniac's intolerance of piety, see Barry Reay, ed., *Popular Culture in Seventeenth-Century England* (New York: St. Martin's Press, 1985), 106; Keith Thomas, *Religion and the Decline of Magic* (New York: Charles Scribner's Sons, 1971), 480; and D. P. Walker, *Unclean Spirits: Possession and Exorcism in France and England in the Late Sixteenth and Early Seventeenth Centuries* (Philadelphia: University of Pennsylvania Press, 1981), 49–52.

CHAPTER 4

The primary source for Alexander Nyndge's case is Edward Nyndge, *A Book Declaring the Fearful Vexation of One Alexander Nyndge* (London, 1578). For corporal restraint of and violence used against the demoniac, see Gregory Zilboorg, *A History of Medical Psychology* (New York: W. W. Norton, 1941), 140–41; Henry Charles Lea, *Materials Toward a History of Witchcraft* (New York: Thomas Yoseloff, 1957), vol. III, 1053–54; Samuel Harsnet, *A Declaration of Egregious Popish Impostures* (London, 1603), 39; and Richard Hunter and Ida Macalpine, *Three Hundred Years of Psychiatry 1535–1860* (London: Oxford University Press, 1963, 177. On conjuration, see Richard Kieckhefer, *Forbidden Rites: A Necromancer's Manual of the Fifteenth Century* (Philadelphia: Pennsylvania State University Press, 1997), 14, 127; James Mason, *The Anatomy of Sorcery Wherein the Wicked Impiety of Charmers, Enchanters, and Such Like is Discovered & Confuted* (London, 1612), 46; Francis Coxe, *A Short Treatise Declaring the Detestable Wickedness of Magical Sciences* (1561), reprinted New York: Da Capo Press, 1972, 9, 11, 18, 25; D. P. Walker, *Unclean Spirits: Possession and Exorcism in France and England in the Late Sixteenth and Early Seventeenth Centuries* (Philadelphia: University of Pennsylvania Press, 1981), 44–45; and James Dalton, *A Strange and True Relation of a Young Woman Possessed with the Devil* (London, 1647), 242. On the significance of a demoniac's demonstration of bestial behavior, see Gregory Zilboorg, *The Medical Man and the Witch During the Renaissance* (New York: Cooper Square, 1935), 96–97; and Keith Thomas, *Man and the Natural World: Changing Attitudes in England 1500–1800* (New York: Oxford University Press, 1983), 43–44, 134–35. On the interrogation of the demon, see Reginald Maxwell Woolley, *Exorcism and the Healing of the Sick* (London: Society for Promoting Christian Knowledge, 1932), 11, 29; Peter Brown, *The Cult of the Saints: Its Rise and Function in Latin Christianity* (Chicago: University of Chicago Press, 1981), 111; Charles Moeller, *Satan* (London:

Sheed and Ward, 1951), xx; John Richards, *But Deliver Us From Evil: An Introduction to the Demonic Dimension in Pastoral Care* (New York: Crossroad, 1974), 168; Reginald Scot, *The Discovery of Witchcraft* (London, 1584), 226; Jesse Bee, *The Most Wonderful and True Story of a Certain Witch Named Alice Gooderidge of Stapenhill* (London, 1597), 11, 15; Richard Baddeley, *The Boy of Bilson* (London, 1622), 25, 39, 40; Jean Bodin, *On the Demon-Mania of Witches* (1580), translated by Randy A. Scott (Toronto: Centre for Reformation and Renaissance Studies, 1995), 108. On dogs, see Mark S. R. Jenner, "The Great Dog Massacre," *Fear in Early Modern Society*, edited by William G. Naphy and Penny Roberts (Manchester: Manchester University Press, 1997), 48–49, 51–56. The discussions of repossession and of possession as a public exemplum are adapted from Kathleen R. Sands, *An Elizabethan Lawyer's Possession by the Devil: The Story of Robert Brigges* (Westport, Connecticut: Praeger, 2002), 29, 38, and 69.

CHAPTER 5

The primary sources for the case of Robert Brigges are two anonymous manuscripts in the collections of the British Library: Harley MS 590, pages 6–63, and Lansdowne MS 101, folios 165–75. This chapter is an abridgement of Kathleen R. Sands, *An Elizabethan Lawyer's Possession by the Devil: The Story of Robert Brigges* (Westport, Connecticut: Praeger, 2002).

CHAPTER 6

The primary source for the cases of Agnes Brigges and Rachel Pindar is the anonymous *The Disclosing of a Late Counterfeited Possession by the Devil in Two Maidens within the City of London* (London, 1574). An edited version of this pamphlet is reprinted in Barbara Rosen, ed., *Witchcraft* (New York: Taplinger, 1969). On the ejection of foreign objects from the body, see Richard Bovet, *Pandaemonium* (1684), edited by Montague Summers (Aldington, Kent: Hand and Flower Press, 1957), 103; C. L'Estrange Ewen, *Witchcraft and Demonianism: A Concise Account Derived from Sworn Depositions and Confessions Obtained in the Courts of England and Wales* (London: Heath Cranton, 1933), 236, 459–460; Gregory Zilboorg, *The Medical Man and the Witch During the Renaissance* (New York: Cooper Square, 1935), 83; Henry Charles Lea, *Materials Toward a History of Witchcraft* (New York: Thomas Yoseloff, 1957), volume III, 1047; Francesco Maria Guazzo, *Compendium Maleficarum* (1608, reprinted New York: Dover, 1988), 108–09; Johann Weyer, *De Praestigiis Daemonum* (*On the Wiles of Devils*, 1593), published as *Witches, Devils, and Doctors in the Renaissance,* edited by George Mora (Binghamton, New York: Medieval and Renaissance Texts and Studies, 1991), 286–7. On the accusation of witches in cases of demon possession, see G. R. Quaife, *Godly Zeal and Furious Rage: The Witch in Early Modern Europe* (New York: Saint

Martin's Press, 1987), 155; Sydney Anglo, ed. *The Damned Art: Essays in the Literature of Witchcraft* (London: Routledge and Kegan Paul, 1977), 63; Richard Bernard, *A Guide to Grand Jury Men* (London, 1630), 52–55; John Brinley, *A Discovery of the Impostures of Witches and Astrologers* (London, 1680), 15–21; D. P. Walker, *Unclean Spirits: Possession and Exorcism in France and England in the Late Sixteenth and Early Seventeenth Centuries* (Philadelphia: University of Pennsylvania Press, 1981), 82; C. L'Estrange Ewen, *Witchcraft in the Star Chamber* (private printing, 1938), 12, 28–36; and Ewen, *Witchcraft and Demonianism*, 81–82. On writing as a prestigious skill, see Tessa Watt, *Cheap Print and Popular Piety 1550–1640* (Cambridge University Press, 1991), 7, 260. On negotiating with demons in cases of possession, see Lea, *Materials toward a History of Witchcraft*, 1040, 1054. On ventriloquism in cases of possession, see Thomas Ady, *A Perfect Discovery of Witches* (London, 1656), 78–79; Ronald Seth, *Children Against Witches* (New York: Taplinger, 1969), 141. On testing demons in cases of possession, see Michel Marescot, *A True Discourse upon the Matter of Martha Brossier,* translated by Abraham Hartwell (London, 1599), 30–31; and Richard Baddeley, *The Boy of Bilson* (London, 1622), 59. On the exaggeration of natural symptoms in cases of possession, see D. P. Walker, *Unclean Spirits: Possession and Exorcism in France and England in the Late Sixteenth and Early Seventeenth Centuries* (Philadelphia: University of Pennsylvania Press, 1981), 16; Bernard, *A Guide to Grand Jury Men*, 46–47; Samuel Harsnet, *A Discovery of the Fraudulent Practices of John Darrel* (London, 1599), 63–64; and Francis Hutchinson, *An Historical Essay Concerning Witchcraft* (London, 1718) 5–9. The discussion of adolescents simulating demon possession was adapted from Kathleen R. Sands, *An Elizabethan Lawyer's Possession by the Devil: The Story of Robert Brigges* (Westport, Connecticut: Praeger, 2002), 74–75. On the public exposure and penance of Agnes Brigges and Rachel Pindar, see John Webster, *The Displaying of Supposed Witchcraft* (London, 1677, 272–73; John Bruce and Thomas Thomason Perowne, eds., *The Correspondence of Matthew Parker, D. D., Archibishop of Canterbury* (Cambridge: Cambridge University Press, 1853), 465; and John Strype, *The Life and Acts of Matthew Parker, the First Archbishop of Canterbury in the Reign of Queen Elizabeth* (Oxford: Clarendon Press, 1822), vol. 2, 373.

CHAPTER 7

The primary source for the case of Sarah Williams is Samuel Harsnet, *A Declaration of Egregious Popish Impostures* (London, 1603). This text is reprinted in F. W. Brownlow, *Shakespeare, Harsnet, and the Devils of Denham* (Newark: University of Delaware Press, 1993). Harsnet, chaplain to the bishop of London and later a bishop himself, was one of the government's most assiduous and effective critics of both Catholic exorcisms and Protestant dispossessions. On the sign of the cross, see Reginald Maxwell Woolley, *Exorcism and the Healing of the Sick* (London: Society for Promoting Christian Knowledge, 1932), 29; Keith Thomas, *Religion and the Decline of Magic* (New York: Charles Scribner's Sons, 1971), 72; Stuart Babbage, *Puritanism and Richard Bancroft* (London: Church Historical Society, 1962), 137; Arthur Dent, *The Plain Man's Pathway to Heaven* (London: 1601), 29; William Monter, *European Witchcraft* (New York: John Wiley & Sons, 1969), 120; John Darrell, *A True Narration of the Strange and Grievous Vexation by the Devil of Seven Persons in Lancashire and William Somers of Nottingham* (1600), reprinted in *A Collection of Scarce and Valuable Tracts*, vol. 3, edited by Walter Scott (London: T. Cadell et al., 1810), 204. On exorcism and other remedies through the nose and mouth, see Sir Thomas Elyot, *The Castle of Health* (n.p., 1539), 79v–80r; Henry Charles Lea, *Materials Toward a History of Witchcraft* (New York: Thomas Yoseloff, 1957), vol. III, 1056–1060; Johann Weyer, *De Praestigiis Daemonum* (*On the Wiles of Devils*, 1593), published as *Witches, Devils, and Doctors in the Renaissance*, edited by George Mora (Binghamton, New York: Medieval and Renaissance Texts and Studies, 1991), 406–07, 424–25; George Rosen, *Madness in Society: Chapters in the Historical Sociology of Mental Illness* (Chicago: University of Chicago Press, 1968), 69–70; Darrell, *A True Narration*, 240; Samuel Harsnet, *A Declaration of Egregious Popish Impostures* (London, 1603); 40, 45; and Michel Marescot, *A True Discourse upon the Matter of Martha Brossier*, translated by Abraham Hartwell (London, 1599), 34. On healing by touch, see Woolley, *Exorcism and the Healing of the Sick*, 11–12, 51, 56–57, 60, 79; Weyer, *De Praestigiis Daemonum*, 426; C. Grant Loomis, *White Magic: An Introduction to the Folklore of Christian Legend* (Cambridge, Massachusetts: Mediaeval Academy of America, 1948), 103–104; Thomas, *Religion and the Decline of Magic*, 192–200; Thomas Alfred Spalding, *Elizabethan Demonology: An Essay in Illustration of the Belief in the Existence of Devils . . . With Special Reference to Shakespeare and His Works* (London: Chatto and Windus, 1880), 79; Henry Foley, ed., *Records of the English Province of the Society of Jesus: Historic Facts Illustrative of the Labours and Sufferings of Its Members in the Sixteenth and Seventeenth Centuries* (London: Burns and Oates, 1877–78), Second, Third, and Fourth Series, 17–18; and Harsnet, *A Declaration of Egregious Popish Impostures*, 73. On the church's attitude toward magic, see Thomas, *Religion and the Decline of Magic*, 36–37, 47–49, 76, 41, 115–17, 153, 160–65, 181, 259, 271, 507; C. L'Estrange Ewen, *Witchcraft and Demonianism: A Concise Account Derived from Sworn Depositions and Confessions Obtained in the Courts of England and Wales* (London: Heath Cranton, 1933), 27; Wallace Notestein, *A History of Witchcraft in England From 1558 to 1718* (New York: Thomas Y. Crowell, 1968), 5–6; Lewis Hughes, *Certain Grievances, or The Popish Errors and Ungodliness of the Service Book Plainly Laid Open* (London, 1642), 168; and Alan Macfarlane, *Witchcraft in Tudor and Stuart England: A Regional and Comparative Study* (New York: Harper and Row, 1970), 107–08.

CHAPTER 8

The primary source for the case of Katherine Wright is Samuel Harsnet, *A Discovery of the Fraudulent Practices of John Darrel* (London, 1599), 279 ff. On hysteria and the rising of the womb, see Audrey Eccles, *Obstetrics and Gynecology in Tudor and Stuart England* (Kent, Ohio: Kent State University Press, 1982), 28, 74–82; Gregory Zilboorg, *A History of Medical Psychology* (New York: W. W. Norton, 1941), 131–32; Nicholas P. Spanos and Jack Gottlieb, "Demonic Possession, Mesmerism, and Hysteria: A Social Psychological Perspective on Their Historical Interactions," *Journal of Abnormal Psychology* 88 (1977): 540; Ilza Veith, *Hysteria: The History of a Disease* (Chicago: University of Chicago Press, 1965), viii; 129, 133, 140; C. L'Estrange Ewen, *Witchcraft and Demonianism: A Concise Account Derived from Sworn Depositions and Confessions Obtained in the Courts of England and Wales* (London: Heath Cranton, 1933), 190–93; Robert S. Kinsman, ed., *The Darker Vision of the Renaissance: Beyond the Fields of Reason* (Berkeley: University of California Press, 1974), 314–15; Edward Jorden, *A Brief Discourse of the Suffocation of Mother* (1603), reprinted in Michael MacDonald, ed., *Witchcraft and Hysteria in Elizabethan London: Edward Jorden and the Mary Glover Case* (London: Tavistock/Routledge, 1991); and Samuel Harsnet, *A Declaration of Egregious Popish Impostures* (London, 1603), 22–23. On fasting and prayer, see John Darrell, *A True Narration of the Strange and Grievous Vexation by the Devil of Seven Persons in Lancashire and William Somers of Nottingham* (1600), reprinted in *A Collection of Scarce and Valuable Tracts*, vol. 3, edited by Walter Scott (London: T. Cadell et al., 1810), 215, 248–250; Reginald Maxwell Woolley, *Exorcism and the Healing of the Sick* (London: Society for Promoting Christian Knowledge, 1932), 24–25; Roger French and Andrew Wear, eds., *The Medical Revolution of the Seventeenth Century* (Cambridge: University Press, 1989), 119; Christopher Hill, *The World Turned Upside Down: Radical Ideas During the English Revolution* (New York: Viking, 1972), 145; W. J. Sheils, ed., *The Church and Healing* (Oxford, 1982), 113; John Barrow, *The Lord's Arm Stretched Out in an Answer of Prayer; or, a True Relation of the Wonderful Deliverance of James Barrow* (London, 1664), 20; John Deacon and John Walker, *A Summary Answer to All the Material Points in Any of Master Darrell His Books* (London, 1601), 94–98, 102; George Lincoln Burr, ed., *Narratives of the Witchcraft Cases 1648–1706* (New York: Barnes and Noble, 1914), 276–77; MacDonald, *Witchcraft and Hysteria in Elizabethan London*, xxix; Thomas, *Religion and the Decline of Magic*, 114–15; Stuart Babbage, *Puritanism and Richard Bancroft* (London: Church Historical Society, 1962, 333; and D. P. Walker, *Unclean Spirits: Possession and Exorcism in France and England in the Late Sixteenth and Early Seventeenth Centuries* (Philadelphia: University of Pennsylvania Press, 1981), 109. On the sexual characteristics of possession and dispossession, see Johann Weyer, *De Praestigiis Daemonum* (*On the Wiles of Devils*, 1593), published as *Witches, Devils, and Doctors in the Renaissance,* edited by George Mora (Binghamton, New York: Medieval and Renaissance Texts and Studies, 1991), 311; Anne Barstow, *Witchcraze: A New History of the European Witch Hunt* (San Francisco: Pandora/Harper, 1994), 72; Jean Bodin, *On the Demon-Mania of Witches* (1580), translated by Randy A. Scott (Toronto: Centre for Reformation and Renaissance Studies, 1995), 169; G. R. Quaife, *Godly Zeal and Furious Rage: The Witch in Early Modern Europe* (New York: Saint Martin's Press, 1987), 56–57; I. M. Lewis, *Ecstatic Religion: An Anthropological Study of Spirit Possession and Shamanism* (Baltimore: Penguin, 1971), 58–59; Samuel Harsnet, *A Declaration of Egregious Popish Impostures* (London, 1603), 75, 122, 141; Sydney Anglo, ed., *The Damned Art: Essays in the Literature of Witchcraft* (London: Routledge and Kegan Paul, 1977), 206; and George Lincoln Burr, ed., *Narratives of the Witchcraft Cases 1648–1706* (New York: Barnes and Noble, 1914), 325–28, 335, 40. The discussion of the significance of witnesses is adapted from Kathleen R. Sands, *An Elizabethan Lawyer's Possession by the Devil: The Story of Robert Brigges* (Westport, Connecticut: Praeger, 2002), 36–38.

CHAPTER 9

The primary source for the case of Thomas Darling is Jesse Bee, *The Most Wonderful and True Story of a Certain Witch Named Alice Gooderidge of Stapenhill* (London, 1597). Bee was one of the witnesses to Darling's affliction and dispossession. The discussion of religious zealotry is adapted from Kathleen R. Sands, *An Elizabethan Lawyer's Possession by the Devil: The Story of Robert Brigges* (Westport, Connecticut: Praeger, 2002), 36–37. On the scriptural authority underlying belief in witches, see Brian Levack, *The Witch-Hunt in Early Modern Europe* (London: Longman, 1995), 113; Alan Macfarlane, *Witchcraft in Tudor and Stuart England: A Regional and Comparative Study* (New York: Harper and Row, 1970), 30; and Peter Burke, "The Comparative Approach to European Witchcraft," *Early Modern Witchcraft: Centres and Peripheries,* edited by Bengt Ankarloo and Gustav Henningsen (Oxford: Clarendon Press, 1990), 436. On the legal process dealing with accusations of witchcraft, see Keith Thomas, *Religion and the Decline of Magic* (New York: Charles Scribner's Sons, 1971), 220–235, 437, 443–45, 460–62, 517; Wallace Notestein, *A History of Witchcraft in England From 1558 to 1718* (New York: Thomas Y. Crowell, 1968), 5–6, 31, 103–04; Christina Larner, *Enemies of God: The Witch-Hunt in Scotland* (London: Chatto and Windus, 1981), 17–18, 22; and Alan Macfarlane, *Witchcraft in Tudor and Stuart England*, 170. The discussion of Darling's case mimicking that of Robert Brigges and the discussion of God's reasons for allowing Satan to possess human bodies are adapted from Sands, *An Elizabethan Lawyer's Possession by the Devil*, 41–42, 60–61. For the events following Darling's dispossession, see Ronald Seth, *Children Against Witches* (New York: Taplinger, 1969), 142; Corinne Hold Rickert, *The Case of John Darrel: Minister*

and Exorcist (Gainesville, Florida: University of Florida Press, 1962), 16; and
D. P. Walker, *Unclean Spirits: Possession and Exorcism in France and England in the
Late Sixteenth and Early Seventeenth Centuries* (Philadelphia: University of Penn-
sylvania Press, 1981), 56.

CHAPTER 10

The primary source for the case of the Starchy household is John Darrell,
*A True Narration of the Strange and Grievous Vexation by the Devil of Seven Per-
sons in Lancashire and William Somers of Nottingham* (1600), reprinted in *A
Collection of Scarce and Valuable Tracts*, vol. 3, edited by Walter Scott (London:
T. Cadell et al., 1810), 170 ff. On Lancashire, see Christina Larner, *Enemies of
God: The Witch-Hunt in Scotland* (London: Chatto and Windus, 1981), 26;
Wallace Notestein, *A History of Witchcraft in England From 1558 to 1718* (New
York: Thomas Y. Crowell, 1968), 118; John Champness, *Lancashire* (Dyfed,
Wales: C. I. Thomas and Sons, n.d.), 5; G. B. Harrison, ed., *The Trial of the
Lancaster Witches* (London: Peter Davies, 1929), xli; and J. J. Bagley, *A History
of Lancashire* (London: Phillimore, 1982), 55. On cunning folk, see Keith
Thomas, *Religion and the Decline of Magic* (New York: Charles Scribner's Sons,
1971), 41–71, 178–191, 263–77, 362, 491; Alan Macfarlane, *Witchcraft in Tudor
and Stuart England: A Regional and Comparative Study* (New York: Harper and
Row, 1970), 115, 121–25, 248, 284; and C. L'Estrange Ewen, *Witchcraft and
Demonianism: A Concise Account Derived from Sworn Depositions and Confessions Obtained in the Courts of England and Wales* (London: Heath Cranton,
1933), 113. On the use of conjuring circles, see Ewen, *Witchcraft and Demonianism* 35, 142, 151, 325–26. On senselessness as a symptom of possession,
see John Deacon and John Walker, *A Summary Answer to All the Material Points
in Any of Master Darrell His Books* (London, 1601), 35. On group possession, see
Henry Charles Lea, *Materials Toward a History of Witchcraft* (New York: Thomas
Yoseloff, 1957), vol. III, 1045, 1051; Johann Weyer, *De Praestigiis Daemonum
(On the Wiles of Devils)*, 1593, published as *Witches, Devils, and Doctors in the
Renaissance*, edited by George Mora (Binghamton, New York: Medieval and
Renaissance Texts and Studies, 1991), 301; George Rosen, "Psychopathology
in the Social Process: Dance Frenzies, Demonic Possession, Revival Move-
ments and Similar So-Called Psychic Epidemics," *Bulletin of the History of Medicine* 36 (1962): 13–14, 36, 43; George Rosen, "Psychopathology in the Social
Process: A Study of the Persecution of Witches in Europe as a Contribution to
the Understanding of Mass Delusions and Psychic Epidemics," *Journal of
Health and Human Behavior* 1 (1960): 204–05; and Gregory Zilboorg, *The Medical Man and the Witch During the Renaissance* (New York: Cooper Square,
1935), 181. On the 1634 witch trial before John Starchy, see Ewen, *Witchcraft
and Demonianism*, 244–51.

CHAPTER 11

The primary source for the case of William Somers is John Darrell, *A True Narration of the Strange and Grievous Vexation by the Devil of Seven Persons in Lancashire and William Somers of Nottingham* (1600), reprinted in *A Collection of Scarce and Valuable Tracts,* vol. 3, edited by Walter Scott (London: T. Cadell et al., 1810), 179 ff. The discussion of servants and apprentices was adapted from Kathleen R. Sands, *An Elizabethan Lawyer's Possession by the Devil: The Story of Robert Brigges* (Westport, Connecticut: Praeger, 2002), 75–76. On Darrel's loss of reputation following his appointment as a preacher, see D. P. Walker, *Unclean Spirits: Possession and Exorcism in France and England in the Late Sixteenth and Early Seventeenth Centuries* (Philadelphia: University of Pennsylvania Press, 1981), 62–63. On the economic impetus behind the early modern accusations of witchcraft, see Mary Brigg, "The Forest of Pendle in the Seventeenth Century," *Transactions of the Historic Society of Lancashire and Cheshire for the Year 1961,* vol. 113 (Liverpool: C. Tinling, 1962), 68–72; G. Youd, "The Common Fields of Lancashire," *Transactions of the Historic Society of Lancashire and Cheshire for the Year 1961,* vol. 113 (Liverpool: C. Tinling, 1962), 9–10; Angus Winchester, *Discovering Parish Boundaries* (Dyfed, Wales: C. I. Thomas and Sons, 1990), 35, 38–39, 42; Keith Thomas, *Religion and the Decline of Magic* (New York: Charles Scribner's Sons, 1971), 65, 88–89, 527, 553–68; Alan Macfarlane, *Witchcraft in Tudor and Stuart England: A Regional and Comparative Study* (New York: Harper and Row, 1970), 30, 105, 173–76, 197, 202; Christina Larner, *Enemies of God: The Witch-Hunt in Scotland* (London: Chatto and Windus, 1981), 7, 93–97; and Norman Cohn, *Europe's Inner Demons: An Enquiry Inspired by the Great Witch-Hunt* (New York: Meridian, 1975), 253–54. On the church commission's investigation of Darrell, see Walker, *Unclean Spirits,* 64; and Samuel Harsnet, *A Discovery of the Fraudulent Practices of John Darrel* (London, 1599), 8.

CHAPTER 12

That part of the summary that covers Mary Glover's case through the trial of Elizabeth Jackson derives primarily from Stephen Bradwell, *Mary Glover's Late Woeful Case, Together with Her Joyful Deliverance* (1603). Bradwell, a member of the London College of Physicians, was one of several physicians who treated Mary Glover. The part of the summary that covers the dispossession derives primarily from John Swan, *A True and Brief Report of Mary Glover's Vexation and of Her Deliverance by the Means of Fasting and Prayer* (1603). Swan, a divinity student, was one of those who participated in the fasting and prayer session on Mary's behalf. Both of these sources are reprinted in Michael MacDonald, ed., *Witchcraft and Hysteria in Elizabethan London: Edward Jorden and the Mary Glover Case* (London: Tavistock/Routledge,

1991). A few of the details of the summary derive from MacDonald's introduction to that same book and from Lewis Hughes, *Certain Grievances, or The Popish Errors and Ungodliness of the Service Book Plainly Laid Open* (London, 1642). The rules of evidence for witch trials derive from Alan Macfarlane, *Witchcraft in Tudor and Stuart England* (New York: Harper and Row, 1970), 18. The discussion of Robert Glover derives from Seymour Byman, "Suicide and Alienation: Martyrdom in Tudor England," *Psychoanalytic Review* 61 (1974): 367–370. The discussion of the demoniac Mercy Short derives from Cotton Mather's account of her case in George Lincoln Burr, *Narratives of the Witchcraft Cases 1648–1706* (New York: Barnes and Noble, 1914), 268–270, 284. The discussion of social alienation and reintegration was adapted from Kathleen R. Sands, *An Elizabethan Lawyer's Possession by the Devil: The Story of Robert Brigges* (Westport, Connecticut: Praeger, 2002), 83.

CHAPTER 13

For the case of Thomas Harrison, see Zachary Taylor, *Popery, Superstition, Ignorance and Knavery* (London, 1698), 10–11; and William Hinde, *A Faithful Remonstrance of the Holy Life and Happy Death of John Bruen* (London, 1641), 149, 152; On the rise of early modern English skepticism concerning possession and dispossession, see D. P. Walker, *Unclean Spirits: Possession and Exorcism in France and England in the Late Sixteenth and Early Seventeenth Centuries* (Philadelphia: University of Pennsylvania Press, 1981), 80, 109; Everett M. Emerson, *English Puritanism from John Hooper to John Milton* (Durham, North Caroline: Duke University Press, 1968), 22–28; Henry N. Paul, *The Royal Play of Macbeth* (New York: Macmillan, 1950), 90–95, 106–07; Stuart Babbage, *Puritanism and Richard Bancroft* (London: Church Historical Society, 1962), 95–101; Rosemary O'Day and Felicity Heal, eds., *Continuity and Change: Personnel and Administration of the Church of England 1500–1642* (Leicester: Leicester University Press, 1976), 183; George Lyman Kittredge, *Witchcraft in Old and New England* (Cambridge, Massachusetts: Harvard University Press, 1929), 301; John Darrell, *The Reply of J. Darrell to the Answer of J. Deacon and J. Walker* (London, 1602), 21–22; and Francis Hutchinson, *An Historical Essay Concerning Witchcraft* (London, 1718), 211. The discussion of *Twelfth Night* was adapted from Kathleen R. Sands, *An Elizabethan Lawyer's Possession by the Devil: The Story of Robert Brigges* (Westport, Connecticut: Praeger, 2002), 91. On the secularization of possession and dispossession, see George Fox, *Book of Miracles* [c. 1640], ed. Henry J. Cadbury (Cambridge: University Press, 1948), 24, 122; Everett M. Emerson, *English Puritanism from John Hooper to John Milton* (Durham, North Carolina: Duke University Press, 1968), 34; and Michael MacDonald, *Mystical Bedlam: Madness, Anxiety, and Healing in 17th-Century England* (Cambridge: Cambridge University Press, 1981), 177. For strokers and Valentine Greatrakes, see Keith Thomas, *Religion and the Decline of Magic*

(New York: Charles Scribner's Sons, 1971), 40; R. Crawfurd, *The King's Evil* (Oxford: Clarendon Press, 1911), 51–57; *The Manner of His Majesty's Curing the Disease Called the King's Evil* (London, 1679); Richard Hunter and Ida Macalpine, *Three Hundred Years of Psychiatry 1535–1860* (London: Oxford University Press, 1963), 151, 181; and Ralph H. Major, *Faiths That Healed* (New York: D. Appleton–Century, 1940), 164–69. Part of the discussion of this subject was adapted from Kathleen R. Sands, "The Doctrine of Transubstantiation and the English Protestant Dispossession of Demons," *History* 85, (July 2000), 461–62. On the inadequacy of modern medical and anthropological explanations for possession and dispossession, see I. M. Lewis, *Ecstatic Religion: An Anthropological Study of Spirit Possession and Shamanism* (Baltimore: Penguin, 1971) 28, 200; and Arnold van Gennep, *The Rites of Passage* (1908), trans. Monika B. Vizedom and Gabrielle L. Caffee (Chicago: University of Chicago Press, 1960), 96. On twentieth-century possession and dispossession under the auspices of the Church of England, see Donald Omand, *Experiences of a Present Day Exorcist* (London: William Kimber, 1970), 9, 11–13; 43, 49; Roger Baker, *Binding the Devil: Exorcism Past and Present* (London: Sheldon, 1974), 4–5, 135, 142, 169; Dom Robert Petitpierre, *Exorcism: The Findings of a Commission Convened by the Bishop of Exeter* (Saffron Walden, Essex: W. Hart and Son, 1972), 9–10, 31–46, 49–52; and Christopher Neil-Smith, *The Exorcist and the Possessed* (Saint Ives, Cornwall: James Pike, 1974), 10, 15–16.

Index

About the Author

KATHLEEN R. SANDS holds a Ph.D. in early modern English literature and history. She has taught at several colleges and universities and currently teaches intellectual history at Temple University in Philadelphia. She has also worked as an educational consultant for a history museum, developing school programs and public presentations on many historical topics. She is author of *An Elizabethan Lawyer's Possession by the Devil: The Story of Robert Brigges* (Praeger, 2002).